THE HEATHFIELD TO EXETER (TEIGN VALLEY) RAILWAY

by

Lawrence W. Pomroy

ARK PUBLICATIONS (RAILWAYS)

First published in 1995 by ARK PUBLICATIONS (RAILWAYS), an imprint of FOREST PUBLISHING, Woodstock, Liverton, Newton Abbot, Devon TQ12 6JJ

British Library Cataloguing in Publication Data
A catalogue record for this book is available from the British Library
ISBN 1–873029–04–7

0–4–2T, No. 1435, with an 'up' train from Heathfield at Alphington Halt on 13th July, 1957.

R. A. Lumber

ARK PUBLICATIONS (RAILWAYS)
Editorial, layout and design by:
Mike Lang

Typeset by:
Carnaby Typesetting, Torquay, Devon TQ1 1EG

Printed and bound in Great Britain by:
BPC Wheatons Ltd, Exeter, Devon EX2 8RP

Cover photographs:

Front — (Top) 0–4–2T, No. 1469, about to leave Heathfield Station with the 1.20 p.m. train to Exeter on 1st April, 1950.

E.R. Shepherd

(Lower) 0–6–0PT, No. 9629, leaving platform 6 at Exeter St. David's Station with the 4.35 p.m. train to Heathfield on 10th February, 1958.

Peter W. Gray

Back – A busy scene at Christow Station on 26th May, 1958 as 2–6–2T, No. 5558, and 0–6–0PT, No. 3606, wait for the 'off' with the 1.16 p.m. train to Exeter and the 1.17 p.m. train to Heathfield respectively.

E. R. Shepherd

CONTENTS

ACKNOWLEDGEMENTS

I would like to thank the many people and organizations who have helped me with my enquiries, for without their help and co-operation, this book could never have been completed. I am especially indebted to Mr D. Lystor, for his interest and kindness in supplying me with information concerning the quarries in the valley, and Mr D. Rouse for his interest and kindness in giving me the benefit of his knowledge of the working of the line.

ARC Ltd, Trusham (Mr P. Hughes, Manager); British Railways Board; Candy Tiles Ltd, Heathfield (Mr E. A. Deaves, Secretary); Devon County Council Libraries (Mr I. Maxted); Devon County Records Office, Exeter; Exeter Cattle Market (Mr R. D. Johnson, Superintendent); Express and Echo, Exeter; GWR Museum, Swindon; Heltor Ltd, Bovey Tracey (Mr A. D. Kingdon, Managing Director); Historical Model Railway Society; Laporte Industries Ltd (Mr R. D. Furness); Ordnance Survey, Southampton (Miss C. Parsons); Public Record Office, Kew (Miss J. Towner); Railway Modeller; Signalling Records Society (Mr G. A. Pryer and Mr R. Caston); Watson Petroleum Ltd (Mr J. Hicks, Manager); Westcountry Studies Library, Exeter; Western Morning News.

A. J. Ball; J. R. Besley; R. M. Booker; Mr & Mrs Borthwick; A. Court; Mr & Mrs J. Cross; L. Crozier; Mrs E. A. Eden; Mrs B. M. Ellis; Viscount Exmouth; B. Gibson; P. Grafton; M. Hale; J. Hanley; G. Howells; W. Hudson; A. R. Kingdom; M. Lang; P. Lindsey; A. Luxton; R. Mann; J. Mills; R. Nash; E. G. Parrott; Mr & Mrs W. Ridgeway; R. C. Riley; E. R. Shepherd; J. N. Slinn; H. Stephens; Capt. P. H. W. Studholme; G. Taylor; Mrs D. Vallance; P. Vipan; W. Williams; J. Wills; R. Zaple.
(Photographs are acknowledged individually in most instances)

Last, but not least, my wife Stella, who recently has had to put up with much burning of the midnight oil, and who has heard little of any subject other than the Teign Valley Railway, but at the same time admits to having thoroughly enjoyed our many visits and explorations into the Teign Valley.

FOREWORD

The first railway journey which I can remember was from St David's, Exeter, to Ide. This long journey must have cost my father a penny, and I thought it was mean of him to make me walk back to Exeter, when for another halfpenny, we could have returned by train. I must, at that time, have been seven years old.

Later on, but before World War I, I was allowed to travel on my own. As I could watch Expresses at St David's, a stones throw from my house, I spent my pocket money on trips along the Teign and Exe Valley Lines. Not only did I enjoy the scenery in these valleys, but I felt that I was an important part of the GWR, for during the day I was one of few passengers, and could talk with the drivers, firemen and guards on almost equal terms. Besides, I loved the little 0–4–2 tank engines and the 'open' coach, in which I rode as if I owned it.

Those Great Western branch lines were a delight. A river, be it the Teign, Exe, Dart or Avon, was never far away, and we used to stop at stations and halts, and listen to the sound of the streams running nearby. Also to be heard was the gossip of the passengers, all of whom knew each other, and the gentle purring of the safety valve of the engine.

I recall that, on one occasion, we ran short of steam on the climb to what we used to call the Haldon Hump, and stopped short of the tunnel; I was allowed to get out of the carriage and pick bluebells, until the shrill whistle called to me. More of the stoppages were caused by the trespassing of a cow or sheep on the line. The passengers never seemed to be impatient.

The trains filled up in the early evenings, and in summer-time I accompanied my schoolfriends to Christow or Trusham, returning solo by the 'up' train from Heathfield.

You will be aware that the Teign Valley line was most useful to the GWR in emergencies, when there was trouble on the sea wall at Dawlish or Teignmouth. The 'up' 'Torbay Express' or 'Cornish Riviera' would slip slowly along the valley, hauled by two 'Bulldog' class locomotives, and as they tackled the bank, their exhausts reverberated in the surrounding hills. At such times, freight trains abounded.

When dark red replaced the chocolate and cream livery on the Great Western coaches, one of the 0–4–2 tanks was painted to match the colour of the coach; this was the only time I saw a red GWR engine.

I had my last journey on the Teign Valley line in the week before it finally closed. Beyond Ide, the line had not changed for fifty years. Sir James Milne, a general manager of the GWR, once said to me that few of the West Country branch lines paid their way, but the company ran them as a social duty. It performed that duty well, and we are much the poorer without those delightful lines

6th August 1981 *Bishop Wilfrid Westall*

PREFACE

During the course of my work for a Berkshire-based building company, whilst living in Exeter, I constantly travelled all around the Westcountry and found traces of many old railway lines long since gone. This had a profound effect, for it quickly rekindled my love and interest of railways, and in 1977 came the turning point where I would soon find myself writing on the subject — I came across a copy of Anthony R. Kingdom's book entitled *The Ashburton Branch.*

After having read and thoroughly enjoyed this excellent work, I then started searching for similar books on other branch lines, especially those in Devon. One of the lines that attracted my particular interest was the Teign Valley Railway that used to run between Exeter and Heathfield. However, after being unable to find any work covering it, I contacted a publisher who produced a very popular series of branchline histories at that time, the Oxford Publishing Company. I was duly informed that as far as it was known nothing at all had been specifically published about this branch line, and the suggestion was subsequently made that as I was living in Devon, and appeared to be extremely interested, I might consider tackling such a project myself.

As a result, and following much deliberation, I first prepared and submitted a synopsis for approval. Then, after a great deal of hard work, coupled with invaluable assistance from many people and organizations, I was ready, in 1981, to submit the completed manuscript, prior to the book being published by the Oxford Publishing Company in 1984. It was entitled *The Teign Valley Line.*

Although this book has now been out of print for a number of years, I still receive letters from readers seeking further information about the line. As a result of this interest, together with a growing demand for the history of Devon's extensive transport system, the proprietors of Forest Publishing and I decided to update and republish this work under its new title *The Heathfield to Exeter (Teign Valley) Railway.*

In most respects, this new edition is a reprint of the original book, using a slightly different format. But, with the benefit of hindsight, a few minor errors have been corrected and some additional information and photographs included, as have maps covering the entire line. We now hope that it will delight and give pleasure to new readers interested in Devon's transport history.

Lawrence W. Pomroy
Warminster
Wiltshire
June 1995

INTRODUCTION

The life of the Heathfield to Exeter branch line was both chequered and varied. Originally authorized in 1863 as a broad gauge line from the embryo Moretonhampstead and South Devon Railway to run to Chudleigh and Doddiscombsleigh, it did not open until 1882. It then ran from Heathfield to Ashton, with a long siding to serve the mine and quarries at Bridford. This

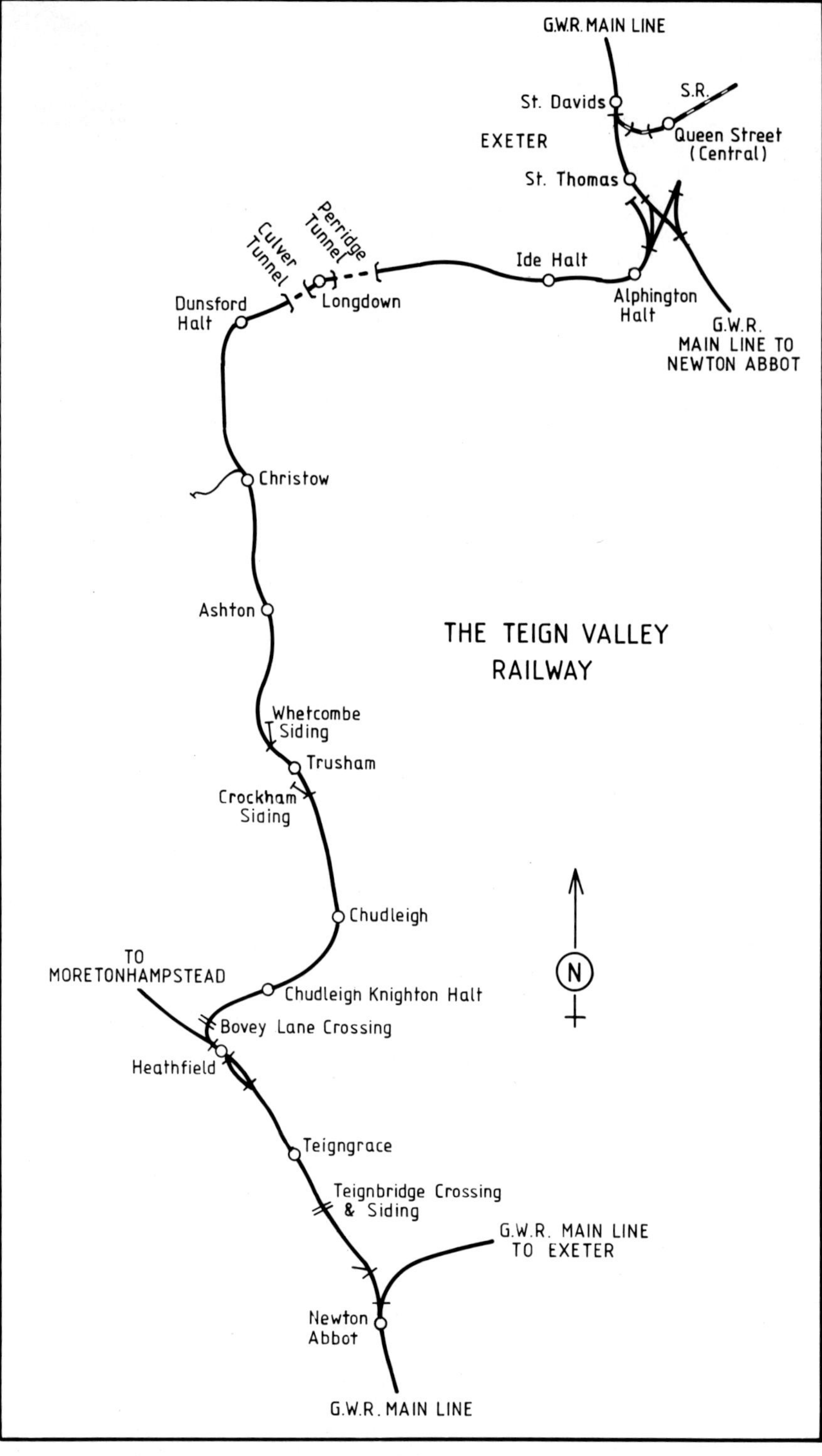
G.W.R. MAIN LINE
S.R.
St. Davids
EXETER
Queen Street
(Central)
St. Thomas
Perridge
Tunnel
Culver
Tunnel
Ide Halt
Alphington
Halt
Longdown
Dunsford
Halt
G.W.R.
MAIN LINE TO
NEWTON ABBOT
Christow
Ashton
THE TEIGN VALLEY
RAILWAY
Whetcombe
Siding
Trusham
Crockham
Siding
Chudleigh
N
TO
MORETONHAMPSTEAD
Chudleigh Knighton Halt
Bovey Lane Crossing
Heathfield
Teigngrace
Teignbridge Crossing
& Siding
G.W.R. MAIN LINE
TO EXETER
Newton
Abbot
G.W.R. MAIN LINE

was known as the Teign House siding. Some years later another company was formed to build a line from Exeter, linking up at what was to become known as Christow Station. The through line, as it became, was opened in 1903. Known as The Teign Valley Line (or Railway), it had an importance all of its own. In addition to serving the needs of the valley, it provided an alternative route from Exeter to Newton Abbot, and was known to carry the main Cornish Expresses at such times as were necessitated by cliff falls and rough seas along the coastal route. It is also reported to have had the honour of sheltering a Royal Train, and its passengers, for a night during official visits to Devon.

The end for passenger traffic came in 1958, after a reported loss of £15,000 per annum, despite protests by people living along the route whose lifeline it was to Exeter and Newton Abbot.

My earliest recollection of the line is of the view from an upstairs window in my parents' house, which overlooked the Haldon Hills. It was often possible to see the white smoke from the little 0–4–2 tank engine shortly after it had left St. Thomas Station and the main line. It would disappear after passing through Alphington. On a clear day the little train would then reappear as it began its ascent to Longdown and the first tunnel. My first actual sight of the train was between Ide Station and the Perridge Tunnel on a summer's day whilst having a picnic with my parents and a cousin. However, my clearest, and certainly most impressive, memory is of the aerial ropeways and elaborate workings at Christow, together with the many stone-carrying wagons, around 1930, on a journey by car through Longdown and the Teign valley.

I have always thought that I never travelled on this line. Prior to being posted overseas during World War II, I made several journeys between Paddington, Plymouth and Bodmin, usually at night. On one occasion I remember arriving very late at Plymouth and being informed that the train had been diverted at Exeter, as the sea wall had been damaged. At the time I imagined that the train had taken the Southern Line through Okehampton and Tavistock. However, on reflection, it is possible that I did travel on the Teign Valley line after all — what a pity that it was at night!

A visit to the beautiful valley, with its graceful little river (which has its beginnings high up on northern Dartmoor) meandering along beneath the surrounding hills, is to be recommended. The current edition of 1:50,000 O.S. maps clearly indicates the course of the disused line. It is very important to remember, however, that the former stations and track-bed are privately owned and should not be explored without permission. On the other hand, some of the remaining old stations, now converted to dwellings, can be seen without risk of trespass.

This book makes an attempt to trace the history of the line, from its early beginnings through to closure. I still repudiate Mr A. A. Camwell's description of the Teign Valley Railway as 'a supreme example of much ado about nothing' in his otherwise excellent article published in *Railway World* of February 1958. In many ways, it is the epitome of the country branch line, terminating in the magnificent train hall of Brunelian design at Exeter St. Thomas Station.

It is a nostalgic look at a line, with a photographic record.

Lawrence W. Pomroy

A scene at Heathfield Station in the early '20s with the Teign Valley train about to leave its bay and being headed by an Exeter '517' class 0–4–2T. On the left of the picture stands a 45XX class and the buildings of Candy & Co. Ltd.

A. R. Kingdom collection

A much later view of Heathfield Station, clearly showing the siding leading off into the Great Western pottery and brickworks of Candy & Co. Ltd., as 0–6–0T No. 7716 prepares for the journey to Exeter on 7th August 1957 — from the 'up' platform on the Moretonhampstead line!

R. A. Lumber

THE ROUTE DESCRIBED

Heathfield to Exeter. The route described in retrospect.

I shall now attempt to describe a trip to Exeter on the Teign Valley Railway as one might have experienced such a journey in the late 'fifties, just before its closure and on which was to be seen one of the most striking examples of the bountiful gifts of nature, and the manner in which they were utilised.

The journey to Exeter commences at Heathfield, adjacent to the A38 trunk road and on the junction with the Moretonhampstead branch, which opened on 4th July 1866. The station is 3 miles 70 chains from Newton Abbot and when first opened in 1874 was named Chudleigh Road; the change of name to Heathfield occurred on 1st October 1882, just prior to the opening of the standard gauge Teign Valley Railway to Ashton on 9th October 1882. It was done so as to avoid confusion with the then new station situated on the outskirts of the small market town of Chudleigh. Initially, because the Moretonhampstead branch was broad gauge, the Teign Valley Railway was completely isolated from the rest of the Great Western system, and Heathfield became an interchange for both the broad and standard gauge trains, with no physical connection between the two, except for adjacent sidings on which goods could be transferred from one wagon to another. Even after 23rd May 1892, when the Moretonhampstead line was converted to standard gauge, the Teign Valley Railway continued in virtual isolation with the only access between the two being provided by a connection facing towards Moretonhampstead and leading into a short bay into which the Teign Valley trains ran, a situation that existed until October 1916 when provision was finally made for a direct connection following extensive alterations to the junction.

After taking the opportunity to take a brief look at the timber-built station and the signal box at the far end of the main platform, it is time to savour the journey ahead. On being given the road by the 'up platform starter', our train pulls slowly out of its own bay, makes a long and sharp curve to the right and sets a course north-eastwards, soon passing over Bovey Lane Crossing, Bovey Marsh Bridge and, a little further on, another, more significant, bridge; this carries the line over the River Bovey, just 1 mile before its waters mingle with those of the Teign. Chudleigh Knighton Heath quickly follows and then, after curving to the right, and only some 5 minutes since leaving Heathfield, the train arrives at Chudleigh Knighton Halt, with its little corrugated Pagoda shelter midway along the single platform and nearby crossing-keeper's cottage. At one time trains of 4 to 5 carriages were filled at this halt, which was added on 9th June 1924, and it provided sufficient traffic to justify its own additional train to Newton Abbot several times a week. But all traces of the group of sidings laid in 1943 have long since disappeared. It is now, just beyond Chudleigh Knighton Halt, that we begin our association with the River Teign, which our train crosses for the first time by means of another substantial bridge. Thereafter, for the next part of our journey, the river

0–6–0PT No. 3606 in charge of the 4.45p.m. train to Exeter on 31st May 1958, depicted just beyond Bovey Lane Crossing on the outskirts of Heathfield.

E. R. Shepherd

Chudleigh Knighton Halt, which was opened on 9th June 1924. The photograph was taken on 30th August 1958.

Michael Hale

The approach to Chudleigh Station.

Author's Collection

Chudleigh Station, on 30th August 1958.

Michael Hale

remains in close proximity to the west: immediately to the east is Bellamarsh Copse and also the B3193 road from nearby Kingsteignton, which is separated from the line by no more than a high wooden fence.

Having now travelled just over 2 miles, the approach is made to the attractive little station of Chudleigh with its single platform and buildings of similar design and wooden construction to those of Heathfield. To the south of the station a loop with a siding caters for the somewhat modest levels of goods traffic, which includes the local coal supplies, and beyond the main station platform lies a wooden platform, reached by a raised gangway from the adjacent roadway; this was designed for use when the River Teign flooded the station approach!

Chudleigh, itself, is a small market town which, at the date of our journey, is situated on the main road between Exeter and Plymouth. In May 1807 it was largely destroyed by fire, but subsequently rebuilt. There are few time-honoured retreats in England that have a more interesting history than that of Chudleigh, nestling among the Devonshire hills. Lovers of the countryside will find here unbroken landscape scenery in all its splendour. Owing to the purity of its air and water, the area was at one time strongly recommended by physicians as a health resort. It has a famous coaching inn, once named 'The Clifford Arms', and now named 'The Old Coaching House'. Indeed, it was at this old coaching house that William of Orange stayed after landing at Torbay, and from one of its windows he addressed the townsfolk, in his broken English. Other guests included two of the exiled Bonaparte Princes, brothers of the exiled Napoleon. The Duke of Clarence, afterwards William IV, often visited here. Nearby, in its great park, stands Ugbrooke. This great and magnificent house is the home of the Clifford family, who still occupy the mansion. After being used as a home, for a school for children evacuated from London's East End in 1939, it was used as a hostel for disabled Polish soldiers of General Ander's Army. The house stood empty from 1952 until 1957, and the downstairs rooms were used to store grain. In 1957 the present Lord and Lady Clifford returned from Australia, and began the long task of restoration. Not far away, towards the station, is a glen with a waterfall, and also Chudleigh Rocks. Little wonder that Ruskin called this spot 'The Virgin Eden of England'.

On leaving Chudleigh Station, our train continues northwards, passing under the road bridge immediately adjacent to the station and staying close to the banks of the River Teign, which winds its way along the beautiful valley bearing its name. Before reaching Trusham, 2 miles up the line, it actually crosses the river on two more occasions in quite rapid succession. Trusham is the most important station on the line, with its full size signal box and adjacent sidings, and traffic from the quarries. The station building is typical South Devon Railway style, built of yellow brick, and next to it, on the main, 'up', platform, is a tin storage shed. Prior to 1943 this, in fact, was the only platform, but as a result of alterations carried out that year, which included the removal of a short loop off the long loop beside the running line, there is also a 'down' platform, on which there is a small concrete shelter. The 'up' and 'down' loops are each 1,500 ft. in length. In addition, there are two sid-

Trusham Station viewed looking towards Heathfield, on 30th August 1958. Towards the top of the picture can be seen part of the nearby quarry buildings.
Michael Hale

ings, facing Heathfield, together with ramified private sidings in the Teign Valley Granite Company's concrete works, while nearby, opposite Doghole Copse, were once the Whetcombe sidings with a loading wharf: these had been removed in the early 'fifties.

Still close to the river, and passing under a road bridge, our train proceeds a further 2 miles to Ashton, which from 1903 until 1914 was distinguished by having the only signal box on the branch at that time, apart from the one at Heathfield. This station, with a building of very similar design and construction to that of Trusham, was also the terminal station of the original line, beyond which it operated a siding to Teign House — later known as Christow, even though the village was some 2 miles away! To the south of the station lie a run-round loop and two sidings, as does a building that was once utilised as an engine shed. This, however, had ceased to function as such as long ago as 1908, and for many years was used as a ganger's store. The signal box, too, had been brought into dis-use in 1914, leaving the level crossing at the north end protected only by distant signals and the track layout controlled by ground frames. Close to the station, on the B3193 road, and on the opposite side of the river, are three cottages, built by a former Lord Exmouth in 1882 for railway employees, and which still bear the name 'Exmouth Cottages'.

With the waters of the River Teign now remaining ever present, our train soon passes the Ryecroft Quarry siding, which was worked by a ground frame locked by key, on the Christow to Trusham electric train staff. It was opened on 10th November 1930 and remained in use for 23 years. This

Ashton Station, pictured on 30th August 1958. The view is towards Heathfield, and the former engine shed can be seen in the distance. Note the milk churns awaiting collection.

Michael Hale

Ashton Station, looking towards Exeter.

Author's Collection

2–6–2T No. 5558 with the 1.16p.m. train for Exeter at Christow Station on 26th May 1958.

E. R. Shepherd

Another view of Christow Station as 0–6–0T No. 7716 stands beside the 'down' platform with the 5.55p.m. Exeter St. David's train to Heathfield on 7th August 1957.

R. A. Lumber

stretch of the line was also originally the siding to Teign House and, after crossing the river twice, our train steams slowly into Christow Station, the adjoining road bridge being the effective boundary between the old Teign Valley and Exeter railways — 7 miles 57 chains from Heathfield and 8 miles 7 chains from Exeter.

At Christow, the station building is found to be of red brick and similar in appearance to those of Ashton and Trusham, but one immediate difference is the roof being hipped as opposed to gable. It is situated on the 'up' platform, beyond which is seen an elevated water tower, fed by a well. Opposite, on the 'down' platform, there is a similarly designed waiting shelter, also with a hipped roof, and at the far end of this platform is a raised timber-built signal box. Immediately beyond the station complex several sidings are apparent, on both sides, as are the Scatter Rock Quarry buildings which, until the quarry closed in 1954, had been fed by an aerial ropeway system from the quarry, situated some 2 miles or so to the west. In the 'thirties excursions were run at weekends to this pretty location, and these were particularly popular in the springtime, when wild daffodils grew in abundance in the vicinity.

Leaving Christow Station, our train now travels on the 'new' line to Exeter, and climbs sharply above the waters of the River Teign which, until now, it has so closely followed, over Leigh Bridge and along the shoulder of the hill, with deep cuttings here and there through the shale. It travels for about a mile, before bearing eastwards towards Exeter, and shortly reaches Dunsford Halt. This halt was opened on 16th January 1928, and has a single

Dunsford Halt, which was opened on 16th January 1928, looking towards Exeter. The photograph was taken on 1st September 1958.

Michael Hale

GREAT WESTERN RAILWAY.

On Monday, January 16th, 1928,

A NEW HALT

WILL BE OPENED AT

DUNSFORD

SITUATE BETWEEN

LONGDOWN AND CHRISTOW.

TRAIN SERVICE. Week-days only.

	M	M	M	M	M	M	M	M	M	M	M
	a.m.	a.m.	a.m.	p.m.	p.m.	p.m.	p.m.	p.m.	p.m.	p.m.	p.m.
Exeter { St. David's .. dep.	7 0	9 30	10 58	12 55	2 45	..	..	5 43	8V45	9J40	11K10
Exeter { St. Thomas .. „	7 4	9 34	11 3	12 59	2 50	..	..	5 47	8V49	9J44	11K15
Ide Halt .. .. .. „	7 12	9 43	11 11	1 7	2 59	..	..	5 55	8V57	9J52	11K23
Longdown .. .. .. „	7 21	9 52	11 20	1 16	3 8	..	..	6 4	9V 6	10J 1	11K32
Dunsford Halt .. .. „	7 25	9 56	11 24	1 20	3 12	..	..	6 8	9V10	10J 5	11K36
Christow .. .. .. „	7 31	10 2	11 30	1 30	3 17	4 13	..	6 17	9V20	10J11	11K42
Ashton .. .. .. „	7 36	10 7	11 35	1 35		4 18	..	6 22	9V25	10J16	11K47
Trusham .. .. .. „	7 44	10 15	11 43	1 43	..	4 26	..	6 30	9V33	10J24	11K55
Chudleigh .. .. .. „	7 50	10 21	11 49	1 49	..	4 32	5 23	6 36	9V39	10J30	12K 1
Chudleigh Knighton Halt „	7 54	10 25	11 53	1 53	..	4 36	5 27	6 40	9V43	10J34	12K 5
Heathfield .. .. arr.	7 58	10 29	11 57	1 57	..	4 40	5 31	6 44	9V47	10J38	12K 9
Heathfield .. .. dep.	8 5	10 35	12 56	2M10	..	5 35	5 35	7 40	9W50	..	..
Bovey .. .. .. arr.	8 14	10 43	1 3	2M15	..	5 44	5 44	7 47	9W57	..	..
Moretonhampstead .. „	8 34	11 5	1 25	3T 55	..	6 5	6 5	8 9	10W19	..	..
Heathfield .. .. dep.	8 20	10 50	12 0	2 3	..	4 45	..	6 49	9V50	..	..
Newton Abbot .. arr.	8 30	11 0	12 10	2 13	..	4 55	..	7 0	10V 0	..	..

	a.m.	a.m.	p.m.		p.m.	p.m.	p.m.	p.m.		p.m.	night
Newton Abbot .. dep.	7 55	10 25	12 46	..	3 15	..	5 25	7 30	..	9J40	9K40
Heathfield .. .. arr.	8 5	10 35	12 56	..	3 25	..	5 35	7 40	..	9J50	9K50
Moretonhampstead dep.	7 55	10 25	11‡35	..	1 40	4 20	4 20	6 25	..	8J20	8K20
Bovey .. .. .. „	8 13	10 43	11‡53	..	2M30	4 38	4 38	6 42	..	8J36	8K36
Heathfield .. .. arr.	8 20	10 50	12 0	..	2M36	4 45	4 45	6 49	..	8J42	8K42
	M	M	M		M	M	M	M		M	M
Heathfield .. .. dep	8 23	10 53	1 0		3 30	5 10	5 40	7 45	..	10J45	12K15
Chudleigh Knighton Halt „	8 28	10 58	1 5	..	3 3[illegible]	5 15	5 45	7 50	..	10J50	12K20
Chudleigh .. .. .. „	8 32	11 2	1 9	..	3 39	5 18	5 49	7 54	..	10J54	12K24
Trusham .. .. .. „	8 38	11 8	1 15	..	3 45		5 55	8 0	..	11J 0	12K30
Ashton .. .. .. „	8 44	11 14	1 21	..	3 51	..	6 1	8 7	..	11J 6	12K36
Christow .. .. .. „	8 50	11U31	1 27	..	3 57	..	6X15	8 13	..	11J12	12K42
Dunsford Halt .. .. „	8 57	11 38	1 34	..	4 4	..	6 22	8 20	..	11J19	12K49
Longdown .. .. .. „	9 0	11 41	1 37	..	4 7	..	6 25	8 23	..	11J22	12K52
Ide Halt .. .. .. „	9 7	11 48	1 44	..	4 14	..	6 32	8 30	..	11J29	12K59
Exeter { St. Thomas .. „	9 16	11 57	1 52	..	4 26	..	6 40	8 38	..	11J40	1K 8
Exeter { St. David's .. arr.	9 19	12 0	1 58	..	4 29	..	6 43	8 41	..	11J43	1K11

J—Saturdays only. Will not run on January 28th. K—Runs Saturday, January 28th only. M—Rail Motor Car, one class only. T—Heathfield depart 3 25 p.m. U—Arrives Christow 11.10 a.m. V—Commences April 2nd. W—Saturdays only until April 28th, daily commencing April 30th. X—Arrives Christow 6.6 p.m. ‡—a.m.

Tickets should be obtained from the Guard on the train.

The Third Class Single Fares from DUNSFORD HALT will be as under :—

	s.	d.		s.	d.
Ashton (Devon)		6	Heathfield	1	3
Christow		4	Ide		7
Chudleigh		11½	Longdown		2½
Chudleigh Knighton Halt	1	2	Newton Abbot	1	9
Dawlish (via St. Thomas)	2	3	Teigngrace	1	6
Exeter, St. David's		11½	Teignmouth (via Newton Abbot) ..	2	5
„ St. Thomas		10	Trusham		9

CHEAP THIRD-CLASS RETURN TICKETS will be issued each week-day by ANY TRAIN—

	s.	d.		s.	d.
To EXETER	1	0	To NEWTON ABBOT	1	9

These Tickets will be available for return on day of Outward Journey by any train.

Parcels and Goods traffic will not be dealt with at the Halt.

Paddington,
January, 1928.

FELIX J. C. POLE,
General Manager.

platform 100ft. in length with a nondescript tin shelter. Passengers without tickets, joining the train at the halt, are booked by the guard. No parcels or goods are dealt with. The guard of the last train calling at the halt is responsible for extinguishing the lights on the platform, and at the top of the nearby steps. The actual halt is 2 miles from Dunsford and it was here that a proposed line to Chagford would have connected.

After Dunsford Halt, our train continues to climb slowly along the shoulder of the hill, through Britton Park and Oxen Park to Midwinter Park and Cotley Wood, where it enters Culver Tunnel. With its gas lamps still flickering, the train emerges from the tunnel into beautiful woodlands and Longdown Station, the highest point on the line. Officially, Longdown does not appear to exist. The name is apparently a description applied to a ridge of hills, stretching from Bakers Hill to Culver Estate, in the parish of Holcombe Burnell. Only in the eyes of the Railway Company, Bus Company, and the Post Office does Longdown exist! It is a most picturesque, red brick-built, station, situated on a curve deeply enfolded in woods between two tunnels, 1 mile from the village. A well-wooded embankment rises behind the station, and leads to Perridge Tunnel. It has a small ground level signal box, and prior to World War II, it had a short loop siding, about 90ft. long between clearance points, and was a 'conditional' goods stop. It appears that the most important freight was the wagon which brought coal for Culver House. Passenger traffic, like so many of these stations, consists of a few commuters to Exeter, and some schoolchildren. In addition to his signalling duties, the signalman acts as booking clerk and porter; he also tends the station garden,

2–6–2T No. 5536 prepares to leave Longdown Station with the 4.35p.m. Exeter to Heathfield train on 28th May 1958.

R. A. Lumber

The approach to Perridge Tunnel, viewed from the platform of Longdown Station on 1st February 1958.

E. R. Shepherd

and in the summer, passengers can often see fresh flowers for sale. A well near the station provides water for the toilets, whilst drinking water is brought by train from Trusham. World War II brought a new lease of life to the line, and its importance as an avoiding line was realized. During the war, when enemy attack seemed inevitable, a passing loop was put in. If, in the event of enemy action, either by sea or air, the sea wall between Starcross and Teignmouth was destroyed, an alternative route was available to Plymouth and Cornwall. It was, in fact, often used when the main line was blocked, mostly by storm damage. The passing loop had remained until 1957. Even the famous 'Cornish Riviera' has been known to use this alternative route. This was not an easy task, on a severely graded single line with its gradients of 1 in 56, and heavy trains generally had to be banked to Longdown, from both directions. In the 'forties a large military hospital was built near Heathfield, and ambulance trains often used the line out of Exeter, almost always at night and in total darkness.

Ide Halt, on 1st September 1958.

Michael Hale

Alphington Halt, which was not opened until 2nd April 1928. The view is towards Heathfield and the photograph was taken on 22nd June 1950.

E. R. Shepherd

City Basin Junction, Exeter, on the approach to the main line to Paddington.
Michael Hale

St. Thomas Station, Exeter, illustrating the distinctive Brunelian roof.
Michael Hale

Immediately after pulling out of Longdown Station, the entrance to Perridge Tunnel appears. Many years ago, someone committed suicide in the tunnel, and during the process was decapitated. Rumour was that a headless ghost was reputed to haunt the station end of Perridge Tunnel, although no-one claims to have actually seen it.

On emerging from the tunnel, our train travels through Perridge Woods, past Perridge House, through Pond Field and Ide Brake, crossing Holscombe Lane, where the deepest cutting is about 50ft. It eventually arrives at Ide Halt which, until 1956, had been designated a station and had had double-ended sidings. These, however, had then been taken up and the station demoted to a halt, appearing on subsequent timetables as such. The original small brick building remains as a shelter. It is quite an important little halt, used by villagers travelling to Exeter to work and to shop, and unlike so many of the stations on this line, it is close to the centre of the village. Just outside stands the 'Railway Inn'.

Leaving Ide Halt, our train crosses the bridge over Ide Lane into beautiful open unspoiled countryside, flanked by trees and blackberry bushes; Constitutional Hill dividing the countryside from Exeter to the left. Alphin Brook runs alongside, with the rolling hills of Haldon to the right and Belvedere standing sentinel. The next and penultimate stop is the timber-built Alphington Halt, which was not opened until 2nd April 1928, but served a village which was fast growing. The halt is reached by a track from a foot-path and, like Dunsford, the platform is 100ft. in length, and, as at Dunsford, the same rules for purchasing tickets apply. Similarly, the guard of the last train is responsible for extinguishing the lights.

Beyond Alphington, our train travels through Marsh Barton to join the main Paddington to Penzance line at City Basin Junction, and into Exeter St. Thomas Station.

So the journey through the Teign Valley branch line ends with just over 16 miles of railway, through some of the most beautiful scenery in the country, having been traversed in about 55 minutes.

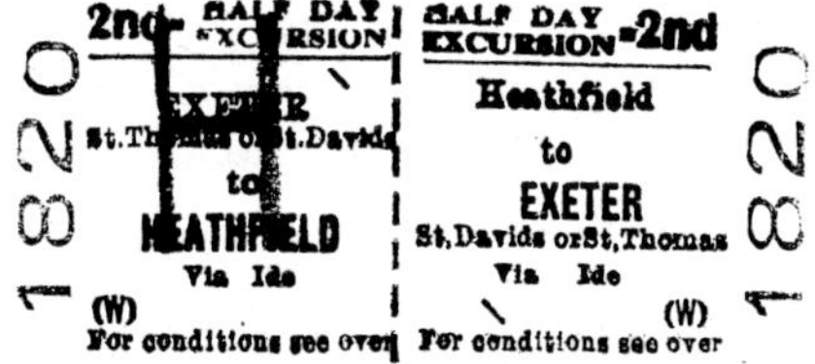

Heathfield to Exeter.

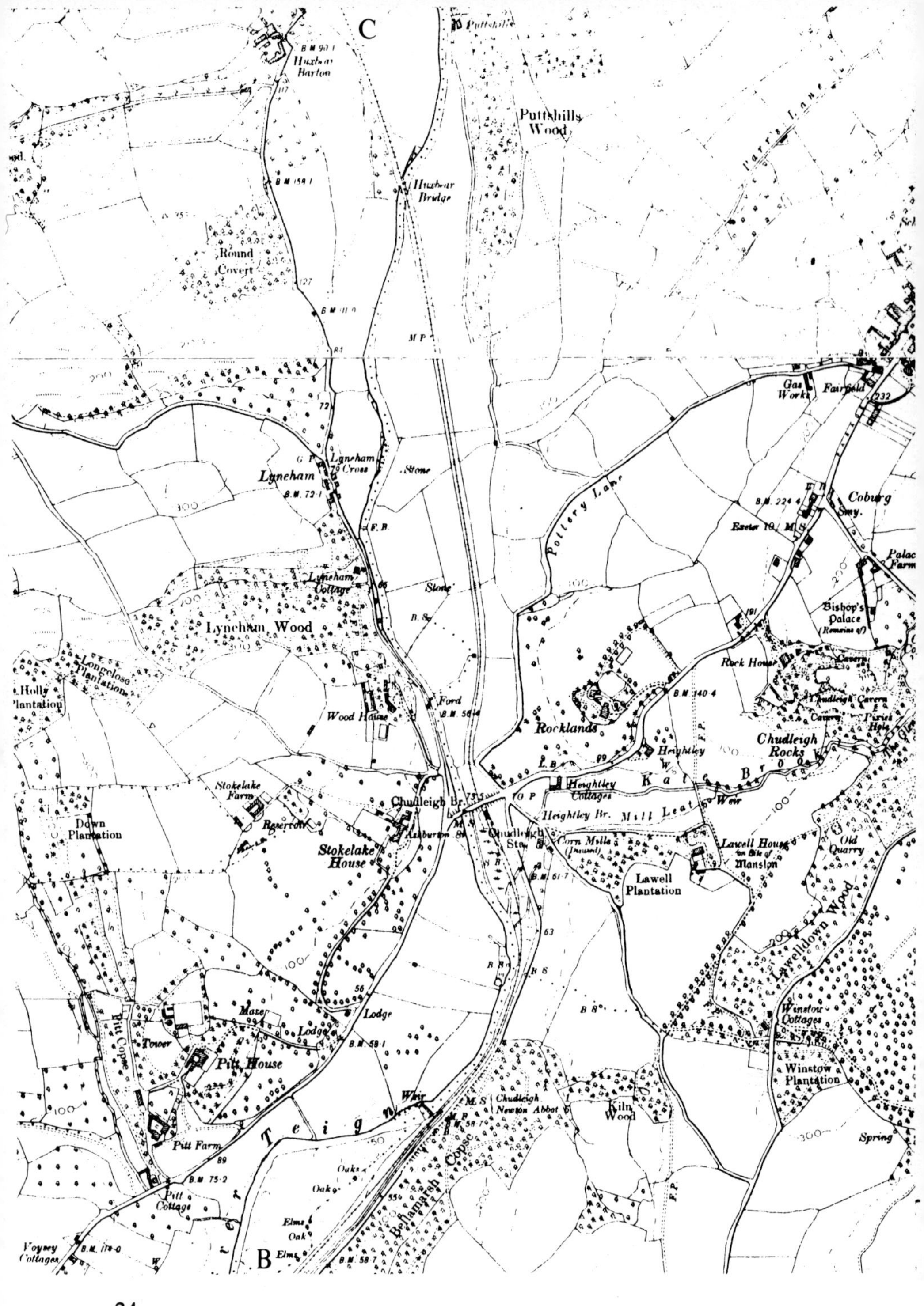
C
Huxbear Barton
Puttshills Wood
Parr's Lane
Huxbear Bridge
Round Covert
Gas Works
Fairfield
Lyneham
Lyneham Cross
Stone
Pottery Lane
Coburg
Lyneham Cottage
Lyneham Wood
Palace Farm
Bishop's Palace (Remains of)
Longclose Plantation
Holly Plantation
Rock House
Chudleigh Cavern
Pixies Hole
Chudleigh Rocks
Ford
Wood House
Rocklands
Heightley
Kate Brook
Stokelake Farm
Reservoir
Chudleigh Br.
Heightley Cottages
Heightley Br.
Mill Leat
Weir
Down Plantation
Stokelake House
Chudleigh Stn.
Corn Mills
Lawell House on Site of Mansion
Lawell Plantation
Old Quarry
Lawelldown Wood
Lodge
Maze
Pitt Copse
Tower
Pitt House
Winstow Cottages
Winstow Plantation
Kiln Wood
Pitt Farm
Teign
Weir
Spring
Pitt Cottage
Bellamarsh Copse
Voysey Cottages
B

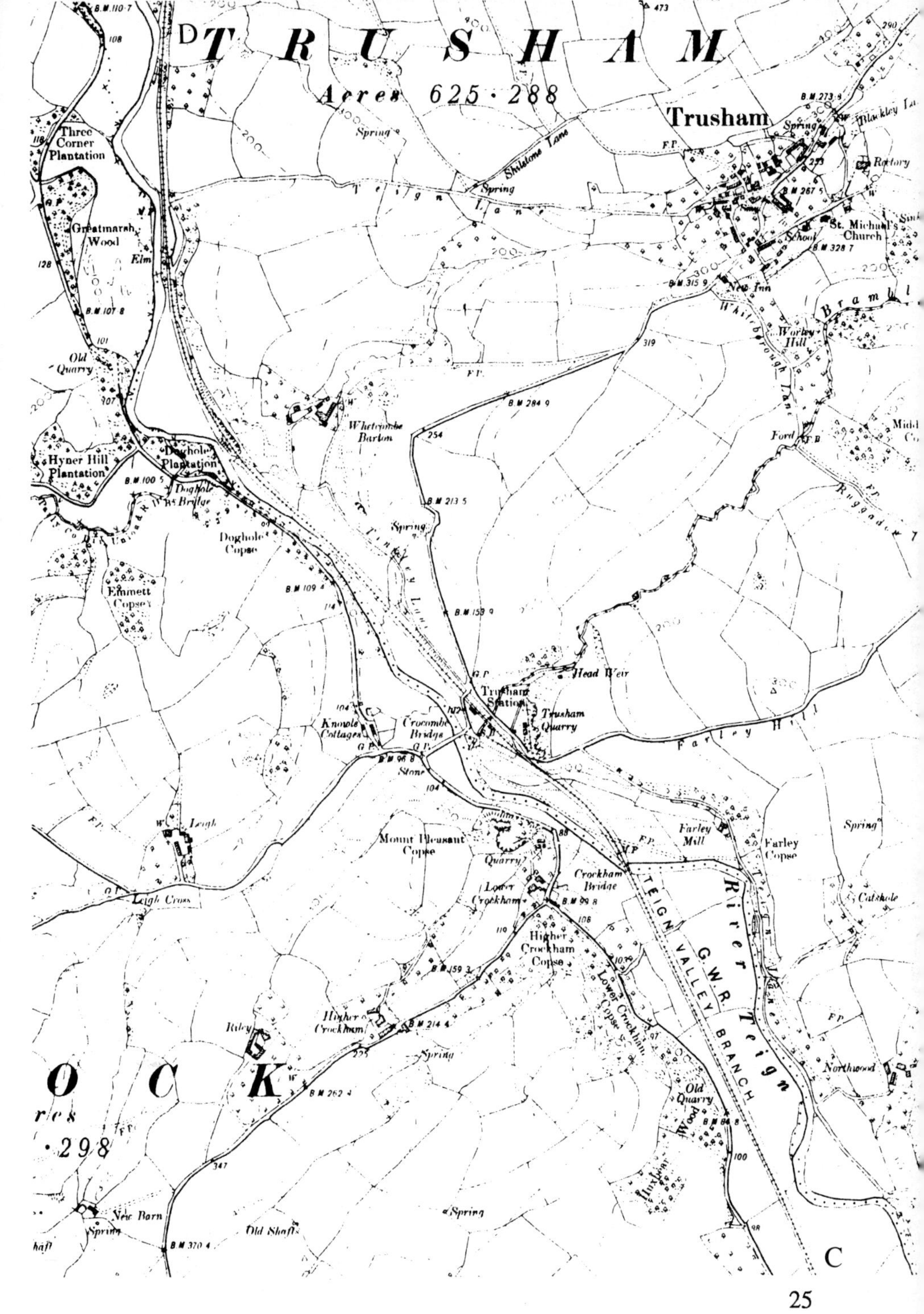
TRUSHAM
Acres 625·288
Trusham
Three Corner Plantation
Greatmarsh Wood
Old Quarry
Hyner Hill Plantation
Doghole Plantation
Doghole Bridge
Doghole Copse
Emmett Copse
Whitcombe Barton
Shilstone Lane
Teign Lane
Spring
Rectory
St. Michael's Church
School
New Inn
Worley Hill
Ford
Head Weir
Trusham Station
Trusham Quarry
Farley Hill
Knowle Cottages
Crocombe Bridge
Stone
Leigh
Leigh Cross
Mount Pleasant Copse
Quarry
Lower Crockham
Crockham Bridge
Higher Crockham Copse
Lower Crockham Copse
Higher Crockham
Riley
Farley Mill
Farley Copse
Catshole
River Teign
TEIGN VALLEY G.W.R. BRANCH
Northwood
Old Quarry Wood
New Barn
Old Shafts
OCK
·298
C

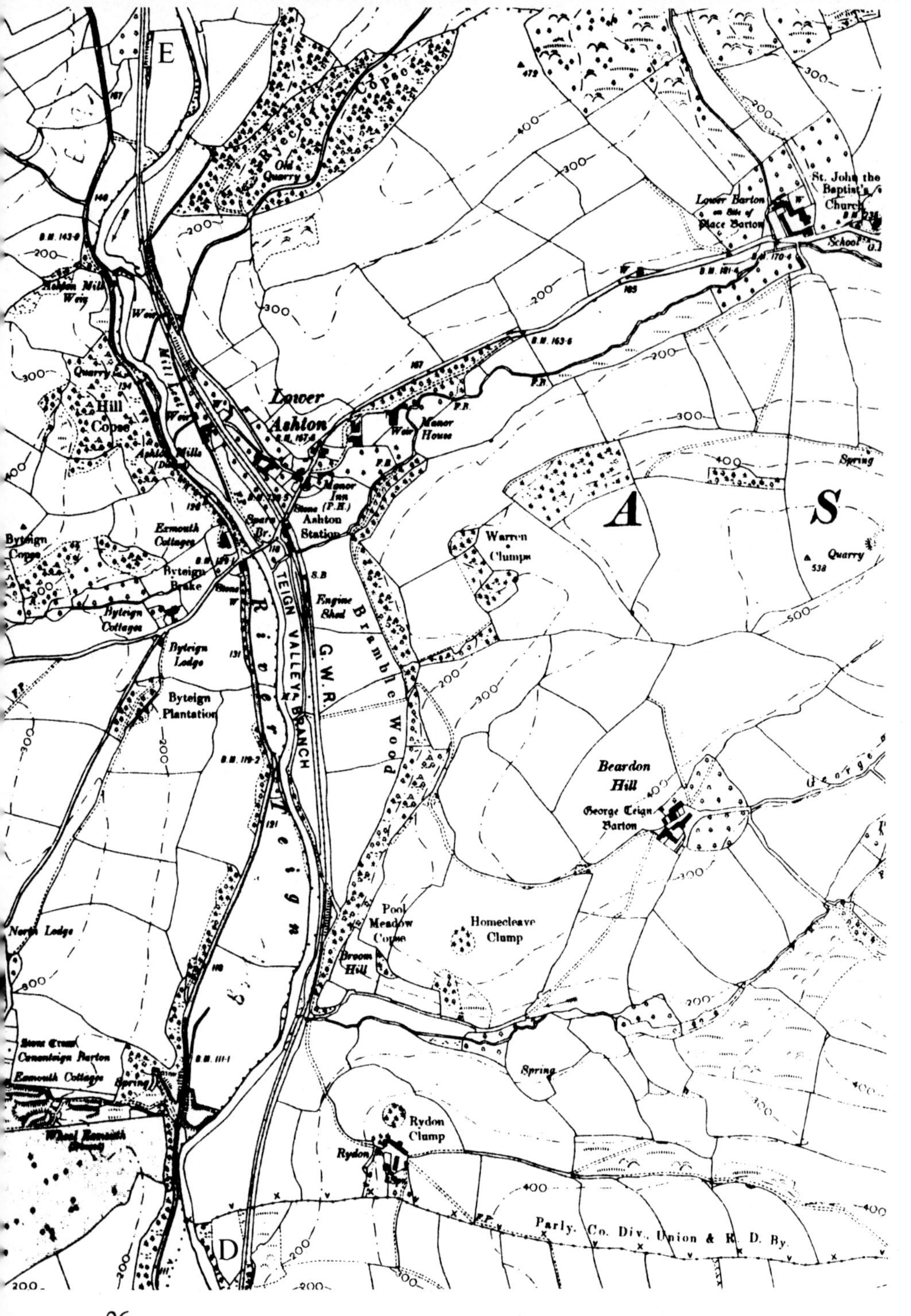
E
Rycroft Copse
Old Quarry
St. John the Baptist's Church
Lower Barton on Site of Place Barton
School
Ashton Mill Weir
Weir
Mill Leat
Quarry
Hill Copse
Lower Ashton
Weir
Manor House
Ashton Mills
Manor Inn
Stone (P.H.)
Ashton Station
Exmouth Cottages
Byteign Copse
Byteign Brake
Byteign Cottages
Byteign Lodge
Byteign Plantation
Engine Shed
TEIGN VALLEY BRANCH
G.W.R.
River Teign
Bramble Wood
A
S
Warren Clumps
Quarry
Spring
Beardon Hill
George Teign Barton
Pool Meadow Copse
Homecleave Clump
Broom Hill
North Lodge
Stone Cross
Canonteign Barton
Exmouth Cottages
Spring
Rydon Clump
Rydon
D
Parly. Co. Div. Union & R. D. By.

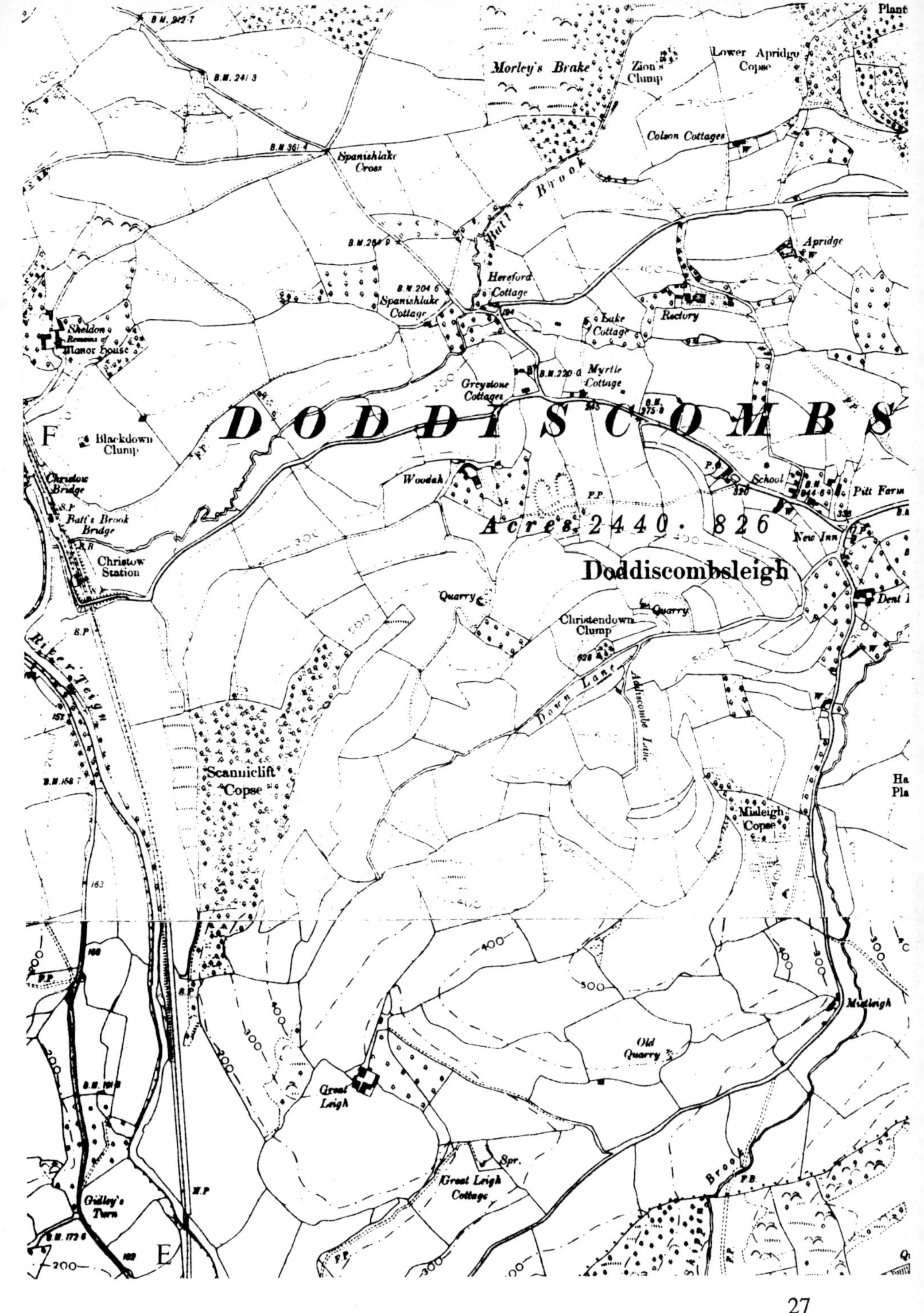

Plant
Morley's Brake
Zion Clump
Lower Apridge Copse
Colson Cottages
Spanishlake Cross
Batt's Brook
Apridge
Hereford Cottage
Spanishlake Cottage
Lake Cottage
Rectory
Sheldon
Remains of Manor House
Greystone Cottages
Myrtle Cottage
DODDISCOMBS
F
Blackdown Clump
Christow Bridge
Woodah
School
Pitt Farm
Batt's Brook Bridge
Acres 2440 · 826
New Inn
Christow Station
Doddiscombsleigh
Quarry
Christendown Clump
Dent
River Teign
Down Lane
Scanniclift Copse
Misleigh Copse
Mistleigh
Old Quarry
Great Leigh
Spr.
Great Leigh Cottage
Brook
Gidley's Turn
E

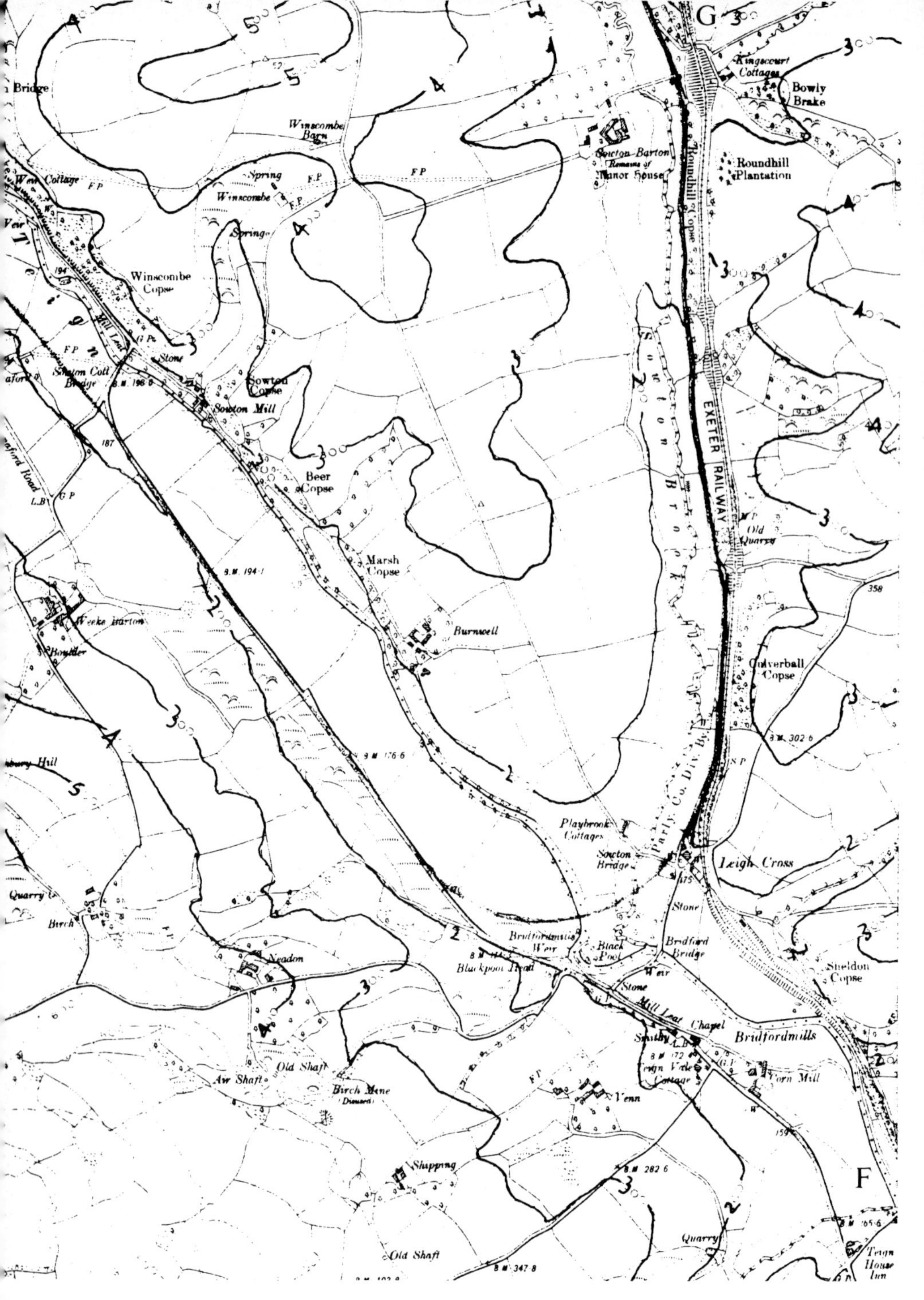

Winscombe Barn
Spring
Winscombe
Weir Cottage
Winscombe Copse
Mill Leat
Sowton Copse
Sowton Mill
Beer Copse
Marsh Copse
Burnwell
Weeke Barton
Sowton Barton
Remains of Manor House
Roundhill Plantation
Kingscourt Cottages
Bowly Brake
EXETER RAILWAY
Old Quarry
Culverball Copse
Playbrook Cottages
Sowton Bridge
Leigh Cross
Bridfordmills Weir
Black Pool
Bridford Bridge
Blackpool Head
Neadom
Mill Leat
Chapel
Bridfordmills
Smithy
Teign Vale Cottage
Corn Mill
Sheldon Copse
Old Shaft
Birch Mine
Venn
Shipping
Quarry
Teign House Inn
Birch
G
F

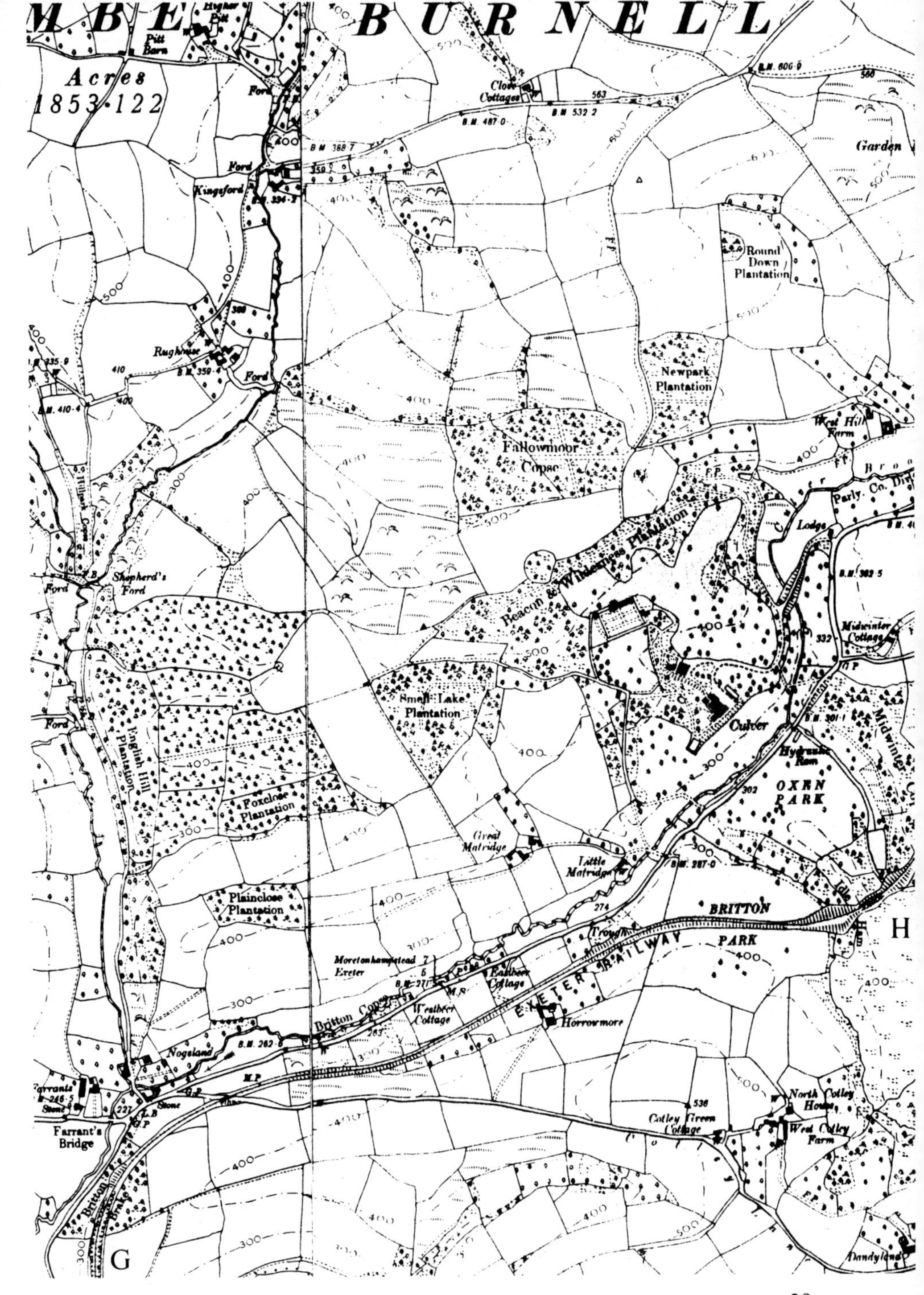

BURNELL
Acres
1853·122
Higher Pitt
Pitt Barn
Ford
Kingsford
Rughouse
Close Cottages
Garden
Round Down Plantation
Newpark Plantation
West Hill Farm
Fallowmoor Copse
Beacon & Wilderness Plantation
Shepherd's Ford
Lodge
Parly. Co. Div.
Midwinter Cottage
Culver
Small Lake Plantation
English Hill Plantation
Foxclose Plantation
Hydraulic Ram
OXEN PARK
Great Matridge
Little Matridge
Plainclose Plantation
BRITTON PARK
Trough
EXETER RAILWAY
Moretonhampstead 7
Exeter 5
Eastbeer Cottage
Westbeer Cottage
Britton Copse
Horrowmore
Nogeland
Farrants
Stone
Farrant's Bridge
North Cotley House
West Cotley Farm
Cotley Green Cottage
Dandyland
Britton Drake
G
H

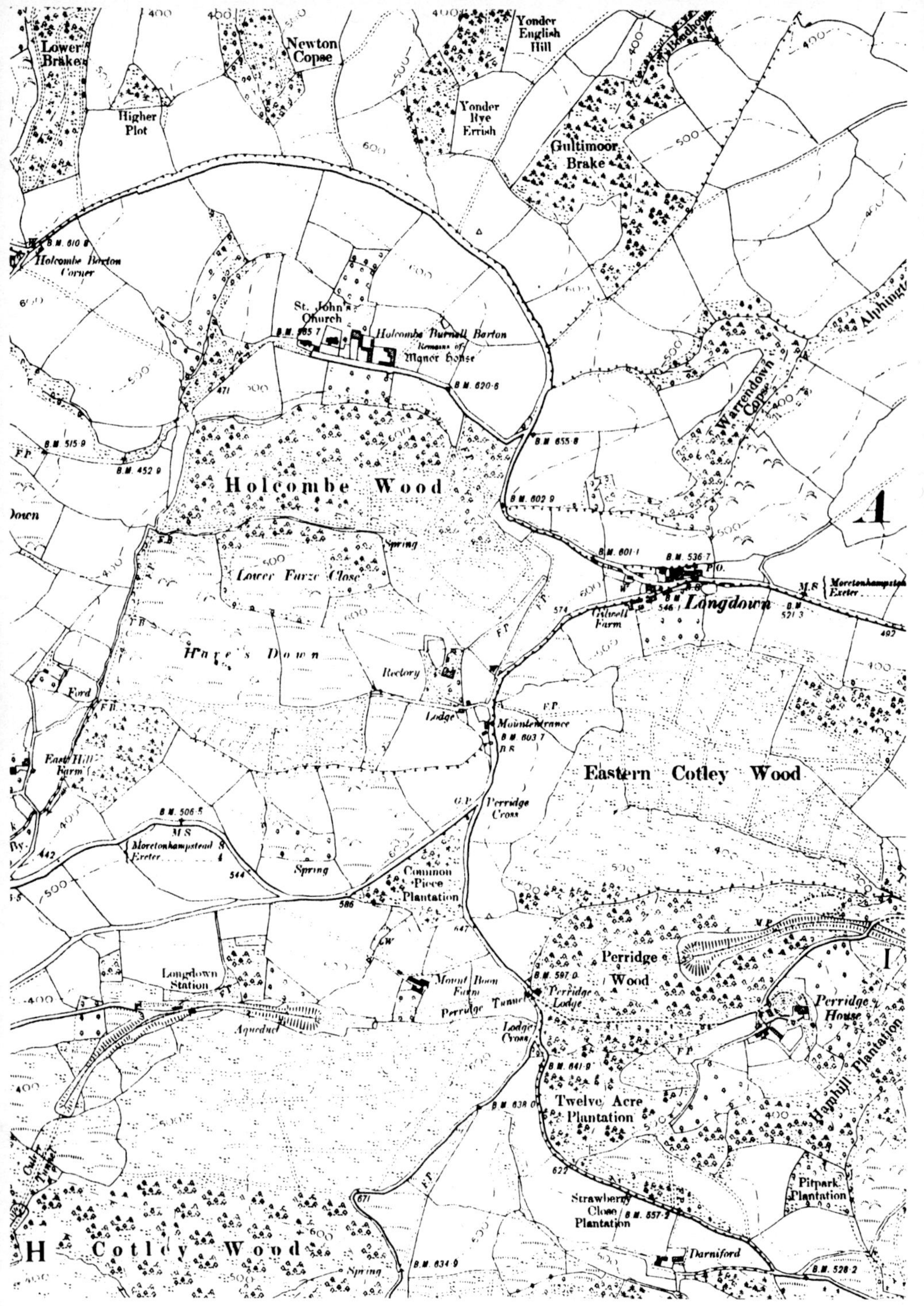

Lower Brakes
Newton Copse
Yonder English Hill
Higher Plot
Yonder Rye Errish
Gultimoor Brake
Holcombe Barton Corner
St. John's Church
Holcombe Burnell Barton
Remains of Manor House
Warrendown Copse
Holcombe Wood
Lower Furze Close
Longdown
Gilwell Farm
Hare's Down
Rectory
Ford
Lodge
Mountentrance
East Hill Farm
Eastern Cotley Wood
Perridge Cross
Moretonhampstead
Exeter
Spring
Common Piece Plantation
Perridge Wood
Longdown Station
Mount Boon Farm
Perridge Tunnel
Perridge Lodge
Perridge House
Aqueduct
Lodge Cross
Twelve Acre Plantation
Hamhill Plantation
Pitpark Plantation
Strawberry Close Plantation
Darniford
Cotley Wood

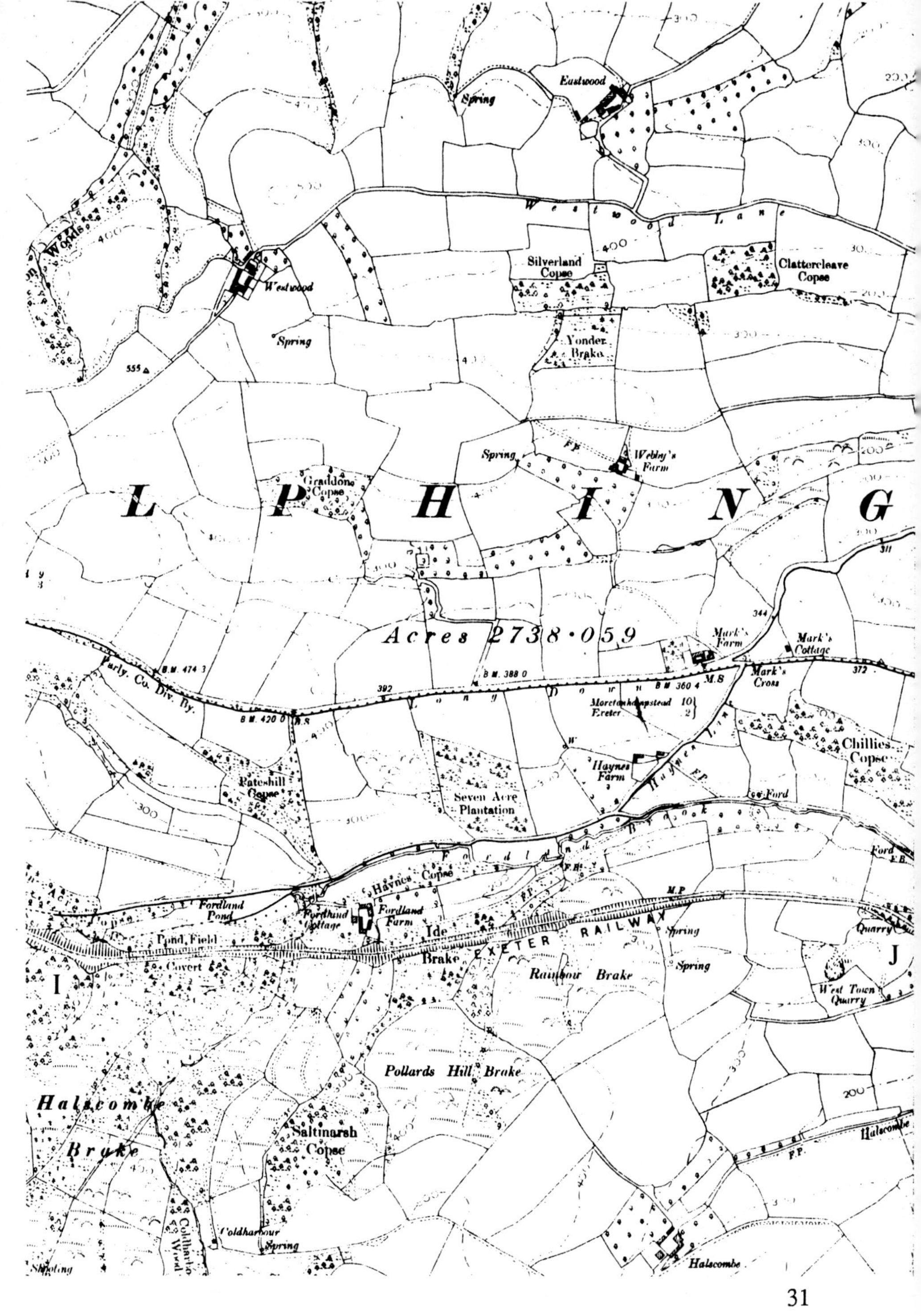
Eastwood
Spring
Westwood
Westwood Lane
Silverland Copse
Clattercleave Copse
Spring
Yonder Brake
555
Spring
Webby's Farm
Graddon Copse
L P H I N G
Acres 2738·059
Mark's Farm
Mark's Cottage
Mark's Cross
Parly. Co. Div. By.
B.M. 474·3
B.M. 420·0
B.M. 388·0
B.M. 360·4
Long Down
Moretonhampstead 10
Exeter 2
Haynes Farm
Chillies Copse
Pateshill Copse
Seven Acre Plantation
Ford
Fordland Pond
Haynes Copse
Fordland Cottage
Fordland Farm
Ide Brake
EXETER RAILWAY
Spring
Quarry
Pond Field Covert
Rainbow Brake
Spring
West Town Quarry
I
J
Pollards Hill Brake
Halscombe Brake
Saltmarsh Copse
Halscombe
Coldharbour Spring
Halscombe

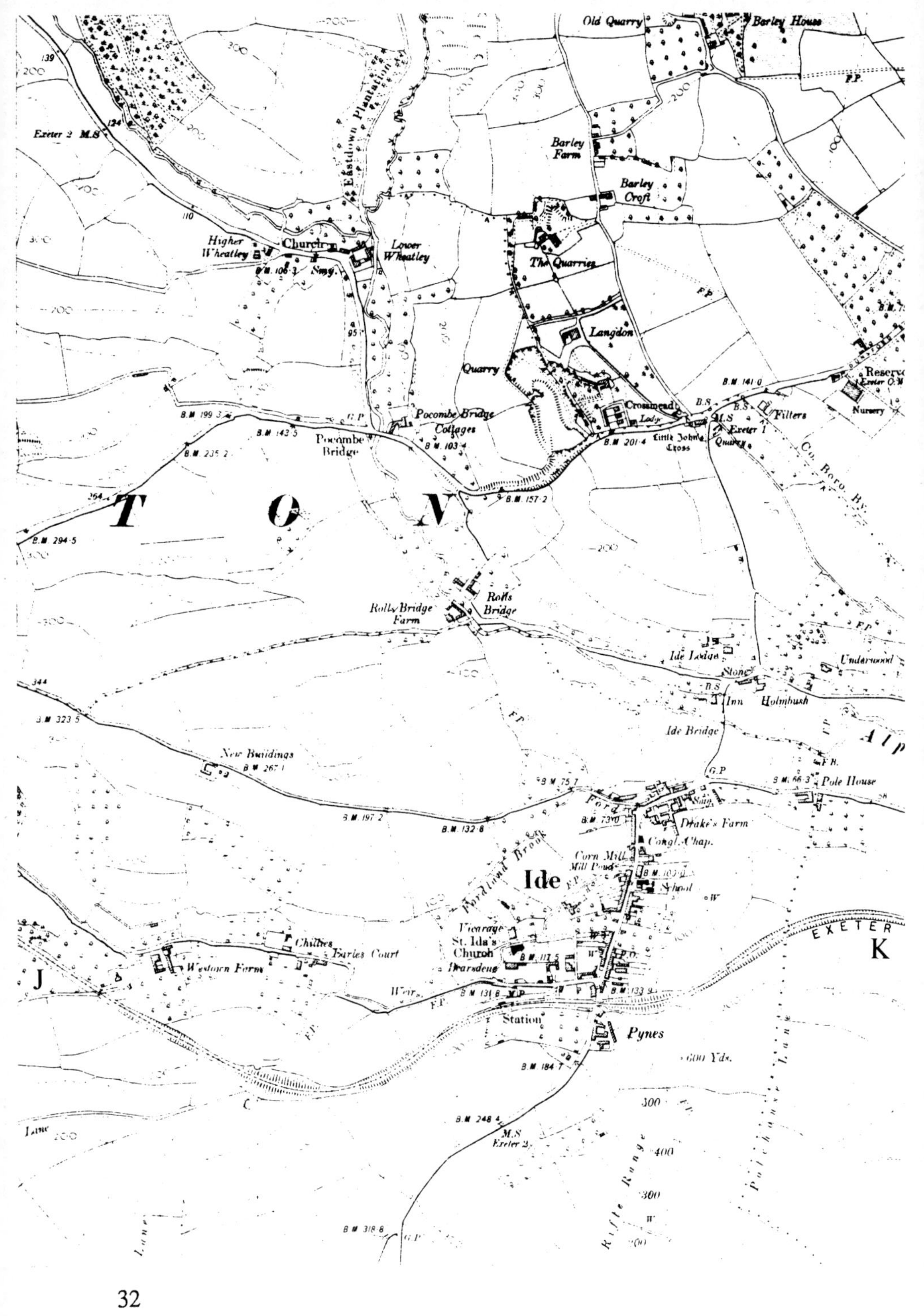
Old Quarry
Barley House
Eastdown Plantation
Exeter 2 M.S
Barley Farm
Barley Croft
Higher Wheatley
Church
Lower Wheatley
The Quarries
Langdon
Quarry
Pocombe Bridge Cottages
Pocombe Bridge
Crossmead
Lodge
Little John's Cross
Filters
Nursery
T O N
Rolls Bridge Farm
Rolls Bridge
Ide Lodge
Stone
Inn
Holmbush
Underwood
Ide Bridge
New Buildings
Pole House
Ford
Drake's Farm
Congl. Chap.
Corn Mill
Mill Pond
School
Ide
Fordland Brook
Vicarage
St. Ida's Church
Chillies
Earles Court
Westown Farm
Station
Pynes
EXETER
K
J
Rifle Range
Pole Lane

Exe Bridge
Ferry
Timber Yard
Slip
Quay
Maltho.
Electricity Works
Engineering Works
South Devon Nursery
Haven Banks
Thomas
Brewery
Gas Works
Swing Bridges
Exe View Cottages
Mission Church
Goods Depot
Cattle Pens
Athletic Ground
The Freehold
Football Ground
Pleasure Grounds
Church
School
Broadmeadow Cottages
Bowhill Gardens
Bowhill
Park House
Franklyn
Haven House
Devon Art Pottery
Nursery
Basin Junction
Filter Bed
Sludge Disposal Works
Exeter Nursery
Spring
Stone Coffin found
Cowick Barton
Cowick Lane
Stonelane Farm
Marsh Barton Lane
Marsh Barton Cottage
Cedar Cottage
Newlands House
Hatherleigh House
Devon Cottage
Manor House
Saint Hill House
Marsh Barton
On Site of St. Mary's Priory
Ball's Farm
Ford
The Briars
Weir
The Elms
Cross
Rock Ho.
Belleville House
Mill Lane
Tannery
Clapperbrook Lane
Clapperbrook
Bridge House
Corn Mill
Mrth. Chap.
Alphington
Water Lane
Alphington Lodge
The Cottage
Spring
Church Inst.
School
St. Michael's Church
Sobey's Farm
Rectory
Aldens Farm
Marl Pit
Railway
K

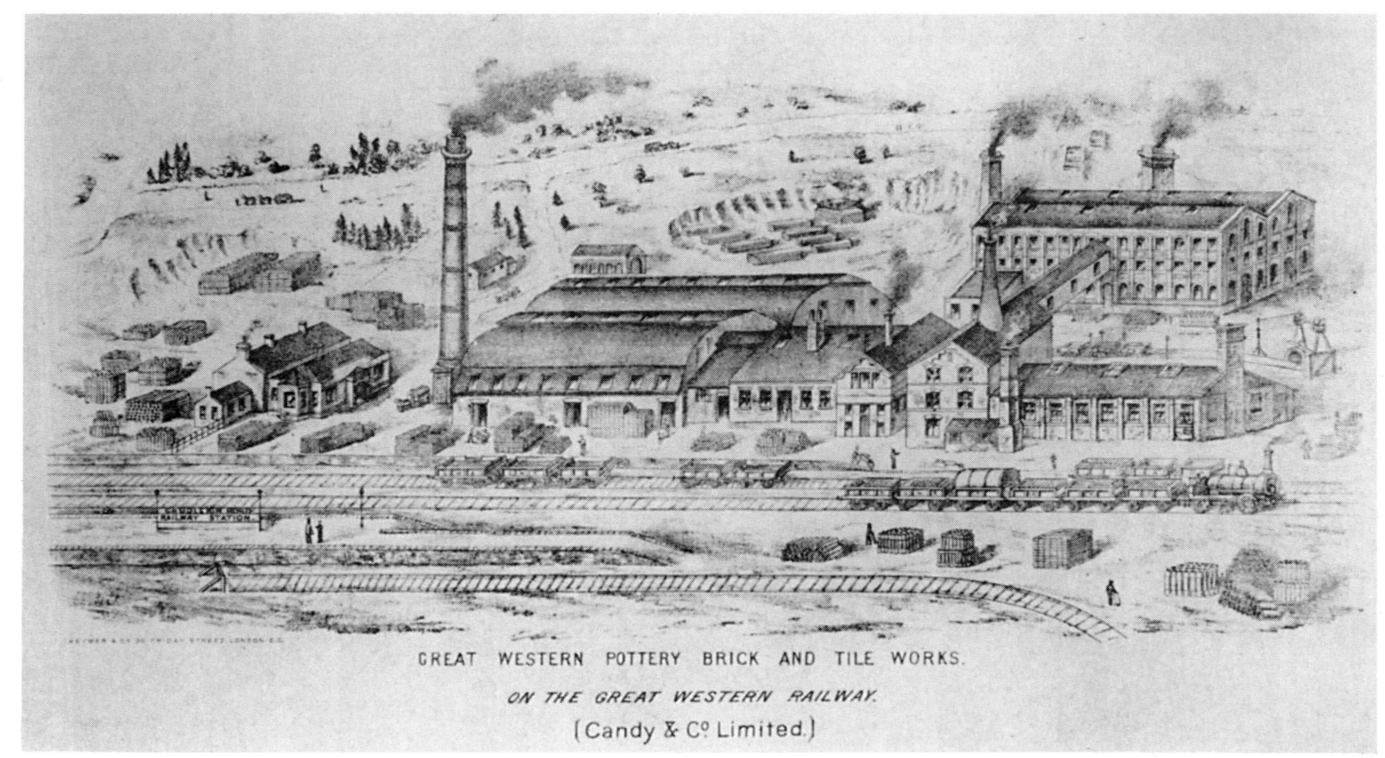

The Great Western Pottery Brick & Tile Works, owned by Candy and Co. Limited. Also pictured is Chudleigh Road Station, on the broad gauge Moretonhampstead branch.

THE TEIGN VALLEY RAILWAY – HISTORY
Part I – The arrival of railways in Devon.

The origin of railways, for the exclusive use of vehicles with flanged wheels, can be traced back to mining practice in medieval Germany, but the development of railways, as a public means of transport, took place entirely in Great Britain.

The first railway opened in Devon on 16th September 1820, and was built by George Templer as a means of transporting stone from quarries owned by him on Haytor Down to other parts of the country, most notably to London for use in the construction of London Bridge. Known as the Haytor Granite Tramway, it was constructed of granite setts, cut with a flange to prevent the flat iron wheels of horse-drawn wagons from leaving the track, and had a gauge of 4ft. 3in. It covered a distance of 8½ miles and had to negotiate a descent of some 1,300 ft. before linking up with the upper terminus of the Stover Canal at Ventiford. There, the granite blocks were off-loaded onto barges and taken down the 2-mile long canal and thence down the Teign estuary to the port of Teignmouth, ready for shipment in sea-going vessels. The canal, itself, had been built in 1792 by James Templer (George Templer's father), principally to improve the means by which local clay bound for the Staffordshire factories and other ports could be transported to the quays of Newton Abbot.

After 1820, a further 24 years were to pass before the first steam train reached Devon. At 12.30 p.m., on 1st May 1844, vast crowds at Exeter welcomed the engine *Actaeon* drawing the six carriages which comprised the train. After a great lunch in the goods shed at St. David's, the return journey to Paddington commenced at 5.30 p.m. Among the passengers on the train was Sir Thomas Ackland, MP; at 10.30 that evening he rose in the House of Commons to say that he had been in Exeter little more than five hours earlier! The Bristol & Exeter Railway had arrived. It had been authorized by Parliament in 1836, at the instigation of a group of Bristol merchants. In the meantime, no sooner had the Act of 1836 been passed than a group of enterprising Plymouth men proposed another railway, to link up at Exeter. Nothing became of this proposal, however, due to lack of support by the Devonshire people to subscribe the necessary capital, and, similarly, several other schemes brought before the public over the next 6 years met with the same fate. By then Isambard Kingdom Brunel had long since surveyed the countryside, and the Haldon range of hills, south-west of Exeter, had compelled him to plan for a line from Exeter to Starcross and along the coast to Dawlish and Teignmouth. Initially, it would then have continued over the River Teign to the neighbourhood of Torquay, thence over the Dart and into the South Hams. But, when the locomotive had shown its capabilities for hill climbing, he had abandoned the idea for a direct run from Teignmouth to Torquay, which would have involved many expensive works, in favour of a line running alongside the Teign estuary to Newton Abbot, and thence over the southern spurs of Dartmoor to Totnes, Ivybridge and Plympton.

Finally, in 1843, the Bristol & Exeter and Great Western Railway companies, together with the Bristol & Gloucester Railway, took up the matter and agreed to subscribe liberally to Brunel's project. This set the project on its feet; in October the prospectus of the Plymouth, Devonport & Exeter Railway – soon to become the South Devon Railway – was issued and the construction of the line was authorized the following July. Furthermore, in less than 2 years, on 30th May 1846, the line was open for traffic as far as Teignmouth and, by the end of that year, it had reached Newton Abbot. Work proceeded, and Plymouth (Laira Green) was reached on 5th May 1848, but this was not its terminus. Mutley Tunnel had to be completed before it reached Millbay, the following year.

The 1860s saw great additions to the railways of Devon. The Moretonhampstead and South Devon Railway was formed by the Earl of Devon, to run from Newton Abbot to Moretonhampstead, 12 1/4 miles away. It was finally opened on 4th July 1866, with stations at Bovey and Lustleigh. Teigngrace was added in December 1867, and Chudleigh Road, in 1874, to be renamed Heathfield in 1882. The line rose from 50 to 588ft., with a maximum gradient of 1 in 50, terminating just below the little market town.

In 1863, the Teign Valley Railway was authorized as a broad gauge line, from the embryo Moretonhampstead & South Devon Railway, to Chudleigh and Doddiscombsleigh.

Part II – (a) The incorporation of the Teign Valley Railway Company in 1863.
(b) 1863 to 1882. Conception to the opening of the line from Heathfield to Ashton, and the siding to Teign House (Christow).

The Act incorporating the Teign Valley Railway Company received Royal Assent on 13th July 1863. It authorized a share capital of £45,000, with borrowing power to the extent of £15,000, for the construction of a railway. It would commence at a junction with the Moretonhampstead & South Devon Railway at Bovey Tracey, and terminate at Doddiscombsleigh. The railway, as authorized by that Act, and a subsequent Act of 1868, was to be 7 miles, 5 furlongs and 1 chain in length.

Before the railway opened it required a total of nine Acts of Parliament, including an Act of 1875, authorizing an extension to Crediton, only to be abandoned by an Act of 1880. The original promoter of the company was Mr William Toogood, a solicitor, and for some time acting manager and secretary of the company. Following his commencement of an action against the company, claiming £20,000, the directors removed Mr Toogood from the position as their adviser, and sought a general account of all monies received by him, and of his dealings with the company's affairs since the commencement of the undertaking. Mr Toogood declined, pending settlement of his claim, to allow access to any papers or documents with the result that the directors subsequently had great difficulty in giving any detailed information as to the early history of the line, as proposed, prior to 1877.

In 1877, a vigorous attempt was made to revive the company and complete the line. A contract was entered into with a Mr Walker, the contractor, to complete the line for £30,000, of which £13,000 was to be paid in cash, and the balance of £17,000 in No. 1 preference shares. Negotiations were entered into to obtain the land, which the directors had been repeatedly assured had long previously been acquired, and arrangements to discharge outstanding liabilities were made. Owing partly to the circumstances mentioned in Mr Jenkins' report (see Appendix I), partly to the additional work required by the GWR, and chiefly to the absence of any protection from the creditors' attacks, the effort proved abortive, and by the end of 1880 the undertaking was little more advanced than it had been in 1877.

Meanwhile, as soon as the directors had withdrawn their confidence in Mr Toogood, they were advised to take immediate steps to protect the company from hostile proceedings, and to secure time for a careful investigation of the company's affairs. A bill of sale over all the company's moveable property, and a mortgage over all their lands, was executed in favour of Lord Haldon, who advanced the necessary money to pay a creditor who had actually seized the company's property. Also a scheme was filed in chancery, which made it impossible for anyone to take proceedings without leave of the court.

The directors then instructed the solicitor to ascertain the condition of the line, and the nature and extent of the company's liabilities, and to advise them on the best course to be adopted.

Mr John Fowler, the company's consulting engineer, examined the line and reported that a sum of around £9,000 would be required to complete the line in accordance with the requirements of the GWR and to open it up for public traffic. A separate and independent report was also made by the engineer of the line, Mr S. W. Jenkins, in whom the board had complete confidence. He reported on 7th February 1881, and estimated the cost of completing all outstanding works to be £8,240. This was an increase of £1,740 over the original estimate.

Under the power conferred by the Act of 1880, the company then entered into negotiation with the GWR whereby the GWR were to work the line for 55 per cent of the gross receipts, and the company be paid £12,000 p.a. as a first charge on the gross receipts. The GWR would also complete the authorized extension to Teign House siding, charging the Teign Valley Railway Company 4 per cent on the actual cost.

The officers of the company at this time were:

Board

The Rt. Hon. Lord Haldon – Chairman
The Rt. Hon. E. A. Palk – Deputy Chairman
J. H. Hiley Wm. Kitson
Captain Gerald F. Talbot

Solicitors

Messrs Lake, Beaumont and Lake, 10 Queens Square Place, Westminster

Consulting Engineer

John Fowler, C. E., 2 Queens Square Place, Westminster

Engineer

S. W. Jenkins, C. E., 5 Victoria Street, Westminster

Secretary

J. Hugh Thompson, 33 Norfolk Street, Strand

As a result of the numerous Acts and steps taken under their authority, the capital of the company in March 1881 consisted of:

£24,000 in 5 per cent debentures falling due on 1st July 1882
£40,000 in 8,000 No. 1, 5 per cent preference shares of £5 each
£22,000 in 4,400 No. 2, 5 per cent preference shares of £5 each
£10,000 in 2,000 No. 3, 5 per cent preference shares of £5 each
£20,740 in 1,037 ordinary shares of £20 each

Tot. £116,740

(In addition to this, the company had power under the Act of 1880 to issue shares to the amount of £40,000, and debentures or other securities to the amount of £13,300)

A further scheme of arrangement was framed as work progressed towards completion (somewhat more quickly than hitherto!), and the line finally opened on 9th October 1882. It ran from Heathfield to Ashton, a distance of 6¼ miles, and continued to a remote siding at Teign House, a further 1¼ miles distant, but, being to standard gauge, was completely isolated from the rest of the Great Western system, the Moretonhampstead line not being converted from broad to standard gauge until 23rd May 1892.

A fine view of Heathfield Station in 1921, and the siding leading off into the Great Western pottery and brickworks of Candy & Co. Ltd.

B. Gibson collection

Chudleigh Station in 1905. An 0–4–2 tank of the 517 class leads a five-coach train of 6-wheeled stock from Heathfield.

Chapman & Son
(Courtesy of A. R. Kingdom)

A view of Trusham Station in 1906, with the arrival of a train from Heathfield headed by the then obiquitous 517 class 0–4–2 tank.

Chapman & Son
(Courtesy of A. R. Kingdom)

Another early view of Trusham Station, looking towards Heathfield.

Chapman & Son
(Courtesy of A. R. Kingdom)

An Heathfield-bound train, headed by a 517 class 0–4–2 tank, arrives bunker first at Ashton Station in 1904.

Chapman & Son
(Courtesy of A. R. Kingdom)

Part III – **(a) The incorporation of the Exeter, Teign Valley and Chagford Railway Company in 1883.**
(b) 1883 to 1903. Conception to the opening of the line from Exeter to Teign House (Christow).

A year after the railway reached Teign House siding from Ashton, in 1882, an Act of Parliament was passed authorizing the Exeter, Teign Valley & Chagford Railway Company to construct a line from Exeter to Christow, connecting with the Teign Valley. A company with a capital of £264,000 in shares, and £88,000 in debentures was incorporated "for the purpose of connecting the city and port of Exeter with the existing Teign Valley line." This afforded direct railway communication with Chagford, which was known as the 'Torquay of the Moors', then 4 miles from the nearest railway. By this proposed route there would be a saving of 1 hour 50 minutes between either London or Exeter and Chagford. The length of the proposed line from Exeter, to the already existing line, was thought to be 8 miles, and of the branch line to Chagford, a further 10 miles. Of the first 8 miles from Exeter to the Teign Valley Railway, sufficient land was acquired for the construction of a double line, including bridges, although at that time both sections were to be constructed as single lines. According to the contracts, the railway would serve a population of 46,372, involving a nominal expenditure of £324,000 (£18,000 per mile).

Once the Act had been passed the GWR, with great foresight, was very enthusiastic in their support of the company, which was to their mutual advantage and, indeed, essential to the Exeter, Teign Valley and Chagford Railway Company if it was to prove viable and succeed. In addition to working the main line for 50 per cent of the gross receipts, the GWR would allow rebates estimated to be worth £5,000 a year, plus the free use of its Exeter station until, in effect, the Exeter, Teign Valley & Chagford Railway was earning not less than £10,450 p.a. Estimates of traffic showed net receipts sufficient to pay 3½ to 6 per cent on the share capital, after allowing 4 per cent on the debentures.

The pleasure traffic to the romantic scenery and bracing air of Fingle and Chagford was estimated to be large. The extensive deposits of china and pottery clays, together with barytes, manganese, tin and copper mines, lime works, greenstone and granite quarries in the district, would also be served by the railway. The distance between Exeter and Moretonhampstead would be reduced from 32 to 24½ miles, and between Exeter and Chagford from 37 to 18 miles.

By means of this company's proposed line to Chagford, yet another line was proposed from Chagford to the then South Western Railway at Okehampton. The GWR would then be 28 miles nearer Bude, that charming Cornish resort where the South Western Railway was busy constructing a railway. Another very important feature was that the new line would be an alternative through route between Exeter and Plymouth, and that by means of proposed railways from Heathfield to Brent, via the Buckfastleigh Railway, it would become a part of the shortest route to Plymouth.

On 1st November 1887 the *Daily Western Times* reported that, on the previous Friday, the Mayor of Exeter had presided at a meeting held at the Guildhall for the purpose of considering a proposal for the immediate construction of the authorized line of railway through the Teign Valley. Those present included the Sheriff of Exeter, Revds F. P. Buckingham, D. B. Clark and J. Bartlett, Major Vanrenen, Messrs F. D. Fulford of Great Fulford, F. Fulford, H. D. Thomas of Exeter, J. E. C. Walkey, S. Jones, J. C. Tuckwell, J. Ponsford of Drewsteignton, E. Wreford of Exeter, Mr Croot of Chudleigh, J. M. Martin, C. E. J. Scanes of Ide, and many other notable and affected persons. Mr C. Hayter-Hames of Chagford and J. L. Thomas of Exeter, were unable to attend, in consequence of other engagements.

The Mayor, Mr A. Burch, in opening the proceedings, said that some time ago an Act of Parliament was passed for the construction of a railway from Exeter to Christow, to join the Teign Valley line, and to proceed from there to Chagford. For reasons which he thought to be mainly pecuniary, the railway had not been constructed, and the time allowed for its completion was rapidly running out. He understood that an offer had been made by a substantial firm of contractors to construct the railway at terms favourable to the shareholders. It was, therefore, up to those interested in the trade and commerce of Exeter, and its neighbourhood, to decide whether they would give the necessary support to enable the company to accept the offer which had been made. He thought that there was no question of the desirability of bringing the important district of Moreton and Chagford in direct communication with Exeter.

Mr W. Lidstone, engineer to the company, was called upon to explain the scheme, which he did with the assistance of a map of the district. As all present were aware, many previous schemes had been submitted to connect Exeter and the Teign Valley with Chagford, and it was his good fortune to be connected with nearly all of them in a similar capacity to that which he now occupied. Not only could he bring into use his knowledge as an engineer, but that of what had been done before. The defects of many of the former schemes accounted for their failure. He then went on to outline the proposed route, decided by the directors. Leaving Exeter, the line went straight to Alphington Cross, round the Ide Valley, running up to the top of the village of Ide, where there would be a station. The line would then take the course of the Ide Valley until it came to Perridge, where there would have to be a tunnel through the Haldon Hills of approximately 700 yards in length, and then on to the Teign Valley line. The upward gradient was 1 in 60, and the downward gradient was slightly shallower. The other gradients were very easy. They would, in effect, have a line of 8 miles in length with very easy grades and very good curves.

They went to Parliament at a very good time to get an Act, for they found that the GWR, instead of offering opposition, was ready to help them, to hold out a hand and give them every facility. The consequence was that they obtained a very excellent working agreement with that company.

Although the GWR was able to meet them on amicable terms with regard to the first section of the line, they were not so generous regarding the Chagford branch, because they already took passengers to Chagford by bus, and did not want that trade interfered with. But this would be no detriment to the scheme.

Many questions were asked; would, on completion of the line, the GWR use the same gauge between Moreton and Newton Abbot and on to Torquay? Because, if not, it would be a great restriction on the goods traffic using the proposed line. Would there be a station at Alphington? Would there be goods traffic to and from Alphington, at the reasonable penny fare? Under the present system of the GWR, it was 1¼d a mile. If trains were run at 1d a mile, the company would gain in the long run.

Mr Lidstone said that in a short time pressure would be brought to bear on the GWR, which would induce them to lay down a narrow gauge line from Bovey to Torquay, which would obviously be to the advantage of the Torquay people. Regarding the station at Alphington, he pointed out that there would be a station at Ide, and it was a little uncertain whether another at Alphington would pay. Still, it was a matter for consideration, and any evidence that could be brought to show the potential amount of traffic would be very valuable and would receive every attention. (In fact, there later was a halt at Alphington). He did not think that the GWR would charge more than a 1d a mile, because they never did on the branches, although they did on the main line.

The Sheriff, Mr G. Colson moved – 'That this meeting is satisfied of the importance of the proposed Exeter, Teign Valley & Chagford Railway which has been authorized by Act of Parliament, and for the construction of which an offer has been received from Messrs Naylor Bros. of Huddersfield, and pledges itself to use its best endeavours to raise the required local subscription of £30,000'. He had been given to understand that the mineral resources of the country, which it was proposed to open up, were very considerable. These included iron-ore of very high quality, silver-lead, manganese and barytes being found in large quantities, to say nothing of granite and other stone, with which the district abounded.

Mr Peters, in seconding the motion, remarked that everyone interested in the commerce of the city should support the Teign Valley Railway. He thought the trade of the canal would be very much benefited, as vessels would then be able to take, in return freights, some of the mineral resources of the district. The resolution was carried unanimously.

Mr. H. Gadd, of Exeter, moved – 'That the following gentlemen be requested to act as a committee to canvas for shares on account of such local subscription and otherwise to further the proposed undertaking, viz: the Mayor, the Sheriff, Messrs W. Peter, S. Jones, J. L. Thomas, H. F. Willey, E. Knapman, W. Pring, W. Easton, J. C. Tuckwell, C. Rowe, C. J. Ross, H. Tapscott, W. Wreyford, J. H. Stanbury, C. Edwards, A. Clements, A. Batt, G. Finch, J. East and W. Norton, with powers to add to their numbers. Mr Gadd remarked that they had heard of the Teign Valley Railway so long, until they had got tired of the title, but if they could proceed from words to acts, Exeter would be benefited. He noticed that the firm who had offered to construct the railway were extremely liberal; the arrangement was that for every £8,000 worth of work, they were to receive £1,000 only in cash which meant that the remaining £7,000 in paper would be absolutely worthless unless the line opened for traffic. They had a very tangible guarantee for the completion of the work. It was essential that there should be a personal canvass, in order to get the £30,000 subscribed.

Mr Easton, of Exeter, in seconding, said that for a long time he had thought Exeter must be asleep in allowing a railway to terminate in a field within 7 miles of the city – a railway leading to a most valuable valley, rich in all sorts of minerals and stones.

Mr Edward Knapman, also of Exeter, proposed a vote of thanks to the Mayor, and said that some years ago they had held a very animated meeting in the city, and then there were rival parties wanting to carry out work on the line. He hoped that there would be no opposition to this line, and that in a short time they would see it successfully carried out.

Mr F. D. Fulford, of Great Fulford, in seconding the vote, said that as a resident in the county, as well as a Freeman of Exeter, he had considerable experience in the promotion of railways to connect Exeter with the Teign Valley. Unfortunately, all those schemes had only got to the committee stage. But now the only thing was to accept the favourable offer made to the directors. The vote was carried, and the Mayor briefly replied, after which the meeting separated.

Seven years after the Guildhall meeting, on 2nd August 1894, a local firm of stockbrokers, W. Mortimer of 14 Bedford Circus, Exeter, issued a prospectus of the Exeter, Teign Valley and Chagford Railway Company. In this document, they stated that the undertaking would be of much interest to all classes in the district, opening up to both traders and pleasure seekers alike, the prospect of a profitable and increasing trade in a locality noted for its charming scenery.

The response to this appeal for investors proved so satisfactory that, despite the supporters having almost lost all hope of the construction of the proposed line, which it was originally hoped to get carried out in Jubilee Year, Parliamentary powers were obtained. A board of directors was composed of Mr David F. Carmichael (Chairman), Lord Exmouth, Lord Norreys, the Hon. C. N. Knatchbull-Hugessen and Messrs Thomas Correy and W. Pring. A contract was entered into with Messrs James and John Dickinson, with whom such favourable terms were made, that a promise could be held of the work being commenced forthwith.

On 7th November 1894, Lady Northcote, wife of the Member of Parliament for Exeter, cut the first sod.

Like all such major enterprises of today, work was not allowed to proceed without its objectors, and on 20th February 1896, *The Times* published a letter of objection from a resident on the route of the line, to which the Hon. C. M. Knatchbull-Hugessen replied on 25th February 1896. The letters were as follows:

EXETER, TEIGN VALLEY, AND CHAGFORD RAILWAY

TO THE EDITOR OF THE TIMES

Sir – Mr Knatchbull-Hugessen thinks I must have private reasons for pointing out the misrepresentations contained in his company's prospectus. Let me tell him, therefore, publicly what my reasons are. (1) I object to a beautiful landscape being spoilt to all time by the banks and cuttings of an abandoned railway; (2) I object to widows and country parsons being encouraged to throw their money into a hole in a hillside; and (3) I object to railway enterprise in England being discredited by one more fiasco of the Didcot and Newbury or Hull and Barnsley character. I am perfectly aware that the inhabitants of Exeter are very anxious to see the line made. Naturally so, for its construction would render once more tributary to the Exeter market a considerable district which the existing Teign Valley line now drains into the market of Newton Abbot. If the inhabitants of Exeter will either themselves make or induce the Great Western Company to make this new line I have not a word to say. But when the outside public are invited to subscribe they are entitled to be told the actual facts. These facts are that the Exeter, Teign Valley, and Chagford Railway was sanctioned by Act of Parliament as long ago as 1883; that under the powers of the present Act of 1894 the first sod was cut in November 1894; that in the 14 months since then a mile and a half of simple and straightforward earthwork has been finished up to formation level; but that the difficult portion of the work has not even been touched. If, knowing this, would-be subscribers agree with Mr Knatchbull-Hugessen in thinking it likely that in the course of the next 18 months a long tunnel, with railway access from one end only, can be driven and completed, and after its completion four miles of line, including a junction on an embankment with the main line of the Great Western, can be taken in hand and completed also, why then by all means let them subscribe their money. But when directors state in generalities that considerable progress has been made in 14 months, and that therefore the whole may be expected to be completed in 18 months more, it is surely fair comment to add this particular fact, that certainly not more than 5 per cent of the work has been accomplished, and that therefore, at the present rate of progress, the line might be expected to be open for traffic about 1920.

I am, Sir, yours obediently,
A resident on the route of the line

EXETER, TEIGN VALLEY, AND CHAGFORD RAILWAY COMPANY

TO THE EDITOR OF THE TIMES

Sir, – Perhaps you will kindly allow me, as chairman of this railway, to reply to your correspondent in today's issue who signs himself 'A Resident on the Route of the Line,' and who is, I venture to suggest, not particularly anxious, for some private reason, to see the line completed.

He throws doubt on the statement that considerable progress has been made with the works, for the reason that only about 1½ miles of the 8 miles of work between Exeter and Lee-cross have been completed. He apparently is unaware that progress in the case of railway construction is not to be measured by the linear yard, but rather by the cubic yard of heavy earthwork in cuttings or on embankments completed. A visit to the cutting and other works in the neighbourhood of Lee-cross would, in the light of the above fact, enable him to see that the statement in the prospectus to which he takes exception is amply justified. As to the tunnel, it is true that the company's Act of Parliament requires the works to be begun at the Lee-cross end of the line, but how this fact affects the general position I do not see. Your correspondent seems to doubt the statement that the directors expect the line to be completed and ready for traffic within 18 months from the date of this issue. That further capital is required is evidenced by the fact that we are asking for it. I may inform your correspondent that the contractors, Messrs James and John Dickson, of London, have undertaken to complete the line, including, of course, the tunnel, on allotment of this issue being made, which will only take place in the event of at least half of this issue being subscribed for; the rest of the contract price being supplied by the issue to them of fully-paid shares and of cash to be realized by issue of debenture. If your correspondent, instead of occupying his time in writing an anonymous letter, had attended the public meeting called yesterday by the Mayor of Exeter in support of the railway, at which a unanimous resolution was passed in favour of the scheme, any doubts as to local opinion on the subject of the railway would have been laid at rest, a satisfactory answer would have been given to his questions, and perhaps he would have followed the lead of influential residents and tried to assist the company instead of attempting, I hope in vain, to injure it by anonymous detraction. Who your correspondent may be I cannot guess; that he is not one of the important local landowners I know.

I am, Sir, your obedient servant,
C. M. Knatchbull-Hugessen

33, Cornhill, E. C., Feb. 25

At around the same time, on 19th February 1896, Mr Edward Byrom, the owner of Culver, wrote to a Mr Drew:

Dear Mr Drew,

It is my intention to attend the meeting at the Guildhall on Monday next about the Teign Valley Railway. I should be very much obliged if you would attend too, as I hope some arrangements may be come to.

My laundry has now been empty for 9 months, in expectation of the Railway Co. buying it. We have had to send our washing to Exwick, as alterations and repairs were required at the laundry before a good washerwoman would stay. This has, of course, been a great inconvenience to us and something must be settled about it at once. The road near Leigh X is most dangerous, and requires fencing before an accident happens. There is a drop from 10 to 20 feet from the road, which runs beside the cutting into the field on the other side.

I hope the Company are going to make the station they promised near Longdown. It would be a great convenience, not only to this parish, but to Dunsford, as the junction is now to be at Teign House instead of Lea X. It is further from here and from Exeter.

I should also wish to have power to stop trains by signal.

I think it is quite decided that the new line will be adopted, running behind my reservoir.

I shall be willing to meet the Company by taking the value of my land in shares if they grant my requests. Will you kindly make this known to them.

Your truly
E. Byrom

(Longdown Station was eventually built alongside the line, between the two tunnel mouths, 1 mile from the village. There is no record that Mr Byrom ever received permission to stop the trains, unlike the Duke of Beaufort at Badminton!)

EXETER, TEIGN VALLEY, AND CHAGFORD RAILWAY.

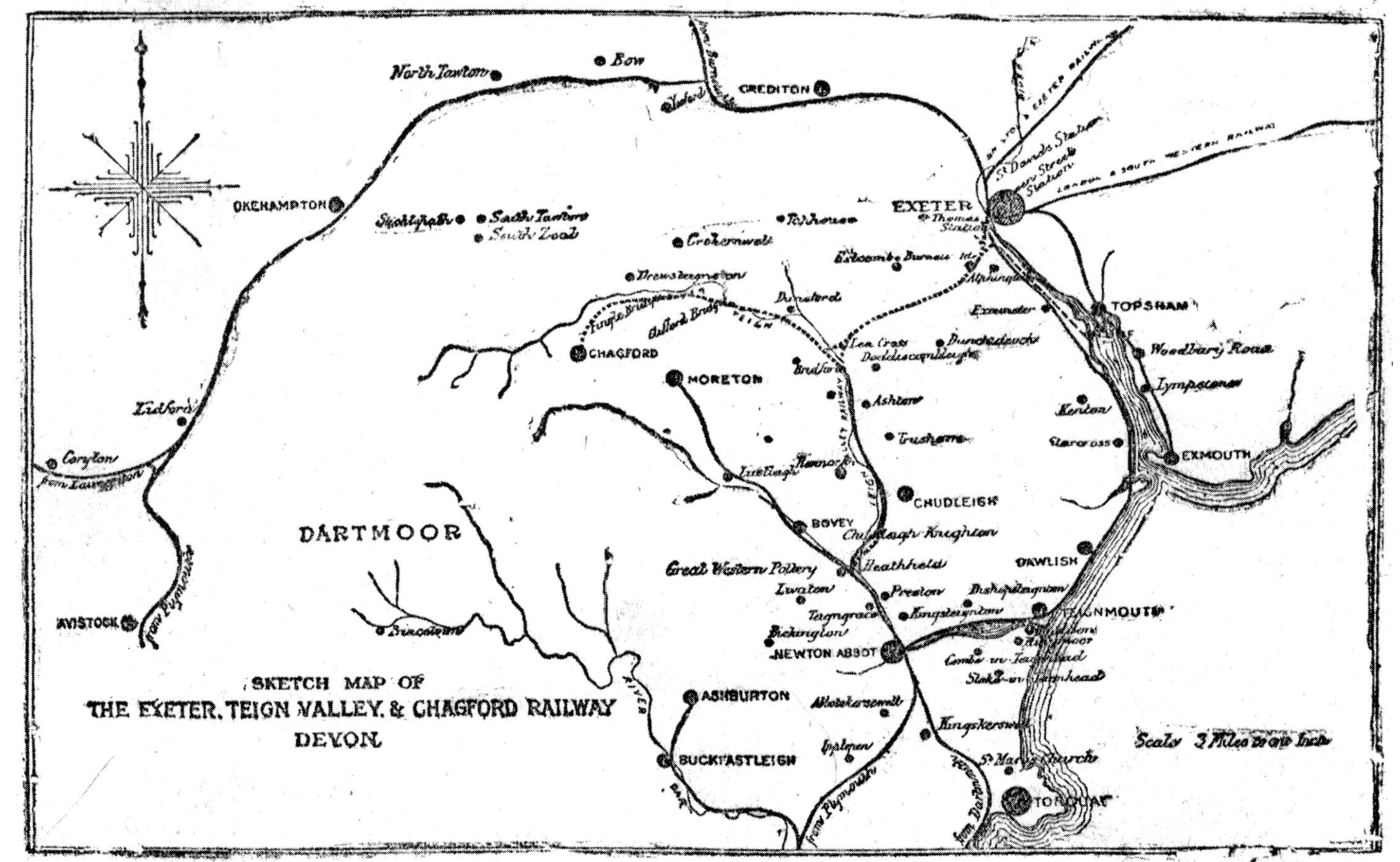

THE PROPOSED NEW RAILWAY IS SHEWN BY A DOTTED LINE ....

2/11/94.

Courtesy of Devon County Council Libraries

The efforts made by the company to raise further capital, as mentioned by the Hon. C. M. Knatchbull-Hugessen in his letter to *The Times*, largely failed to produce the needed response from the local populace, and it was partly for this reason that in 1897 the company obtained Parliamentary permission to abandon the Chagford branch, and to change the nomenclature; it would now simply be called The Exeter Railway Company. Nevertheless, construction work on connecting Exeter to the Teign Valley line continued throughout, and progress was reasonably satisfactory, even though the work involved the removal of some 600,000 cubic yards of earth and rock. Two tunnels had also to be bored, for in addition to the Perridge Tunnel (ultimately to be of 1,056 yards) already mentioned at the Exeter meeting in 1887, a further tunnel of 330 yards in length was required at Culver. Work on these subsequently commenced simultaneously as soon as the railroad from Lea Cross to Culver, including the construction of some bridges, had been completed.

The next major development towards completion of the line came in March 1899 with the completion of the boring of the two tunnels – within a few days of one another. The first to be completed was Culver, and the occasion was marked by an opening ceremony. After all the necessary preparations were made by the contractors, six shots were fired – the first by Mrs Byrom, followed by Mrs Buckingham, Mrs Smee, of Perridge, Mr Edward Byrom and Miss J. Byrom. The sixth and final shot, which completely demolished the remaining rock between the two headings, was fired by Mrs Byrom. After drinking the health of the contractors, the assembled company expressed their pleasure at finding that so much progress had been made with the tunnel and work generally, and looked forward to the completion of the railway.

The ceremony continued with the company entering the tunnel to inspect the result of the firing. This completed, they re-emerged, spent some time watching, with great interest, the miners at work and were then conveyed on trolleys through the tunnel, which was brilliantly illuminated by candles. Upon their return to the tunnel-mouth, a most interesting and enjoyable incident in the history of the construction of the railway was brought to a close.

Four days later, a similar ceremony was enacted after the Mayoress of Exeter, Mrs Pople, had accepted an invitation by the contractors to fire the charge to complete the boring of the Perridge Tunnel. Among those who travelled out from Exeter were the Mayor and Miss Pople, Walter Pring, a director, Mrs Pring, Mr C. R. Collins, Mr & Mrs Gratwicke and Mr W. Easton – who, 20 years before, had given evidence before the House of Commons in favour of a line in this district. Also among those present were Mr L. Thomas, Mr C. Sanders, Mr John Gidley (the under sheriff, whose father worked for years in connection with the line), Mr T. S. Mortimer, Mr Eadie, Mr M. Dunsford (for a considerable time the local secretary), Mr Milton, Mr Cummings, Mr Brett, Mr Scott, Mr W. R. Lisle, Mr F. Newcombe, Mr Besley, Mr Flint and Mr Pett. (The Sheriff, Mr Wilson, was prevented from being present due to a prior engagement.) In addition, at Perridge, were Mrs and Miss Smee, Mr Atherton Byrom, The Revd. & Mrs F. Buckingham, the

Revd., Mrs and Miss Lloyd, and others. The visitors were received by Mr J. Dickinson, Mr Harvey Dickinson and Mr Bluett, the engineer.

The contractors had worked from both ends, and the lines were so well laid that the parties had met within inches of each other. Even so, the work had been far from easy and had, in fact, been compounded by the workmen coming across some bastard granite, which had necessitated the use of large charges of dynamite. All that was needed now to clear the passage, however, was the removal of a small remaining piece of rock in the centre of the tunnel, for which purpose a battery attached to a cable for conveying current to some dynamite had been placed on a specially constructed platform about 500 yards in.

The Mayor, at the invitation of Mr Dickinson, fired the first charge, followed by Mrs Smee and Miss Smee. The fourth charge was fired by the Mayoress; immediately after, a current of air surged through the tunnel and, amid cheers, it was seen that the passage had been cleared. Further charges were fired by Mrs Pring, Miss Buckingham and Mr Atherton Byrom, which widened the passage. After the debris had been cleared, the party, which entered from the Exeter side, passed through the tunnel to emerge at the Culver side.

The party were then invited by the contractors to take refreshments. Afterwards, congratulatory speeches were made, and the health of the Queen was loyally toasted. Mr James Dickson, in the course of an interesting speech, mentioned that although the expectations held out to them had not been realized, his brother and himself meant business, and were doing their best to construct the line in a manner which would be satisfactory to all concerned. People outside had done much more in the way of taking shares, than had either the people of Exeter or the district, and now the time had come when those residing in the locality must show that they felt it was to their personal interest to assist in getting the line completed. Up to the present time, £58,000 had been spent, but of the promised subscription of £114,000, there was no less than £73,000 outstanding. He expressed the hope that the landowners between Perridge and Exeter would meet the company in a liberal manner and, seeing how greatly their properties would be benefited, he thought they might well take the value of their land in shares. This would be an encouragement to those who had already given considerable help to the undertaking. He felt sure that there was a good future for the line and, in addition to dividends, its existence would bring a very substantial reward to the people of Exeter in the shape of additional business. Messrs H. Dickinson and W. Easton also spoke. The concluding toast was that of the press, coupled with the name of Mr Gratwicke. On leaving Perridge Tunnel, the party visited Culver Tunnel. Everyone who was present dwelt with satisfaction on the progress which had been made, and the contractors were spoken of in the highest terms as businessmen who were doing their very utmost, despite difficulties, to carry to completion the undertaking, which was of such financial importance to the district.

The line had now to be carried from Perridge to Exeter, through the property of Mr Walkey, Sir William Walrond, the Ecclesiastical Commissioner, and the Devon Estate, a distance of 3½ miles to St. Thomas. Compared to the work already carried out, this appeared to be easy even though it was going to involve heavy cutting, banking, bridging and culverting. However, protracted negotiations with the Ecclesiastical Commissioners and the Earl of Devon, for the purchase of the necessary land, led to further delays and two years later, in early 1901, a company report stated that still only 4½ miles of the permanent way from Teign House had been laid, although five-sixths of the two tunnels had been completed and optimism was expressed as regards the completion of the remainder of the works. At the same time the company reported that, as at 31st December 1900, £193,960 of the share capital (£198,000 in ordinary shares of £10 each) and £54,200 four per cent debenture stock (out of a total of £66,000) had been issued, the calls due having been £32,951 and cash in hand £2,232 10s 8d. The Report then went on to say 'The Great Western Railway Company have entered into an exceptionally favourable working agreement with this Company, by which they undertake to maintain and work this line in perpetuity at 50 per cent. of the gross receipts, and also agree to allow this Company: (1) The free use of their Exeter Station; (2) Rebates not exceeding 10 per cent. between Bristol and Plymouth, and 5 per cent. on the rest of the Great Western Railway system upon the gross receipts from all classes of traffic on their system passed to or from this Company's Railway, so long as this Company's nett receipts shall not be sufficient to pay a dividend at the rate of 5 per cent. upon £165,000 of Share Capital after payment of interest at a rate not exceeding 4½ per cent. on £55,000 of the Debenture Debt of this Company.'

It continued 'The importance of the Rebates will be appreciated when it is understood that the result will be that a third-class passenger to or from this Company's line will earn for this Company, in addition to 50 per cent. of the local fare, 7½d. in rebate on a journey to or from Bristol, and 1s. on a journey to or from London. These rebates apply to all goods and mineral traffic, as well as passengers. The pleasure traffic to the lovely valley of the Teign and the adjacent moors is bound to be very considerable. The Great Western Railway Company have requested this Company to provide accommodation for a large coal traffic in its Exeter Goods Yard in response to numerous applications from merchants on account of its advantages to the growing districts of St. Thomas and Alphington. There will also be a considerable traffic in road stones with the canal basin to provide return freights.

The junction at Heathfield being 7½ miles nearer Exeter by this Company's route than by the existing one, it follows that all traffic between these points will be sent over this Company's line.

A check upon the traffic passing Heathfield Junction gives the following estimated result:

Merchandise and Minerals 108,000 tons per annum, of which about 72,000 tons is traffic with the east.
Passengers 212,160 per annum.

The Great Western Railway Company should find it to their interest to pass at least half of their special through traffic consisting of fish, vegetable and excursion trains over this Company's route so as to relieve the congestion of traffic on the piece of single line at Dawlish. This traffic is estimated at 1,490 trains per annum.

The merchandise and mineral traffic originating or terminating on this Company's railway should exceed 45,000 tons per annum; and the local and through passenger traffic should not be less than that on the Moretonhampstead branch, or say 200,000 per annum, but will probably exceed 500,000, including excursionists to the Moors and the lovely valley of the Teign.'

The following estimate of traffic on the company's line, based on the foregoing, was given:

	£	s.	d.
72,000 tons Through Merchandise and Mineral Traffic with the Teign Valley and Moretonhampstead Branches at 1s. 11d.	£6,900	0	0
745 Special Through Trains between Exeter and Newton Abbot at 4s. 6d. per train mile	1,341	0	0
45,000 tons Local Merchandise and Mineral Traffic at an average rate of 1s.4d. per ton	3,000	0	0
200,000 Passengers at an average fare of 6d. each	5,000	0	0
Parcels, Horse Carriage and Dog Traffic, at say £100 per mile per annum	800	0	0
Mails, at say £30 per mile per annum	240	0	0
Gross Traffic	17,281	0	0
Less 50 per cent. Working Expenses	8,640	10	0
	8,640	10	0
Balance required from Rebates to make up 5 per cent. on £165,000 Share Capital and 4 per cent. on £55,000 Debenture Stock as per agreement with the G.W.R. Company (these Rebates are estimated to be worth £5,000 a year)	1,809	10	0
Net Receipts, including Rebates	£10,450	0	0

The Report was concluded with reference being made to a connection between the Teign Valley line (when completed) and a proposed Brent, Ashburton and Heathfield (Mid-Devon) Railway, which, it was observed, would form part of the shortest route between Exeter and Plymouth, effecting a saving of about 6 miles, besides affording much easier gradients. It added that 'it is also important to consider the prospective increase of traffic between Plymouth and London and the great commercial centres of England, consequent upon the additional dock and harbour accommodation at Plymouth, involving an expenditure of £3,460,000, and the shortening of the Great Western Railway between Paddington and Exeter, which works are in course of construction. It is therefore reasonable to assume that a large volume of the Plymouth through traffic will ultimately be passed over this

Company's Railway, which would be an addition to the above estimate.'

(It should be noted that the Act authorizing this proposed railway called for two lines to be constructed, the first running from a junction with the Teign Valley line and crossing the Moretonhampstead branch to Ashburton – a total length of 7 miles, 3 furlongs and 7 chains – and the second running from Ashburton to Brent, via Buckfastleigh. Neither of these lines came to fruition, however, and the plans, as deposited with the Devon Authorities, are now in the Devon Records Office in Exeter)

The officials and officers of the company at the time of this report were:

Directors
The Hon. C. M. Knatchbull-Hugessen (Chairman)
R. J. Jenkins, Esq., C.E., J.P.
Walter Pring, Esq., J.P.
G. F. S. Warne, Esq.
Vincent W. Yorke, Esq.

Engineers
R. Elliott-Cooper, M.I.C.E. (Consulting Engineer)
Frederick Bluett, A.M.I.C.E. (Engineer)

Solicitors
Messrs. Mayo & Co., 10, Draper's Gardens, London, E.C.

Secretary & Offices
Frank Faulkner, 63, Queen Victoria Street, London, E.C.

Auditors
W. P. Campbell-Everden, F.C.A.
Robert Warner, F.C.A.

Thereafter, progress speeded up somewhat with work finally being completed by the summer of 1903 – almost 9 years after Lady Northcote had cut the first sod! The long delay in the completion of the railway had, to some extent, been occasioned by the protracted negotiations with the Ecclesiastical Commissioners and the Earl of Devon, for the purchase of the necessary land, as already mentioned. But the longest delay had been caused by financial difficulties, brought about by the misrepresentations of the promoters. To have overcome all the difficulties brought about by no fault of theirs, reflected the highest possible credit on the contractors, James and John Dickson. These people had stuck to the enterprise with the tenacity of a limpet to rock, despite the meagreness of local support complained of by James Dickson after the completion of the initial boring of the Perridge Tunnel.

The line was officially opened on Wednesday 1st July 1903, the ceremony being preceded by a luncheon, which was presided over by Sir Edgar Vincent and held in a marquee at the goods station in Alphington Road. The Mayor and the Sheriff, Mr Pring and Mr Warne (directors of the line), Mr Dickson and representatives of the London shareholders were present, as was Mr Sheepshank, who had done so much to assist the completion of the line, and his agent and solicitor, Messrs Tiplade and Barber. An excellent menu was provided by Messrs Palmer and Edwards, who catered for the meal, music being provided by the Band of the 1st Royal Devon Imperial Yeomanry. Toasts were few – 'Success to the railway', 'Prosperity to Exeter' and'The Health of the directors' being the only other ones outside the loyal toast. The GWR placed a special train at the disposal of the Committee of the Exeter Chamber of Commerce, who had made the arrangements; these had included invitations being sent to every shareholder in Devon, and to members of the Chamber of Commerce, who had been requested to signify, by the 25th June 1903, whether they intended to join in the celebrations. In the event, the acceptances had swallowed up nearly all the tickets. The *Western Morning News*, of 26th June 1903, had reported that 'Lady shareholders were among those who were in the party of acceptors and would attend the luncheon and ride on the special train'!

The official train left St. Thomas Station at 3.40p.m., and arrived at Ide Station at 4 p.m., where the Parish Council presented an address to the directors. After the address had been received and acknowledged, the train proceeded to Longdown and on to Christow. After another address by the council of that parish, the visitors, numbering nearly 500, were entertained to tea by the committee. Sports were held, to which the Chamber of Commerce Committee contributed prizes, and the Band of the Yeomanry combined with the Christow Band to provide the music. The return train to Exeter left at 7p.m., but the festivities continued for another hour!

Together with the Moretonhampstead line, it formed an alternative route, albeit single line, between Exeter and Newton Abbot, which was to prove invaluable in the years ahead. The complete Exeter St. Thomas to Heathfield route then generally became known as the Teign Valley Railway, and was worked by the GWR as one unit, though some short-distance locals were run.

At this point it is interesting to reflect that although leased and worked by the GWR, the Exeter Railway Company remained in existence until 1923, when it merged with the GWR, and was the last remaining independent company within Great Western territory.

For each £100 stock held, company stockholders were entitled to GWR stock as follows:

'A' – 4 per cent debenture	£100 – 4 per cent debenture
1884 – 4 per cent	£100 – 4 per cent debenture
'B' – 4 per cent	£80 – 5 per cent consolidated preferential (£50) cash
'C' – 4 per cent	£80 – GWR 5 per cent consolidated preferential

No. 1 – 5 per cent preferential	£14 cash
No. 2 – 5 per cent preferential	£9 cash
No. 3 – 5 per cent preferential	£6 cash
Ordinary	£5 5s 0d (£5.25p) cash

Ide Station, in the early 1900s.

P. R. Madge

Christow Station, in 1905. An 0–4–2 tank of the 517 class is pictured with a three-coach train from Exeter, with the station staff in attendance.

Chapman & Son
(Courtesy of A. R. Kingdom)

THE RAILWAYS OF SOUTH DEVON

A 14XX class 0–4–2T, No. 1405, leaving Chudleigh Knighton Halt with the mid-morning train to Exeter on 10th June 1957.

E. R. Shepherd

TIME TABLES AND BRANCH WORKING
Part I – Motive Power

History does not record any details of the locomotive that hauled the first train over the Teign Valley line, except for a brief reference to the fact that a single engine with side tanks worked several six-wheeled coaches five times a day during its early years. The earliest class recorded as being used on the line was the 517 front-coupled 0–4–2 tank; in 1901, the engine shed at Ashton was recorded as being allocated 0–4–2 tank, No. 540, and it is possible that this was the engine that hauled the first train. This class of locomotive, incidentally, was a prime example of GWR policy of carrying out successive improvements and modifications to the original design over the years in preference to branching out into something entirely new.

For several years, until being withdrawn in the mid-thirties, steam railmotors were also a common sight on the line.

Eventually, in 1932, the 517 was superseded by the introduction of the 4800 class (to be renumbered into the 14XX series in 1946) 0–4–2T push-pull fitted locomotive, designed by C. B. Collett. As a result, the earlier 517 class locomotives were gradually phased out over the next 6 years, and prior to nationalization, in 1948, Exeter's allocation of the newer locomotives represented the largest concentration of the 14XX class on the GWR system. It included Nos. 1405/29/35/40/49/51/68 & 69, and all except No. 1429 were allocated there from new.

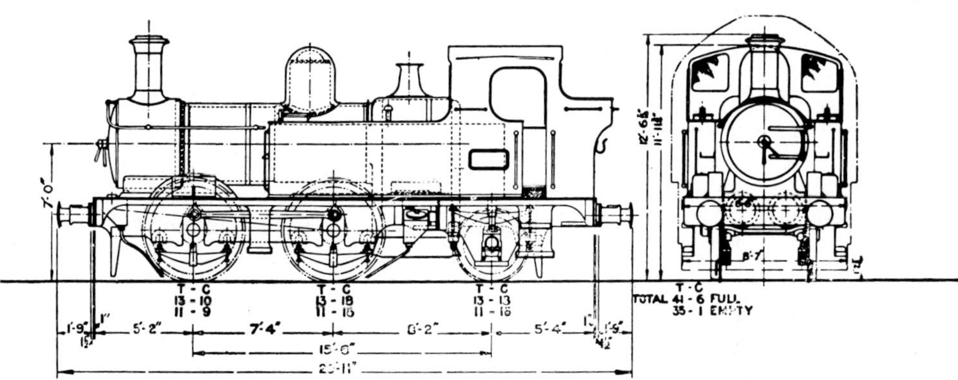

4800 Class (Auto. engines) 5800 Class (Non-auto. engines)

Weight:	41 tons 6 cwt.
Pressure:	165lb sq. in.
Cylinders:	16in. x 24in.
Wheels:	Coupled 5ft. 2in, Trailing 3ft. 8in.
Tractive effort:	13,900lb

Unlike the 517 class locomotives, the 4800 (14XX) class locomotives were not extensively modified, the only major change being the addition of top feed from around 1948, and even then only a few carried these boilers. However, whilst the former 517 class type of boilers were largely retained, with the regulator in the dome, the modified engines could be recognised by the oil cock, which lubricated the regulator on top of the dome cover. One such engine at Exeter was No. 1429. These locomotives were normally employed on auto-train services, and were very popular, as they were light on track, coal and maintenance.

Another Collett-designed engine used on the line was the 57XX class 0–6–0PT. Originally designed in 1929, it was developed from the 'Dean' 655 class. Other locomotives of this class, with modifications, were introduced in 1930 and 1933, including Nos. 3600/59, 9623/33/68/78 from Newton Abbot, used for quarry trains at Trusham. Exeter-based 57XX class locomotives also worked passenger services, and these included Nos. 3603/6/77, 3794, 5760, 7716/71.

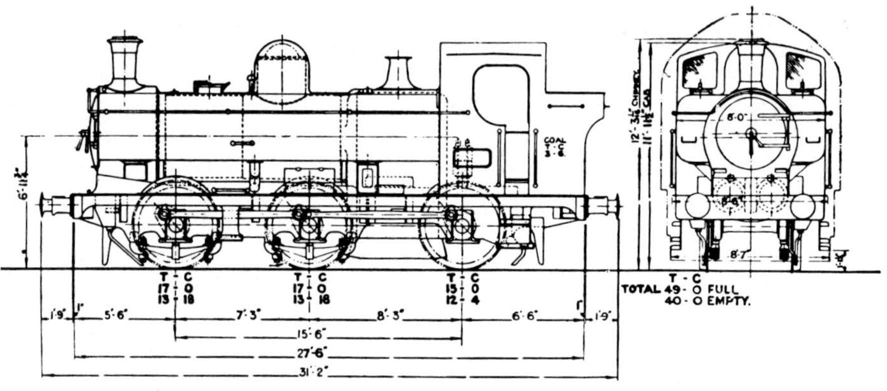

5700 Class

Weight: .... 49 tons (1933 model)
Length: .... 31ft. 2in.
Pressure: .... 200lb sq. in.
Cylinders: .... $17^1/2$in. x 24 in.
Wheels: .... Coupled 4ft. $7^1/2$ in.
Tractive effort: 22,515lb

Larger engines used on the line included the 45XX class 2–6–2T locomotives originally introduced in 1906 for light branch line passenger traffic, and of Churchward design. The original design had flat-topped side tanks, but later, in 1927, larger capacity sloping side tanks were utilised.

A 57XX class 0–6–OPT, No. 3677, departs from Longdown Station with the 5.55p.m. Exeter to Heathfield train on 3rd July 1957.

R. A. Lumber

A 45XX class 2–6–2T, No. 5571, at Christow Station in the late 'twenties.

Chapman & Son
(Courtesy of A. R. Kingdom)

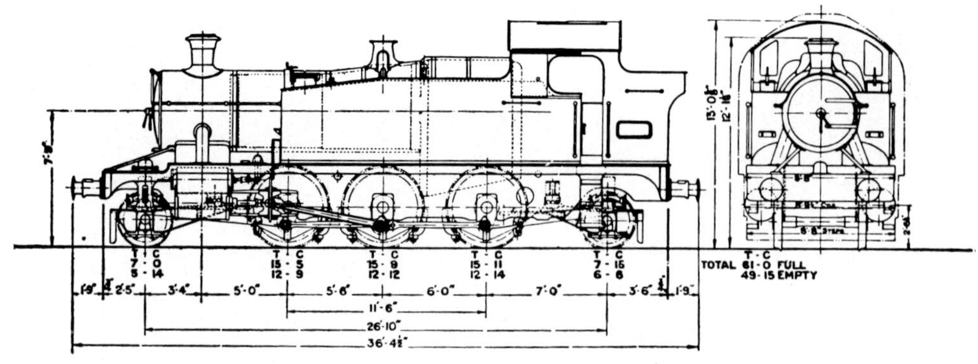

4500 Class

Weight: ....61 tons (loaded)
Length: ....36ft. 4½in.
Pressure: ....200lb sq. in.
Cylinders: ....17in. x 24 in.
Wheels: ....Pony Truck 3ft. 2 in., Coupled 4ft. 7½in., Pony Truck 3ft. 2 in.
Tractive effort: 21,250lb

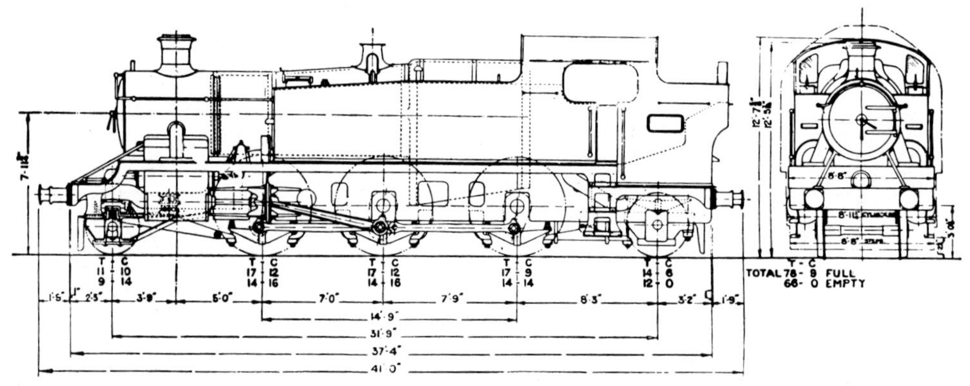

5100 Class

Weight:...76 tons, 11 cwt (loaded)
Length:... 41ft.
Pressure:.. 200lb sq. in.
Cylinders:.. 18in. x 30in.
Wheels:............ Pony Truck 3ft. 2in., Coupled 5ft. 8in., Radial Truck 3ft. 8in.
Tractive effort: 24,300lb

A 51XX class 2–6–2T, No. 4148, pictured at Trusham Station on 24th March 1962. This was not an 'original' Newton Abbot engine, but a relative newcomer.

J. R. Besley

The even larger 51XX class locomotives only appeared after the line had been cut back to Trusham, and they were employed solely on the quarry trains. As far as is known, no locomotives of BR designs were employed.

The heaviest class of engine permitted, except under emergency conditions, was the 78XX 'Manor' class, but there is no record of any of this class of locomotive ever being used. When diversions such as the 'Limited' were made, 53XX class engines were used to provide power, and 45XX class locomotives were used for banking, invariably Nos. 4530 or 5525.

In the 1950s, the marshalling yards at Newton Abbot employed four yard and two carriage pilots. Three of the yard engines were employed in the Hackney marshalling yard, which lay between the racecourse and the River Teign. The fourth shunted in the new yard to the west of the Moretonhampstead branch, after its junction with the main line. The new yard was the town's goods depot, built on reclaimed ground during the 1920s, at around the time of the building of the new station.

Pilot No. 1 was the new yard engine, which was off shed each day at 6 a.m., relieving the previous day's engine, which then went to shed. In the 1950s the yard had a pilot 24 hours a day, Monday to Saturday. One of the people employed on this duty was Mr David Rouse, who recorded his experiences:

'Shunting would commence almost immediately, every road being dealt with in accordance with a pre-conceived plan, which seldom varied. The idea was that wagons would be ready for the traders when they commenced work, and that the incoming goods would be ready for immediate unloading without any delays. Added to this, the branch goods trains were required to be made ready for their booked departure times, not to mention transfer trips to Hackney, which could only run at their booked times due to other services. The branch trains included the Moretonhampstead, which left at 08.30 a.m., and the Trusham, leaving at 11.00 a.m.

After the Moretonhampstead train had left, it was time for breakfast, and the shovel (which had been prepared by polishing it well with a piece of cotton waste) would be well larded, and frying would commence; a practice by no means confined to the yard. The cabin in the new yard was a brake van shorn of its running gear, and on a winter's morning this would become a very welcome haven with its stove and seats, even though some of the tobacco smoke still pervaded the atmosphere. After this break shunting would continue again until 11 a.m., when the shunter's loud telephone bell would ring. This call was the East box asking for the road into the yard for the transfer goods trip from Hackney and was, in fact, the Trusham goods combined with the wagons for Newton Abbot, to make one train. This time the pilot would stand clear of the incoming points, while the shunters would reset the road for an empty siding. Very soon a long line of wagons would curve their way down into the yard, with either a pannier tank or a 55XX class locomotive head. As soon as the transfer engine was clear of the pilot, it would stop and cut off from its train, and then take refuge in another siding. The pilot would couple to the train and then haul it up so that the Trusham engine could recouple at the front. The pilot would then stand clear of the yard exit points and the Trusham train would be propelled out of the yard on to the branch, wait for the signal, and then set off on the journey for Heathfield and on to the Teign Valley line.

During race meetings at Newton Abbot, pilot No. 3 was one of the most popular duties, as from the siding in which it worked there was an uninterrupted view of the racecourse. Shunting was worked out so that as each race was due there was a pause, during which operations were suspended to allow everyone to watch. On these occasions the platelayers seemed to find that a lot of work was required on the sidings in the vicinity, so that there were quite a few onlookers when the racing took place! Unfortunately, it happened too late for the Trusham travellers to observe.'

Although the scene at the Newton Abbot yard seldom varied, occasionally something exceptional would occur. One morning in the early 1950s, whilst Mr David Rouse was sitting on pilot No. 2, a heavily loaded Trusham/transfer pulled out and Mr Rouse noticed that one of the wagons was off the road, just short of the diamond crossover, at the point where it crossed the shunting neck. As he grabbed the brake whistle chain, a second wagon dropped off, quickly followed by a third. By the time they had reached the diamond, they were rearing and jumping all over the place, although still staying in line. A 'R.O.D.' 2–8–0 locomotive, freshly painted out of Swindon, was standing on the other side of the derailment, and was also blowing its brake whistle, but the crew on 4575 class 2–6–2T, No. 5552, heading the transfer, apparently heard nothing, despite the effect on their train. But just as the fourth wagon to be derailed, a covered van, came to the diamond and very nearly overturned, they must have realised something was amiss, and stopped. A hasty conference took place, and the Trusham train was sent on its way, lighter by over half of its former load! David Rouse and his colleagues were trapped on the shunting neck, but had a water column beside them, and sat there for the remainder of the turn. The breakdown vans appeared in the charge of a 'Grange' class locomotive and, with packing and jacks, the gang set to work to re-rail the wagons. By the time that David Rouse went off duty two of the four trucks were back on the rails, but it was well into the afternoon before the yard was back in business again. The 'R.O.D.' was retrieved by courtesy of pilot No. 3, who hauled her train back and out of the yard on the 'down' main line. She was then able to go to shed, using one of the reception sidings normally used by 'up' trains.

All the goods yard pilots did their work coupled to shunter's trucks, which were otherwise known as 'Dummys' or 'Chariots'. The shunters rode on the chariots, which were used for carrying re-railing ramps, spare shunting poles and tail lamps, and they were coupled to the engines using their 'instanter' coupling, with the centre link in the short position to lessen the jerking that would otherwise take place at every move. It was the fireman's duty to place lamps on the vehicle as when coupled to the engine it was regarded as one unit, rather like an engine and tender.

Although 'Chariots' gradually went out of use, in some instances to be replaced by goods brake vans, they did not become extinct as several were preserved. These included No. 41873, built at Swindon in 1896, which was acquired by the Dart Valley Railway at Buckfastleigh, and an ex-van underframe, converted by BRC in 1955, which came under the ownership of the Great Western Society at Didcot.

The only station on the Teign Valley line with its own engine shed was Ashton, the terminus of the original line. It was brick built, of gable style, with timber trusses under a slate roof and was 56ft. 8in. in length and 17ft. wide, inside measurements. Its facilities included a timber coaling platform 30ft. by 10ft. and a store 14ft. 6in. by 6ft. There was a 50ft. pit inside the shed, with a 25ft. pit in front of the coal platform. On 1st January 1901, its allocation was 0–4–2T No. 540. This engine, of the 517 class, was built at Wolverhampton in 1869.

In 1908 the shed was closed, after which it was used as a gangers' store. It was finally demolished in 1960, despite the offer of the local coal merchant to purchase it, although the adjoining store still stands to this day.

The engine shed at Ashton, looking towards Heathfield.

Author's collection

DO NOT LOOK OVER OR PASS
ALONG THE SIDE OF THIS
CAB WHEN NEAR BRIDGES
TUNNELS LOADGAUGES OR
COAL STAGES JAN 1909

A cast iron plate, such as the one illustrated, was carried in the cab of each locomotive

Part II – Rolling Stock.

The GWR had, in service over the Teign Valley line, many wagons of several different types, which were generally used by the motive and permanent way departments. They included open wagons, ballast and sand wagons, covered vans, cattle wagons, brake vans and, in addition to these, private owner wagons. Until nationalization, private owner coal and stone wagons were a familiar sight on the railways, and the Teign Valley line was no exception. Often, other railway companies' wagons were to be seen on the line, as after 1916 all conventional box and open wagons were put into a pool by the major companies, which resulted in considerable economies, as wagons would be used by any company, irrespective of ownership. The GWR kept a strict check on its vehicles, and gave each a code name for easy identification.

As the quarries provided the bulk of the goods traffic, open wagons and hoppers were the most common type to be used. The standard four plank open wagons, finished in the livery of the Teign Valley Granite Co. and the Scatter Rock Quarries, were to be seen at the Trusham and Christow sidings, as were the five plank wagons.

Railway ballast was traditionally conveyed in wagons holding about 6 tons, and then shovelled out prior to being placed on the track. Towards the end of the nineteenth century, however, various companies began using hopper wagons to convey ballast from the quarries to the site, which enabled them to unload the ballast directly onto the track. The GWR was the first railway in Great Britain to use this idea, and two men taking ten minutes, could do work previously taking several hours, and needing a gang of 30 or more men. The hoppers were coded 'P'.

Between 1902 and 1906 extensive reconstruction took place, when the wagons were first increased in capacity to 20 tons and then converted to automatic vacuum and dual-control brakes. The pattern for these changes was the P6, which was a one-off 20 ton ballast hopper, built in 1902. The covered vans used for general goods were code named 'Mink', and those with all-metal bodies were known as 'Iron Mink'.

The GWR, along with other railway companies, owned relatively few tank wagons, most of these being privately-owned. Nevertheless, a few water, oil and creosote tankers were built for the company's own use, these being originally flat and not cylindrical. Privately-owned tankers could be seen at the Chudleigh siding and in the Teign Valley Granite Company's quarry at Trusham.

No goods train was complete without a brake van. They were code named 'Toad' and, unlike most wagon stock, this code was never branded on the vans. The basic single verandah design was used from the 1880s into nationalization, although most other companies had brake vans with verandahs at both ends. The tonnage of the 'Toads' increased over the years from 10 to 20 tons. At the turn of the century there were six-wheeled 'Toads' of 25 tons, but 20 tons later became standard. The weight was obtained by having hollow chassis filled with scrap-iron or concrete. The weight was vital because the van had to be of sufficient weight to hold a train of wagons on a gradient when no locomotive was attached. This would occur during shunting, or when running with unbraked wagons to assist the locomotive brake, or to hold the train and avoid snatching of the loose couplings on falling gradients.

Many 'Toads' were restricted to particular areas or trains and were branded with the name of the home depot, and had to be returned there. The livery of the 'Toads' was standard GWR grey with hand-rails picked out in white. A guard often kept the same van for several years and some of them were maintained in immaculate condition.

Another vehicle, without which the line's goods traffic could not operate, was the shunter's truck. These were usually kept in the marshalling yard and have already been described.

No carriages, except trailers, were used regularly on the line, as passenger trains were only of scratch sets made up from spare stock. Trailer No. 215 was the last one used regularly. Two other trailers, Nos. 147 and 156, were often to be seen on the line, propelled by 0–4–2T No. 1440.

In 1934 camping coaches were introduced and one was sited at Ashton; by 1939, Chudleigh and Ide also had them. At the outbreak of World War II these coaches were used as mess and sleeping vans. One, No. 9993 of 1885, remained in use until 1967, and another was purchased by the Bristol Museum. For a few years after the war camping coaches were used again at Ashton and Chudleigh.

An example of a camping coach, similar to those used on the Teign Valley line.
Author's collection

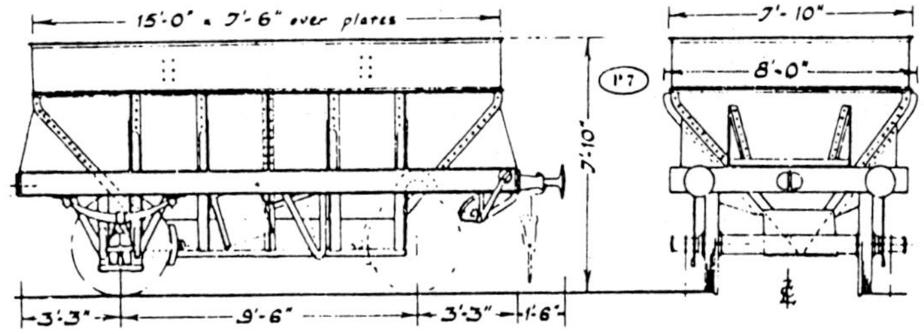

A 20 ton Ballast Hopper Wagon of P6 pattern.

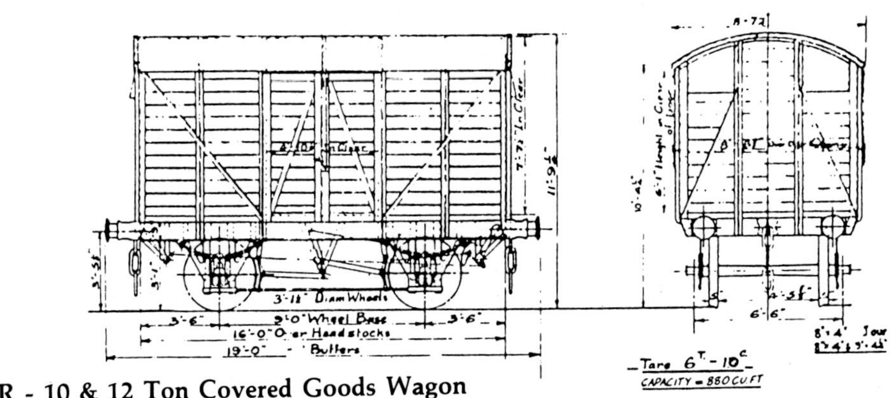

GWR - 10 & 12 Ton Covered Goods Wagon

GWR - 12 Ton Covered Goods Wagon

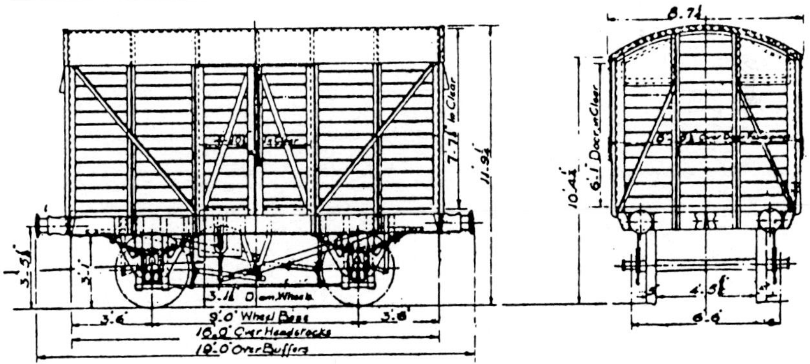

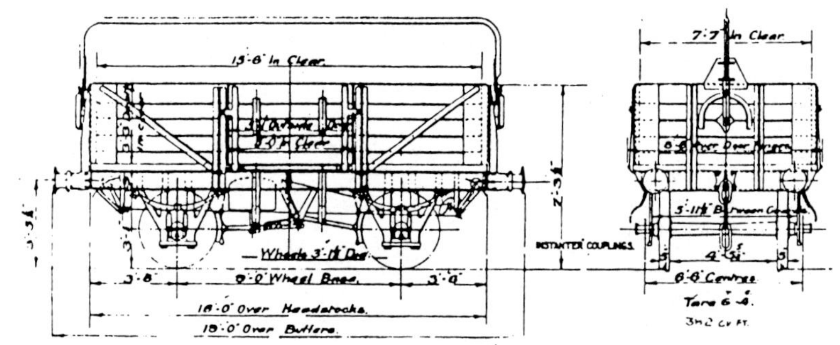

GWR (Swindon) - 10 Ton Open Goods Wagon

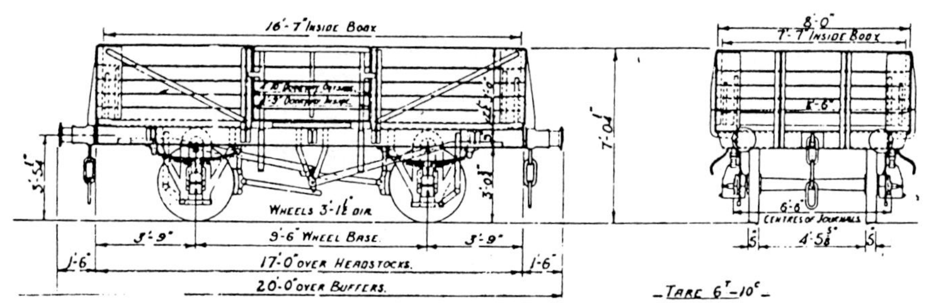

GWR - 10 & 13 Ton Open Goods Wagons

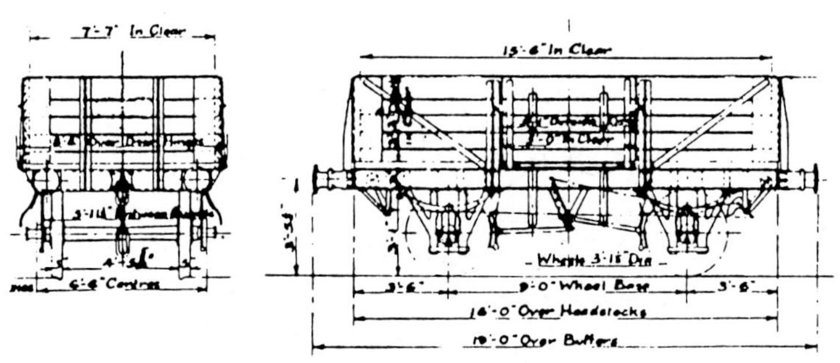

GWR - 13 Ton Open Goods Wagon

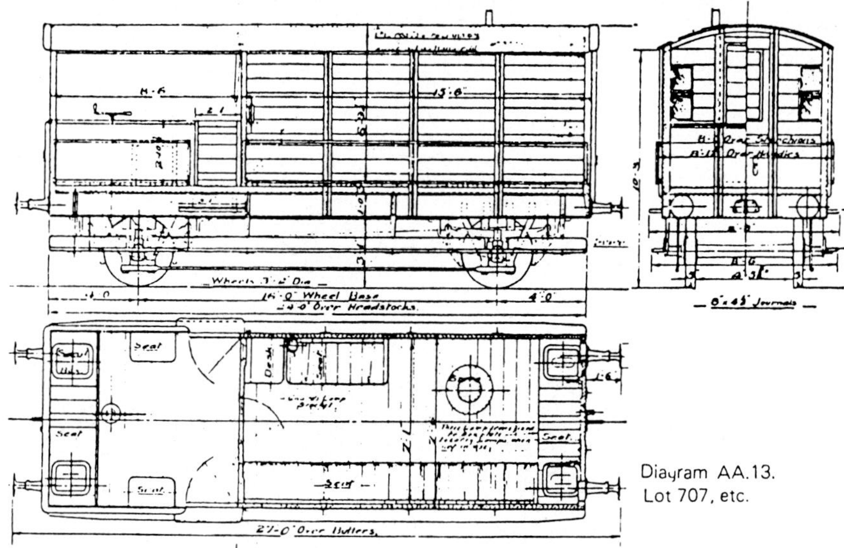

GWR - 20 Ton Goods Brake Van

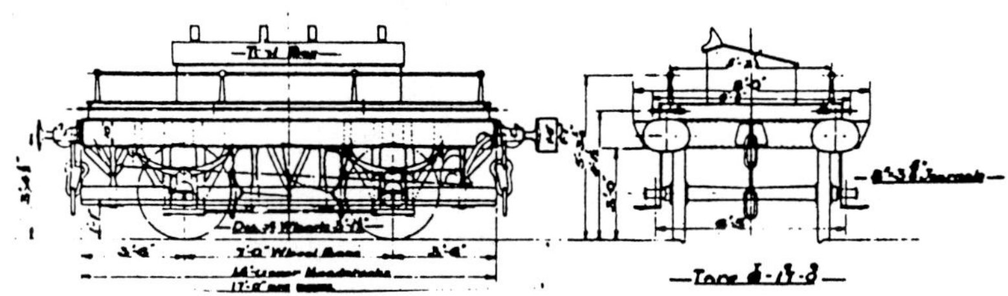

GWR - Shunting Truck
(Only used at Newton Abbot marshalling yard)

A 20 ton ballast hopper wagon of P6 pattern, with 10 in. solebars. It is photographed when built in 1902, in broad gauge style livery. Dust covers are fitted over the springs and axle boxes. Handed brake-blocks are also fitted.

J. N. Slinn collection

Two private owner wagons of the Teign Valley Granite Co.

Courtesy of W. Hudson

Length:	15' 0"
Width:	7'6"
Depth, floor to top:	2'4"
Wheelbase:	9'0"

This wagon was built in May 1910, and was one of a batch of thirty numbered 700 to 845, rising in 5s. The order for these wagons specified: 'The floor planks to be very good as material carried is almost a powder'. Sides were cut from 3in. thick planks.

Length (over headstocks):	15' 6"
Width:	7' 5"
Depth, floor to top:	2' 4"
Wheelbase:	9' 0"

(Note the old postal address on the side of the wagon)

Two examples of large cattle wagons with the lettering on the ends as well as the sides. A partition, placed against the 'S' mark, reduced accommodation to that of a small cattle wagon, the 'M' to that of a medium.

J. N. Slinn collection/British Rail

An early 6-wheeled coach, used on the Teign Valley line, seen in various photographs of trains in stations.

British Rail

Auto-coach, No. 147.

P. J. Garland

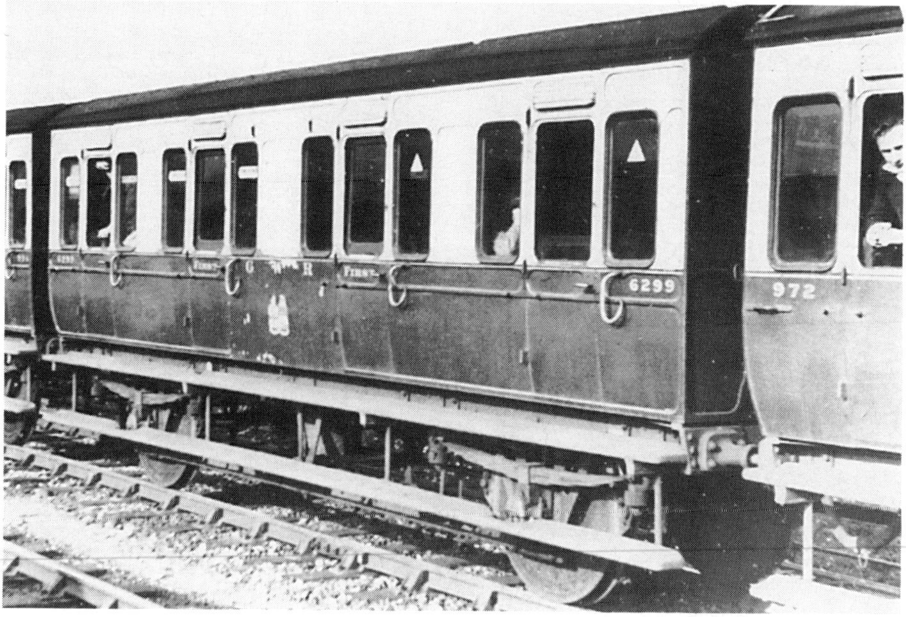

Two early GWR coaches, which were used on the Teign Valley line.
J. N. Slinn collection

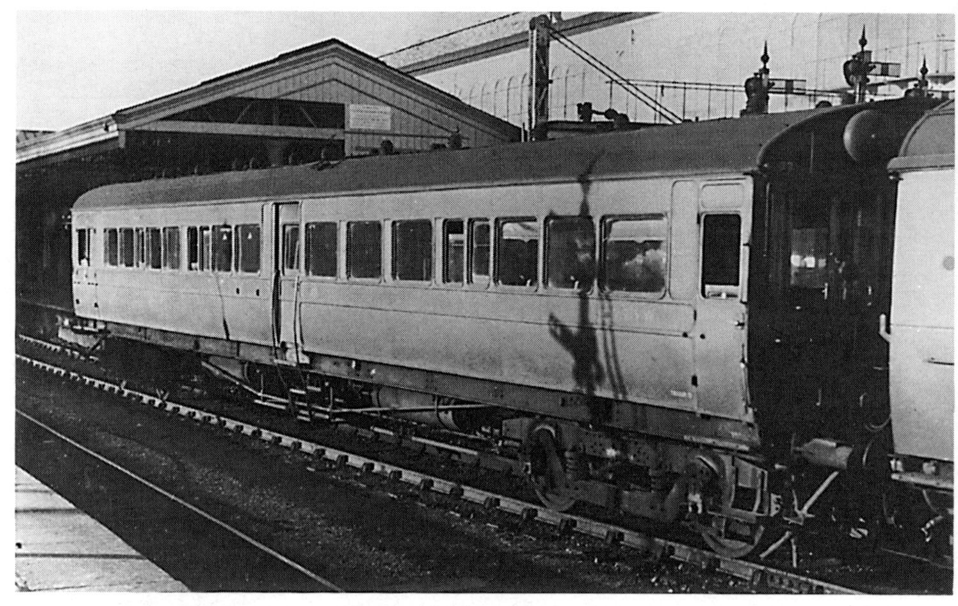

Another auto-coach, this time No. W 215W.

J. N. Slinn collection

Part III — Goods Traffic.

The largest customer for goods traffic on the line was the Teign Valley Granite Company, which owned and operated quarries at Trusham from before the turn of the century. In fact, by 1900, this company was already working at full capacity and employing some 130 operatives, under the management of Mr. R. Bathurst. At that time orders were flowing in from corporations, urban and rural district councils, and other public bodies, as well as from private individuals.

The main works were at Crockham Quarry, which was effectively operated at two levels, loosely referred to as the lower quarry and the upper quarry. The lower quarry, where the rock was generally in larger blocks than that of its counterpart, had a face of about 60 feet. Here the rock was drilled both by hand and by steam drilling machines, and blasted with dynamite and ammonal, before being hammered down to the size required for two steam crushing machines, driven by a 20hp engine; this same engine also drove the steam drills. Afterwards the stone was loaded into skips, which, in turn, were raised by a travelling steam crane, and then tipped into the crushers, where it was broken down to 2½ inches. The stone was then taken up by outside elevators and passed through revolving cylindrical ('Poole') screens before being loaded directly into empty wagons on the company's adjoining railway

Two views of Crockham Quarry, Trusham, looking towards Chudleigh.
Courtesy of ARC Ltd

GREAT WESTERN RAILWAY.

(1392)
(Copyable Ink.)

(2,000- 10—6-14.) W. & S. Ltd.

ENGINEER'S OFFICE, PADDINGTON,

B. 39012. November 8th, 1916.

BALLAST REQUIREMENTS FOR WEEK ENDING November 18th, 1916.

Please arrange to load the following trains at Trusham.

on the days mentioned.

For W. W. GRIERSON,

Messrs Teign Valley Granite Co.,
Hennock,
Bovey Tracey
DEVON.

TEIGN VALLEY GRANITE COMPANY LTD. 10 NOV. 1916 HENNOCK, BOVEY TRACEY

Day.	Ballast.	Destination of Train.	Advice to be sent to	Account to be sent to
Saturday ...	Crushed 12	Lustleigh	Mr. H.D. Smith	Mr. H.D.Smith.
Monday ...				
Tuesday ...				
Wednesday				
Thursday ...				
Friday				

sidings, although any rejects were subjected to the crushing procedure a second time and broken down from between 1/2 inch and dust. In addition to this, there was an automatic arrangement for separating the smaller stone, which was used for the manufacture of concrete slabs, and whenever large blocks or rough stone was required this was loaded direct from the quarry into the railway wagons manually or, as was the case in later years, mechanically.

The upper quarry had a face of about 120 feet and was worked in a similar manner, although the stone, instead of being conveyed to the crushers by a travelling steam crane, was loaded into timber trucks, pushed down to the bottom of an incline, and hooked on to a wagon before being tipped into the crushers.

The company had a total of three travelling steam cranes, including another used for shunting, and it employed its own fitters, smiths and carpenters. Indeed, some idea of the size of this concern can be gleaned from the fact that even as early as 1900 some 500 tons of stone, including ballast for the permanent way, were being despatched every working day, necessitating the use of four special trains, and that the railway sidings could accommodate upwards of 50 wagons, many of which were company-owned. Furthermore, this was without taking into account the stone quarried at the nearby

Whetcombe Quarry, opposite Doghole Copse, which this same company worked until 1931.

In addition to supplying stone, another important branch of the business was the manufacture of Targranix. This, which was claimed would make a model road, consisted of a mixture of granite chippings blended with a special tar mixture so as to form an adhesive conglomerate. The tar mixture was laid on the granite metalling, before the roller was applied, in the proportion of one tarred material to three of the roadstone. A finer quality was prepared for playgrounds and parks. Both these mixtures were sent to all parts of Devon,

Telegrams:- ENGINEER, PADDINGTON STAT.
Telephone:- Nº 4901 PADDINGTON.

Great Western Railway.

B 91012
L 619/86 5

Engineer's Office,
Paddington Station,
London, W.

1st.March 1909

Dear Sirs,

Ballat Supplies.

Will you please arrange to forward 150 tons of ballast to Mr J.N.Taylor, Kingsworthy Station, this week and oblige. The advice notes and account should be sent to Mr.Taylor, Paddington, in due course.

Entered Book Order 114

Yours truly,
For W.W.Grierson,

The Teign Valley Granite Coy.
Hennock, Bovey Tracey,
Devon.

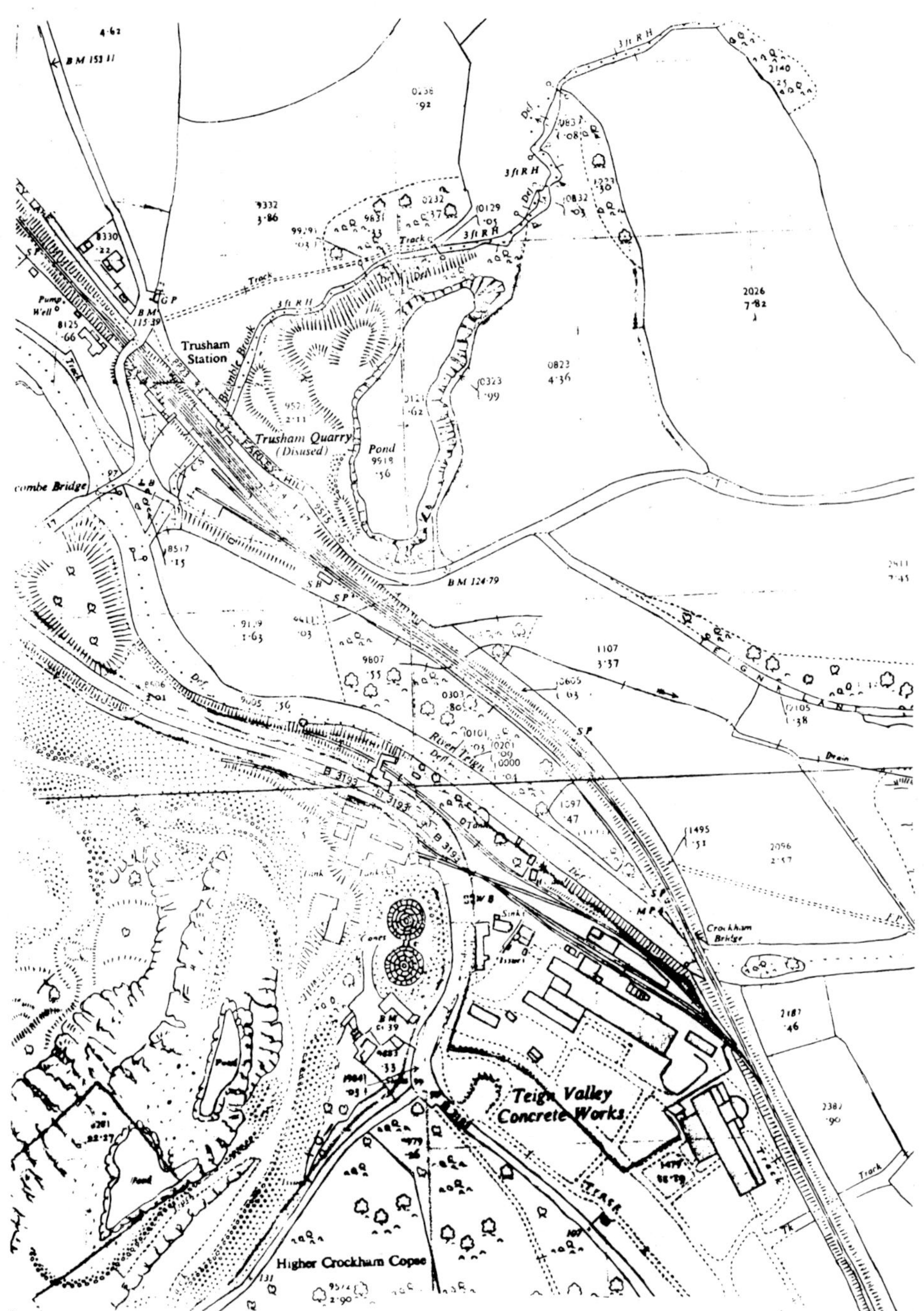

A map of the Trusham area, showing the track layout at Trusham Station and the sidings into Crockham Quarry.

Somerset, Gloucestershire, Dorset, Wiltshire, Berkshire, Hampshire, Buckinghamshire, Oxfordshire, Surrey and Sussex. At this point it should also be mentioned that the railway siding to Crockham Quarry passed through and served the adjacent Teign Valley Concrete Works, which specialised in the manufacture of cement, concrete blocks and pre-cast beams.

Many other business concerns operating in the Teign Valley were also served by the railway over the years. At Trusham, these included the Devon Basalt & Granite Company, which, for many years, operated the original Trusham Quarry owned by Paddy Dixon, while above Trusham, in the hills to the west of Hennock, the Ferrubron Manufacturing Company owned and operated the Great Rock Mine. This mine produced micaceous haematite, which was used in protective paints, and was re-opened in 1902 after having been worked for many years, up until 1890, by the Hennock Iron Steel and

One of the tar plants at Crockham Quarry.

Courtesy of J. Hanley

Whetcombe Quarry, part of the Teign Valley Granite Co. Ltd. This was known as the Whetcombe 'Ton per minute' plant.

Courtesy of ARC Ltd

Whetcombe Quarry and sidings, looking towards Exeter. Note the network of lines in the quarry.

Courtesy of ARC Ltd

Tin Mining Company. It was worked at six levels, five of them being rail served, and there were also three adits on the opposite side of the hill at Beadon Lane, which were connected through the hill. The track gauges of the mine's internal railway system were 1 ft. 6 in. and 2 ft. 0 in., on alternate levels, and two purpose-built locomotives were employed. In addition, a mill was located on the second level, from where the product was piped to drying sheds prior to the ore being transported, by road, to Trusham Station and loaded on to railway wagons destined for Bristol or London Docks, from where a large proportion was then sent abroad. The mine was closed in 1969, when the company went into voluntary liquidation.

For a few years, from 1930, the Mills family provided yet another source of revenue to the railway by operating the Ryecroft Quarry, situated between Christow and Ashton, for the purpose of extracting basalt. A bridge, which remains to this day, was built over the River Teign to provide access to the quarry, and the stone was initially sent away by road. However, towards the end of 1930, a private railway siding was laid and a level crossing provided, and thereafter the bulk of the stone was taken away in railway wagons. Unfortunately, though, there was not a lot of good quality stone in this particular hill, and too much waste material to make the venture profitable. As a result, the Mills family decided eventually to close the quarry, in 1939, and sell the plant.

Of far greater importance was the goods traffic provided by the mines and quarries around Bridford, a village larger than most of the upland villages of the Teign Valley because of the amount of work available in the area. The largest quarry was Scatter Rock, which was operated over a considerable period until 1954, when the cost of crushing the stone (renowned for being of a particularly hard quality) became prohibitive. Up until then the stone was extracted in a manner similar to that employed at Crockham Quarry, both from the top quarry and the lower quarry. However, whereas the stone from the lower quarry was seldom crushed, but taken direct to Christow Station by road in large blocks, where it was weighed and loaded straight on to railway wagons, the stone from the upper quarry was broken down from $2^1/_2$ inches to dust, as at Crockham. Furthermore, it was transported to Christow Station by an entirely different method. First it was removed from the quarry face and taken down an incline in wagons operated on a conveyor-belt type of system whereby there would always be four full wagons going down the incline and four empty wagons coming back up. Then, after being crushed and screened, the stone would be loaded into skip-type buckets, each capable of carrying upwards of half a ton, and hauled to Christow Station on an elaborate aerial ropeway system; this worked on principles similar to that of a pulley and was capable of moving 20 buckets in each direction. On arriving at Christow Station, the contents of each bucket were then tipped into purpose-built containers alongside the company's sidings and subsequently loaded into railway wagons, a large proportion of which were owned by Scatter Rock Macadams.

The Devon Basalt & Granite Company, in addition to operating the original Trusham Quarry, also owned and operated a quarry in this same area

C.A 12)

(587)

GREAT WESTERN RAILWAY

CA 83/192
8/3/3

Please address your reply to
D. W. B. PRICE,
AUDIT ACCOUNTANT

Audit Office,

Paddington Station, W.,

8th March 1913

Gentlemen

I have to inform you that a Monthly Ledger Account at Christow *Station has been opened in your name, subject to the conditions annexed.*

Please to acknowledge receipt of this advice.

Yours truly,

D W B Price

Encl.

The Scatter Rock Macadams Ltd
Clarence House
Arthur St
E.C

prior to World War II. In this instance a siding, the original Teign House Siding, ran westwards from Christow Station, across the River Teign and the B3193 road to a point below Scatter Rock. An incline then ran to the quarry, high up in the hills, to complete the connection.

As already mentioned, mines were also operated around Bridford. Of these, the most significant was the Bridford Barytes Mine, which, until 1948, was owned by the Devonshire Barytes Company and subsequently, until being closed in 1953, by Laporte Industries. The barytes extracted from this mine was used for the manufacture of barytes chemicals and, after being transported by road to Christow Station, was loaded into standard GWR trucks and conveyed to Luton.

In concluding this chapter it must be stressed that whilst the operators of the various mines and quarries undoubtedly provided the bulk of the goods traffic they were by no means alone, as was evidenced by the movement of such commodities as coal, timber and oil along the line. Indeed, for a number of years, up until 1967, the siding at Chudleigh Station was used by Liquid Fuels (the Texaco distributors) as an off-loading point for oil from rail-cars to road tankers, added to which several of the stations, including those at Chudleigh, Trusham and Ashton, were used as a base by the local coal merchants. In the early days of the line, especially, milk churns standing on the station platforms from the nearby farms were also a common sight, whilst Christow Station had the added distinction of having its own cattle pen to cater for the movement of cattle to and from Exeter market, which, from 1939, was situated at the western side of Marsh Barton and served by a siding fed from the Alphington Road sidings on the Teign Valley line near City Basin Junction.

Scatter Rock Quarry siding at Christow Station, showing the company's own wagons in the 1920s and the gantry carrying the aerial ropeway.

Courtesy of ARC Ltd

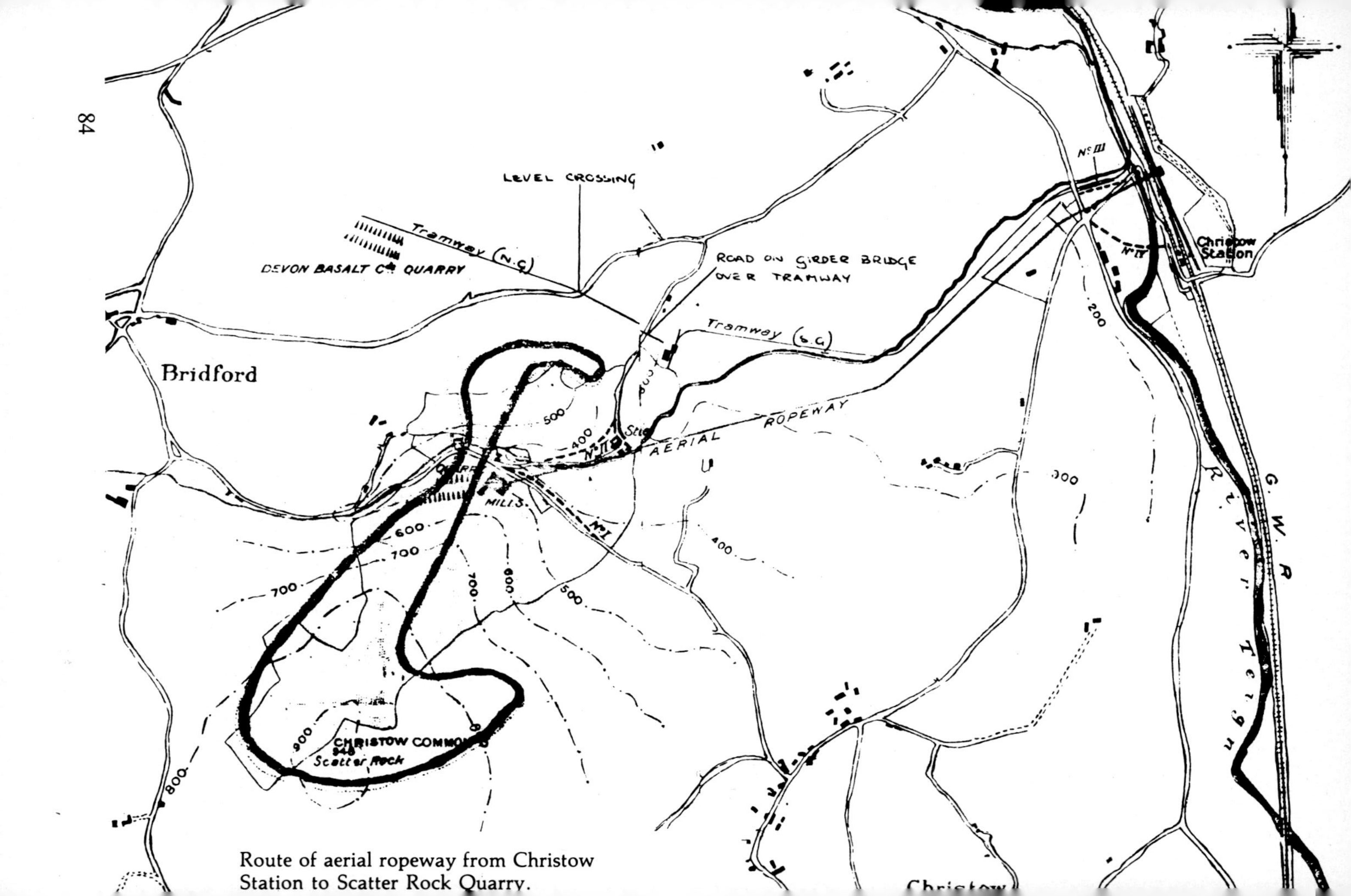

Route of aerial ropeway from Christow Station to Scatter Rock Quarry.

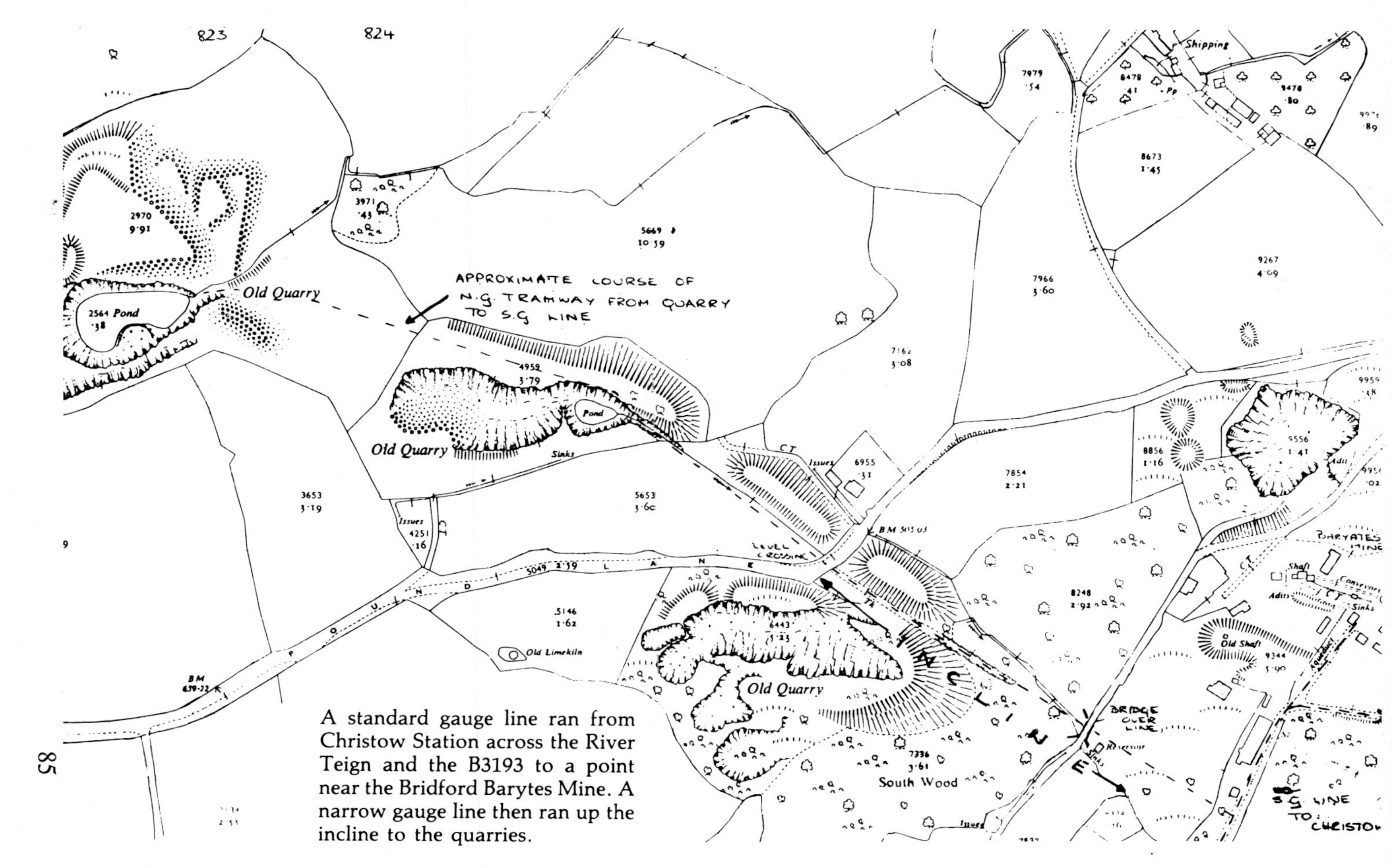

A standard gauge line ran from Christow Station across the River Teign and the B3193 to a point near the Bridford Barytes Mine. A narrow gauge line then ran up the incline to the quarries.

Part IV — Passenger Services and Public Time Tables.

Immediately prior to the opening of the through line in 1903, the passenger service between Heathfield and Ashton consisted of five trains daily in each direction, on weekdays only, there being no trains at all on Sundays. Of these, the 10.25 a.m. service from Ashton was run as a 'mixed' train, as was the 6.05 p.m. service from Heathfield, for which an additional 10 minutes was allowed over and above the normal journey time of 25 minutes. The first departure of the day was the 7.05 a.m. train from Ashton and the last evening departure was from Heathfield at 9.20 p.m., the engine shed of the Teign Valley line being situated at Ashton at that time.

When the line did open from Exeter, the passenger service was integrated with that of the Teign Valley Railway, and it was not until 1924 that any further significant changes were made to the time table, when one additional train was added. It was in the early 'thirties, though, that the peak was reached with seven daily services provided each way between Heathfield and Exeter, plus extra trains on certain days. Moreover, it was during this period that passenger workings were at their most varied with steam railmotors, auto-trains, two-coach (bogie stock) trains and *ordinary* trains all being employed to operate the weekday services. However, despite having been employed on the branch for several years by now, the steam railmotors were not a great success and, in 1935, they gave way to the more familiar push and pull auto-trains used extensively on Great Western branch lines throughout the system.

During World War II passenger services between Heathfield and Exeter were reduced to just four trains daily in each direction, Sundays excepted, and, whilst this was increased to five after the war, it soon became increasingly clear that the branch was going into decline as more and more people took to the motor car as an alternative means of transport, a pattern that was now developing nationwide. Furthermore, even the periodical introduction of slightly revised time tables failed to stem the flow from the railway with the result that the branch declined still further until BR finally withdrew passenger services on 9th June 1958 — some four years before the commencement of the 'Beeching Era'.

6337
Gt Western Ry Gt Western Ry
Ashton (Devon Ashton (Devon
TO
HEATHFIELD
THIRD CLASS
9d. Fare 9d.
Issued subject to the conditions & regulations set out in the Company's Time Tables Bills & Notices
Heathfield Heathfield
6337

7716
Gt Western Ry Gt Western Ry
Christow Christow
TO
ALPHINGTON HALT
Via Ide
THIRD CLASS
1/2 C Fare 1/2 C
Alphington Halt Alphington Halt
FOR CONDITIONS SEE BACK W.B.
7716

A Heathfield-bound train, headed by an unidentified 0–4–2T, passing through Perridge Wood in January 1958.

Courtesy of Western Mercury News Ltd

July, 1903 until further notice

'Down' Trains - Week Days Only

St. David's	*5.40	9.40		1.00	3.10	6.12
St. Thomas		9.47	Goods	1.10	3.15	6.19
Ide	6.03	9.54	when	1.21	3.22	6.20
Longdown	6.25	10.03	wanted	1.30	3.32	6.36
Christow	6.44	10.13	*a.m.*	1.39	3.44	6.54
Ashton	*7.05	10.25	11.40	1.45	3.55	7.06
Trusham	7.13	10.35	11.55	1.53	4.03	7.14
Chudleigh	7.21	10.43		2.01	4.10	7.22
Heathfield	7.29	11.00	12.05	2.09	4.20	7.30
Newton Abbot	*7.45	11.20		2.25	4.40	7.50

**** 5.40a.m. Goods only from Exeter to Christow : Passenger from Ashton to Newton*

'Up' Trains - Week Days Only

Newton Abbot	8.13		12.00	2.48	5.45	8.58*
Heathfield	8.35	11.05	12.20	3.10	6.05	9.20
Chudleigh	8.45		12.30	3.19	6.20	9.29
Trusham	8.53	11.23	12.38	3.27	6.33	9.37
Ashton	9.01	11.30	12.45	3.36	6.47	9.44*
Christow	9.08	Goods	12.53	3.43	7.02	10.20
Longdown	9.18	when	1.03	3.53	7.12	10.40
Ide	9.25	wanted	1.10	4.00	7.19	10.55
St. Thomas	9.30		1.15	4.05	7.24	
St. David's	9.36		1.21	4.11	7.30	11.10*

*** 8.58p.m. Passenger from Newton to Ashton : Goods only from Christow to Exeter

Period 12th July, 1913 to 30th September 1913

84 **EXETER, ASHTON AND HEATHFIELD.** **(Week Days only.)**

	n'g't		a.m.	a.m.		a.m.	p.m.
London (Paddington) dep.	*12*G*0*	...	...	7 30		11 50	1 30
Bristol (Temple Meads) ,,	*3*A *9*	.	6 15	10 23		1 10	4 0
Taunton ,,	*4*A*13*	...	7 41	11 46		1 12	5 16
Exeter (St. David's) arr.	*4*A*53*	.	8 30	12 25		2 50	5 55
	a.m.		a.m.	p.m.		p.m.	p.m.
Exeter St. David's dep.	6 35	...	9 45	1 12		3 17	6 12
Exeter St. Thomas ,,	6 39	.	9 50	1 17		3 22	6 20
Ide ,,	6 47	...	9 58	1 25		3 30	6 28
Longdown ,,	6 56	.	10 7	1 34		3 39	6 37
Christow arr.	7 5	...	10 16	1 43		3 48	6 46
Christow dep.	7 6	.	10 34	1 44		3 50	6 48
Ashton ,,	7 11	...	10 39	1 49		3 55	6 53
Trusham ,,	7 19	.	10 48	1 58		4 4	7 2
Chudleigh ,,	7 25	...	10 54	2 4		4 10	7 8
Heathfield arr.	7 31	.	11 0	2 10		4 16	7 14
Heathfield dep.	8 20	...	12 15	3 12	*5*R*11*	6 4	9 18
Bovey arr.	8 29	.	12 22	3 19	*5*R*18*	6 11	9 25
Moretonhampstead ,,	8 53	...	12 45	3 42	*5*R*41*	6 35	9 50
Heathfield dep.	7 34	...	11 9	2 15	...	4 20	7 24
Newton Abbot arr.	7 45	.	11 20	2 26	.	4 31	7 35
Newton Abbot dep.	7M50	...	11 30	2 43	...	4 45	7 54
Torquay arr.	8M 7	.	11 50	3 1	.	4 55	8 13
Kingswear ,,	9 10	...	12 35	3 35	...	5 48	9 46
Newton Abbot dep.	8 12	...	12 1	3 35	...	4 51	8 1
Plymouth (Millbay) arr.	9 37	.	1 24	4 59	.	5 55	9 22
Falmouth ,,	12 30	...	4T50	8 30	...	9 4	
Penzance ,,	1 10	.	5 5	9 5	.	9 32	.

	a.m.	a.m.		a.m.		a.m.	p.m.		p.m.	p.m.
Penzance dep.	...	...	...	6 35	...	10 0	1 15	...	2 0	...
Falmouth ,,	.	.	.	7 9	.	10 15	1 30	.	3 28	.
Plymouth (Millbay) ,,	6 15	...	...	10 40	...	12 52	4 15	...	7 20	..
Newton Abbot arr.	7 38	.	.	11 48	.	2 15	5 38	.	8 50	.
Kingswear dep.	6 40	...	...	10 56	...	1 50	4 40	...	7 21	...
Torquay ,,	7 9	.	.	11 27	.	2 20	5 11	.	8 41	.
Newton Abbot arr.	7 32	...	...	11 46	...	2 40	5 30	...	8 56	...
Newton Abbot dep.	8 10	.	.	12 3	.	3 0	5 52	.	9 8	.
Heathfield arr.	8 20	...	...	12 15	...	3 12	6 4	...	9 18	...
Moretonhampstead dep.	7 10	*8*K *7*	.	10 45	.	1 50	5 55	.	7 0	*8*R *0*
Bovey ,,	7 27	*8*K*26*	...	11 2	...	2 7	6 12	...	7 18	*8*R*16*
Heathfield arr.	7 34	*8*K*31*	.	11 9	.	2 15	6 18	.	7 24	*8*R*22*
	a.m.			p.m.		p.m.	p.m.		p.m.	
Heathfield dep.	8 33		...	12 22	...	3 22	6 20	...	9 25	
Chudleigh ,,	8 40		.	12 29	.	3 29	6 27	.	9 32	
Trusham ,,	8 46		...	12 35	...	3 35	6 33	...	9 38	
Ashton ,,	8 52		.	12 41	.	3 41	6 39	.	9 44	
Christow arr.	8 57		...	12 46	...	3 46	6 44	...	9 49	
Christow dep.	8 58		.	12 47	.	3 49	6 47	.	9 50	
Longdown ,,	9 8		...	12 57	...	3 59	6 57	...	10 0	
Ide ,,	9 16		.	1 5	.	4 7	7 5	.	10 8	
Exeter St. Thomas ,,	9 25		...	1 14	...	4 17	7 15	...	10 17	
Exeter S. David's arr.	9 28		.	1 17	.	4 20	7 18	.	10 20	
Exeter (St. David's) dep.	10 15		...	1 45	...	4 50	7 47	...	*1*H*52*	
Taunton arr.	10 53		.	2 58	.	5 38	8 45	.	*2*H*32*	
Bristol (Temple Meads) ,,	12 2		...	3 57	...	6 47	9 45	...	*3*H*37*	
London (Paddington) ,,	1 30		.	4 45	.	8 40		.	*6*H*45*	

A—Monday mornings excepted. **G**—Saturday nights excepted. Sunday nights depart 9.50 p.m. **H**—Sunday mornings excepted.
K—Wednesdays only. **M**—Rail Motor Car, one class only. **R**—Will not run after September 13th.
T—Arrive 4.5 p.m. on July 31st, August 1st, and on Saturdays, August 2nd to September 20th inclusive.

Period 20th July, 1931 to 13th September, 1931

EXETER, ASHTON AND HEATHFIELD. **(Week Days only).**

RAIL MOTOR CAR, ONE CLASS ONLY.

			a.m.	a.m.	a.m.	a.m.	p.m.	p.m.	p.m.	p.m.	p.m.	p.m.	p.m. Saturdays only.
Exeter St. David's * dep.	....	....	7 0	7 20	9 25	11 25	12 55	2 45	....	..	6 15	8 45	*9 42*
Exeter St. Thomas ,,	..	..	7 4	7 24	9 29	11 30	12 59	2 50	..	4 30	6 19	8 49	*9 48*
Alphington ,,	....	....	7 9	7 29	9 34	11 37	1 4	2 55	....	4 35	6 23	8 54	*9 54*
Ide Halt ,,	..	..	7 14	7 34	9 39	11 42	1 9	3 0	..	4 40	6 28	8 59	*9 58*
Longdown ,,	....	....	7 23	7 43	9 48	11 51	1 18	3 9	....	4 49	6 36	9 8	*10 8*
Dunsford Halt ,,	..	..	7 28	7 48	9 53	11 56	1 23	3 14	..	4 54	6 41	9 13	*10 13*
Christow ,,	....	....	7 35	7 54	10 2	12 3	1 31	3 25	4 35	5 0	6 50	9 20	*10 23*
Ashton ,,	..	..	7 40		10 8	12 9	1 37	3 31	4 41		6 56	9 27	*10 30*
Trusham ,,	....	....	7 48	....	10 14	12 15	1 43	3 37	4 47	....	7 2	9 33	*10 36*
Chudleigh ,,	..	..	7 54	..	10 20	12 21	1 49	3 43	4 53	..	7 8	9 39	*10 42*
Chudleigh Knighton Halt ,,	....	....	7 58	....	10 24	12 25	1 53	3 47	4 57	....	7 12	9 43	*10 46*
Heathfield* arr.	..	..	8 2	..	10 28	12 29	1 57	3 51	5 1	..	7 18	9 47	*10 50*

			a.m.	a.m.	a.m.	p.m.	p.m.	p.m.	p.m.	p.m.	p.m.	p.m. Saturdays only.	
Heathfield* dep.	....	....	....	8 23	10 35	1 0	2 57	5 10	....	7 45	9 55	*10 55*	....
Chudleigh Knighton Halt ,,	..	..	..	8 28	10 40	1 5	3 2	5 14	..	7 50	10 0	*11 0*	..
Chudleigh ,,	....	....	....	8 32	10 44	1 9	3 6	5 18	..	7 55	10 4	*11 4*	....
Trusham ,,	..	..	..	8 38	10 50	1 15	3 12	5 23	..	8 0	10 10	*11 10*	..
Ashton ,,	....	....	....	8 44	10 56	1 21	3 18	5 29	....	8 6	10 16	*11 16*	....
Christow ,,	..	..	8 0	8 50	11 4	1 31	3 25	5 35	7 0	8 12	10 22	*11 22*	..
Dunsford Halt ,,	....	....	8 8	8 57	11 12	1 38	3 33	5 42	7 8	8 20	10 29	*11 29*	....
Longdown ,,	..	..	8 13	9 2	11 17	1 43	3 38	5 47	7 13	8 25	10 34	*11 34*	..
Ide Halt ,,	....	....	8 20	9 9	11 24	1 50	3 45	5 54	7 20	8 32	10 41	*11 41*	....
Alphington Halt ,,	..	..	8 25	9 14	11 29	1 55	3 50	5 59	7 25	8 37	10 46	*11 46*	..
Exeter St. Thomas ,,	....	....	8 32	9 20	11 35	2 0	3 56	6 5	7 30	8 42	10 51	*11 51*	....
Exeter St. David's * arr.	..	..	8 35	9 23	11 38	2 3	4 1	6 11	7 33	8 45	10 54	*11 54*	..

* For other Services between Exeter and Heathfield and connecting trains to and from Heathfield, see next page.

A steam railmotor standing at the timber-built Alphington Halt, c. 1930.
A. R. Kingdom collection

1947

EXETER, CHRISTOW AND HEATHFIELD. (Week Days only. Third class only.)

	a.m.	a.m.	a.m.	p.m. (Saturdays only)	p.m.	p.m.	p.m.	p.m.	p.m. (Saturdays only)
Exeter St. David's dep.	6 30	7 0	9 45	12 5	12 50	4 30	...	6 30	9 55
Exeter St. Thomas ,,	6 34	7 4	9 49	12 8	12 54	4 34	.	6 34	9 58
Alphington Halt ... ,,	6 38	7 9	9 54	12 13	12 58	4 38	...	6 38	10 3
Ide Halt ,,	6 42	7 14	9 58	12 17	1 3	4 43	.	6 43	10 8
Longdown ,,	6 49	7 22	10 6	12 25	1 12	4 51	...	6 51	10 17
Dunsford Halt ,,	6 53	7 26	10 9	12 29	1 16	4 55	.	6 55	10 20
Christow ,,	6 58	7 33	10 15	12 35	1 25	5 2	5 52	7 0	10 26
Ashton ,,	7 4	7 38	10 19	12 40	1 28	5 6	5 57	7 4	10 31
Trusham ,,	7 10	7 44	10 25	12 46	1 37	5 11	6 2	7 9	10 37
Chudleigh ,,		7 49	10 29	12 51	1 44	5 16	6 6	7 14	
Chudleigh Knighton Halt ,,	...	7 53	10 33	12 55	1 48	5 20	6 10	7 17	...
Heathfield arr.	.	7 57	10 38	1 0	1 52	5 24	6 15	7 22	.
Newton Abbot ... arr.	...	8 25	10 51	...	2 8	5 51	...	7 34	...

D—Saturdays excepted and change at Bath.
F—For Brean Sands and Lympsham.
L—Bristol (Temple Meads) depart 5.45 p.m., via Badminton.
S—Saturdays only.
a—See page 132.
Ⓣ—Third class only.

HEATHFIELD, CHRISTOW AND EXETER. (Week Days only. Third Class only.)

	a.m.	a.m.	a.m.	p.m. (Saturdays only)	p.m.	p.m.	p.m.	p.m.	p.m. (Sats. only)
Newton Abbot ... dep.	...	7 50	11 5	12 50	3 10	4 35	6 10	8 10	...
Heathfield dep.	.	8 20	11 15	1 20	3 25	5 27	6 30	8 22	.
Chudleigh Knighton Halt ,,	...	8 25	11 20	1 25	3 30	5 32	6 35	8 27	...
Chudleigh ,,	.	8 29	11 24	1 30	3 34	5 35	6 40	8 31	.
Trusham ,,	7 45	8 34	11 29	1a45	3 39	5 40	6 46	8 36	10 45
Ashton ,,	7 50	8 39	11 34	1 52	3 44	5 44	6 51	8 42	10 50
Christow ,,	8 0	8 45	11 39	1 55	3 49	5 49	7 0	8 48	10 55
Dunsford Halt ,,	8 6	8 51	11 45	2 2	3 55		7 7	8 55	11 1
Longdown ,,	8 11	8 56	11 50	2 6	4 0	...	7 11	9 0	11 6
Ide Halt ,,	8 17	9 2	11 57	2 12	4 7	.	7 18	9 7	11 12
Alphington Halt ... ,,	8 21	9 6	12 0	2 16	4 11	...	7 21	9 12	11 16
Exeter St. Thomas ,,	8 26	9 12	12 6	2 21	4 17	.	7 26	9 20	11 21
Exeter St. David's arr.	8 31	9 15	12 10	2 25	4 20	...	7 30	9 24	11 25

D—On Saturdays, depart 3.15 p.m.
F—For Brean Sands and Lympsham.
X—Third class only (limited accommodation).
Ⓣ—Third class only
a—Arrive 1.35 p.m.
‡—Yatton arrive 9.14 p.m.
¶—Yatton arrive 8.35 p.m.
*—a.m.

Table 88

EXETER, CHRISTOW and HEATHFIELD

WEEK DAYS ONLY (Second class only)

Miles		am	am	pm	pm	pm	pm S
	Exeter (St. David's).. dep	**7 30**	**9 25**	**12 45**	**4 35**	**5 58**	**9 30**
¾	„ (St. Thomas)	**7 33**	**9 28**	**12 48**	**4 38**	**6 1**	**9 33**
2	Alphington Halt	7 38	9 33	12 53	4 43	6 6	9 38
3¼	Ide Halt	7 43	9 38	12 58	4 48	6 11	9 43
6	Longdown	7 51	9 47	1 6	4 56	6 19	9 52
7¼	Dunsford Halt.......	7 55	9 51	1 10	5 0	6 23	9 56
9¼	Christow	8 3	9 58	1 17	5 7	6 38	10 1
0¾	Ashton	8 8	10 4	1 23	5 12	6 44	10 6
2¾	Trusham	8 14	10 10	1 29	5 18	6 50	1012
4¾	Chudleigh........	8 19	10 15	1 34	5 23	6 55	1017
6	Chudleigh Knighton Halt..	8 23	10 19	1 38	5 27	6 59	1021
7	**Heathfield** .... arr	**8 28**	**10 24**	**1 43**	**5 32**	**7 4**	**1026**
0¾	90 Newton Abbot .. arr	8 38	10 50	1 55	5 42	7 14	1035
Miles		am	am	pm	pm	pm	pm S
	90 Newton Abbot .. dep	7 30	10 30	12 40	4 35	6 5	8 0
—	**Heathfield** .... dep	**7 40**	**10 43**	**12 49**	**4 44**	**6 15**	**8 9**
1	Chudleigh Knighton Halt..	7 44	10 47	12 53	4 48	6 19	8 13
2¼	Chudleigh........	7 48	10 51	12 57	4 52	6 23	8 17
4¼	Trusham	7 53	10 56	1 2	4 57	6 28	8 22
6¼	Ashton	7 58	11 1	1 7	5 2	6 33	8 27
7¾	Christow	8 4	11 8	1 16	5 8	6 40	8 32
9¾	Dunsford Halt.......	8 10	11 14	1 23	5 15	6 45	8 40
1	Longdown	8 15	11 19	1 28	5 20	6 50	8 45
3¾	Ide Halt	8 22	11 26	1 35	5 27	6 57	8 52
5	Alphington Halt	8 26	11 30	1 39	5 31	7 1	8 56
6¼	**Exeter** (St. Thomas)	**8 31**	**11 35**	**1 44**	**5 36**	**7 6**	**9 1**
7	„ (St. David's).. arr	**8 35**	**11 41**	**1 48**	**5 40**	**7 10**	**9 5**

S Saturdays only

For OTHER TRAINS between Exeter (St. David's) and Exeter (St. Thomas), see Table 81

(For further information on passenger services see also working time tables on pages 109 to 111)

0–4–2T, No. 1451, arrives at Ide Halt with an Exeter-bound train in 1956.
Chapman & Son
(Courtesy of A. R. Kingdom)

Part V – Signalling and Train Working.

The whole of the Teign Valley route was controlled by electric train staff instruments, except the Trusham to Heathfield section, which was key token from 1943. This system was first introduced in 1901, and the Dawlish to Parsons Tunnel box was the first section to use it. In January 1914 a modification of the apparatus was brought into use on the Great Marlow branch. This worked on the same principle as the electric train staff system, but the instruments were much smaller, and the rather clumsy staffs were replaced by small key-shaped implements, known as tokens. Afterwards this system was adopted as standard and gradually supplanted the electric staff as those instruments became due for renewal.

As already mentioned, the junction at Heathfield was originally connected with one platform signalled for both directions. However, in 1916 certain track alterations were made for taking out the section from the 'up' Moretonhampstead siding to the Teign Valley line platform, and also the crossover to the back siding. The formation would be replaced with a direct lead from the 'up' siding to the Teign Valley branch, and the crossover would be moved further down to lead into the Teign Valley branch, in the same direction.

This gave two new facilities. Firstly the back siding, parallel to the Teign Valley platform line, could now be used as a 'run-round' facility; secondly the Teign Valley trains could now run direct to and from the Moretonhampstead line platform.

Further engineering works were carried out at Heathfield during 1927. A new platform, 320ft. in length, with a new loop line, 1,030ft. long, was constructed, having facilities for both 'up' and 'down' trains, and the original platform was extended to a length of 413ft. Between 22nd and 24th May 1927 the following new signals were brought into use:

Date	Form	Description	Position	Distance from Box
May 23rd	1 2	1. Down Main Home. (To be temporarily kept at danger). 2. Down Main to Up Main Home. (Temporary Down Main Home).	Down side of Line.	296 yards.
May 24th		Up Main Starting.	Up side of Line.	214 yards.

The existing Down Main Home and Down Main to Branch Home will be taken out of use, and Up Main Starting will become Up Main Advanced Starting.
Occupation of the following Signals will be required:-
Up Main to Goods Loop Home } Bracket Signal.
Up Main Home

The new platform and loop line was opened on 9th June 1927, and the following signal alterations were brought into use:

NEW SIGNALS

Form	Description	Position	Distance from Box
* 	1. Down Main Starting.	Down side of Down Loop.	130 yards.
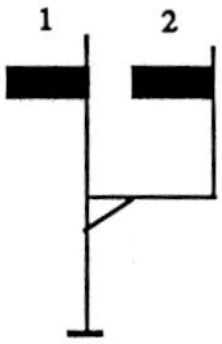 1 2	1. Down Main Home. 2. Down Main to Up Main Home.	Down side of Line.	296 yards.
* 	Down Main to Up Main Starting.	End of New Platform.	108 yards.
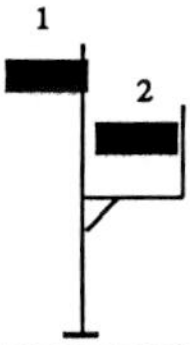 * 1 2	1. Down Main to Up Main Advanced Starting. 2. Down Main to Siding Starting.	Down side of Loop.	190 yards.
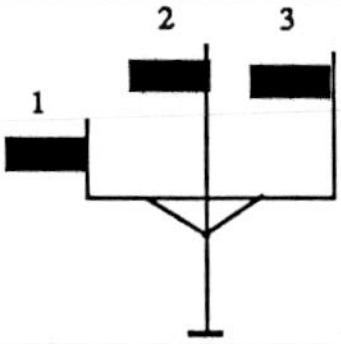 1 2 3	1. Up Main to Goods Loop Home. 2. Up Main Home. 3. Up Main to Down Main Home. (Nos. 1 and 2 already in use).	Between Main Line and Siding.	275 yards.
*	Up Main to Down Main Starting.	Between Main Line and Siding.	138 yards.

* — Train Waiting Indicators will be fixed at these Signals.
The existing Up Main Inner Home Signal will be taken out of use, and the Down Main Starting will become the Down Main Advanced Starting.

Sixteen years were to pass before further major works were carried out. By 1943 preparations for the invasion of Europe were well under way and extensive alterations were necessary to accommodate military stores trains. The loop was extended to form a double track for some distance either side of Heathfield, and a double junction was put in. The loops for trains on the Moretonhampstead line were 1,520ft. long and the loops for trains on the Teign Valley line were 1,100ft. in length. The Bay line was 385ft. long. Work commenced on these alterations on 28th March 1943 and was completed on 11th May 1943.

The new works necessitated the following signal alterations:

NEW SIGNALS

Form	Description	Position	Distance from Box
A 	1. Down Main Home.	Down side of Line.	471 yards.
B 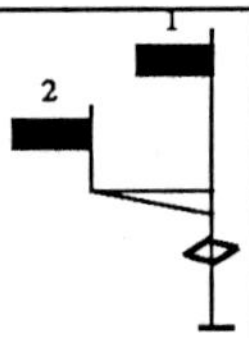 (1, 2)	1. Down Main Intermediate Home. 2. Down Main to Candy's Siding Intermediate Home.	ditto.	261 yards.
C 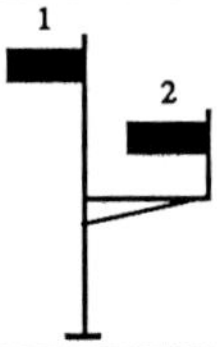 (1, 2)	1. Down Main Inner Home. 2. Down Main to Up Branch Inner Home. (Signal No. 2 to be brought into use Sunday, May 9th)	ditto.	4 yards.
D 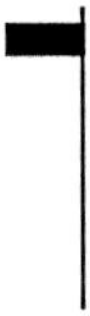	Bay to Up Branch Starting.	Between Bay and Up Main.	26 yards.

Heathfield Signal Box

Michael Hale

At the same time as the engineering works were being carried out at Heathfield, sidings were laid at Chudleigh Knighton to serve a military stores on Knighton Heath.

On 22nd August 1943 the Signal Engineers brought into use a new ground frame, which was known as Chudleigh Knighton ground frame and was situated on the 'up' side of the line between Heathfield and Trusham. The ground frame controlled a 'down' facing connection to the sidings, also situated on the 'up' side of the line, and the ground frame was released by the electric train token of the Heathfield to Trusham section. An intermediate token instrument was provided at the ground frame to permit a train to be shunted in and out of the siding, and this instrument was worked in accordance with the standard instructions of the *Book of Train Signalling Regulations.*At the same time a telephone was provided on the Exeter to Heathfield omnibus circuit, and the existing electric train staff apparatus between Heathfield and Trusham was substituted by the electric train token system; occupation of the ground frames at Crockham, Chudleigh North and South were required for the purpose of changing ground frame locks to the electric train token pattern.

Earlier that year, on 16th April, alterations were made to the signal box at Trusham. The 'down' main and 'down' main to loop homes bracket signal were taken down and re-erected on the same side of the line, 16 yards further from the signal box, making it 268 yards from the signal box. The 'up' main and 'up' main to loop homes bracket signal were also taken down and re-erected 16 yards from the signal box, making it 281 yards from the signal box.

Between 4th and 8th July 1943 alterations were carried out to the loop and the new 'down' platform at Trusham. The existing 'up' and 'down' goods loop was converted to a 'down' passenger loop, and a new platform 150ft. in length on the 'down' side of the line was brought into use. The 'up' and 'down' loops were each 1,050ft. in length.

The following new signals were brought into use:

NEW SIGNALS

Form	Description	Position	Distance from Box
	Down Home.	Down side of Down Main Line.	275 yards.
	Down Main Starting.	Down side of Down Main Line.	180 yards.
	Down Advanced Starting.	Down side of Down Main Line.	600 yards.

No major works or alterations appear to have been carried out at Ashton.

Further along the line, between Ashton and Christow, 6 miles and 50 chains from Heathfield, a private siding to Ryecroft Quarry was opened on 10th November 1930. The siding was worked by a ground frame, locked by key. An appointed man from the Christow Station staff had to accompany the train and assist the guard at the siding. In addition a telephone was provided between the level crossing and the Christow signal box for the protection of the line when exceptional traffic passed over the Quarry Company's level crossing.

In the spring of 1943 both the 'up' and 'down' loops at Christow were extended to 1,100ft. with a capacity of 47 wagons, engine and van, per loop. Between 16th and 21st May 1943 extensive works were made to the signalling system, which resulted in the following new signals being installed, whilst some were removed from use, and others altered.

NEW SIGNALS

Form	Description	Position	Distance from Box
A	Down Main Home.	Down side of Single Line.	326 yards.
B	Down Main Advanced Starting.	Ditto.	494 yards.
C	Up Main Starting.	Up side of Up Main.	235 yards.
D	Up Main Advanced Starting.	Up side of Single Line.	442 yards.

SIGNALS TO BE TAKEN OUT OF USE

The following signals will be taken out of use:
Up Main Inner Home. Up Main Starting. Up Main Advanced Starting. Down Main Home. Down Main Inner Home.

ALTERED POSITIONS OF SIGNALS

The Up Main Home Signal will be taken down and re-erected on the same side of the line, 9 yards further from the Signal Box, with no other alterations. Present distance 207 yards. New distance 216 yards.

NEW INDEPENDENT DISCS AND CONNECTIONS, ETC.

Alterations to the lay-out and additional Independent Discs will be brought into use as shown on diagram.

SPEEDS

Speed Restrictions will apply as under:
All Up and Down trains entering Station Loops — 15 m.p.h.
Particulars appearing in No. 5 Service Books to be amended accordingly.

TRACK CIRCUITS TAKEN OUT OF USE

The existing Track Circuit to the rear of the Down Main Home Signal will be taken out of use.

OCCUPATION OF LOCKING FRAME

The Signal Engineer will have occupation of the Locking Frame for alterations and testing.

Christow Signal Box

J. R. Besley

Longdown Signal Box

Michael Hale

On 19th September 1943 a new 'up' main inner home signal was brought into use:

NEW SIGNAL

Form	Description	Position	Distance from Box
	Up Main Inner Home.	Up side of Line.	22 yards.

Following completion of more engineering works, on Sunday, 19th September 1943, Longdown became a 'crossing station' when a new 'down' loop was brought into use, together with ground frames and signals. The 'up' and 'down' platform was 1,100ft. long, as was the 'down' loop. A new nine lever frame was provided in the signal box, situated on the 'up' side of the line controlling the following new signals and ground frames:

NEW SIGNALS

Form	Description	Position	Distance from Box
B A	A. Down Main Home. B. Down Main to Down Loop Home.	Down side of Single Line at entrance to Loop.	228 yards.
	Down Main Starting.	Up side of Up and Down Main Line.	184 yards
	Down Loop to Down Main Starting.	Down side of Down Loop at exit from Loop.	184 yards.
	Up Main Home.	Up side of Single Line.	263 yards.

NEW AUXILIARY GROUND FRAMES

LONGDOWN EAST LOOP GROUND FRAME. A two-lever Ground Frame situated on the Up side of Line at 5 m. 72 ch. controlling entrance to the new Down Loop, electrically released from Station Ground Signal Box.

LONGDOWN WEST LOOP GROUND FRAME. A two-lever Ground Frame situated on the Down side of the Down Loop at 6 m. 7 ch. controlling exit of the new Down Loop, electrically released from Station Ground Signal Box.

LONGDOWN EAST SIDING GROUND FRAME. A two-lever Ground Frame situated on the Up side of the Up and Down Main Line at 5 m. 78 chs. controlling the Eastern end of the Up Siding, released by Annetts Key from Station Ground Signal Box.

LONGDOWN WEST SIDING GROUND FRAME. A two-lever Ground Frame situated on the Up side of the Up and Down Main Line at 6 m. 1 ch. controlling the West end of the Up Siding, released by Annetts Key from Station Ground Signal Box.

For some years before World War II Exeter City Council had planned a new cattle market, and as it was not possible to extend the existing market in Bonhay Road a new site was found at Marsh Barton, adjacent to the Teign Valley line. Siding facilities were constructed, with connections to and from the Alphington Road sidings, which were close to the City Basin Junction. The new sidings necessitated permanent way and signal alterations, which were carried out between 14th and 19th October 1939. The existing connections, leading from the branch to Alphington Road goods yard, and the connection leading from the branch to City Basin sidings, were connected and were worked from the City Basin Junction box. New independent disc signals were provided at both connections. The existing City Basin Junction ground frame, together with point discs and catch point in connection, leading from Alphington Road goods yard to the branch, were taken out of use. The 'up' branch stop board was moved to a new position 12 yards further from the box and fixed at the 'up' branch home signal. The new position was 328 yards from the box, as shown below:

Form	Description	Position	Distance from Box
	Down Branch Advanced Starting.	Up side of Branch Line.	538 yards.
2 1 3	1. Up Branch to Alphington Road Goods Yard Home. 2. Up Branch Home. 3. Up Branch to City Basin Sidings Home.	Up side of Up BranchLine.	328 yards.

The existing 'up' branch home signal was taken out of use and the 'up' branch distant signal was moved to a new position 112 yards further from the box, on the same side of the line. The new position was 1,328 yards from the box. In addition, a telephone was provided in the checker's hut at the cattle market, connected to the Exeter and Heathfield telephone circuit.

LIST OF SIGNAL BOXES—continued.

Distance to Box M.	Distance to Box C.	NAME OF BOX.	Week Days. Opened. Mondays.	Week Days. Opened. Other Days.	Week Days. Closed at	Sundays. Opened at	Sundays. Closed at	Whether provided with Switch.
—	—	City Basin Junction	6. 0 a.m.	—	—	—	9.50 p.m	Yes
4	58	Longdown	First Train.	First Train.	Last Train.	—	—	No.
3	25	Christow						
3	41	Trusham						
4	20	Heathfield						

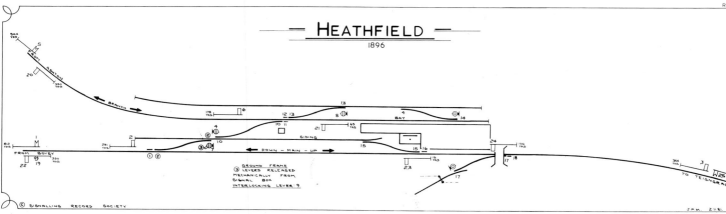

(The times for Longdown, Christow, Trusham and Heathfield are printed once, against a brace covering all four boxes.)

RD

— HEATHFIELD —

1896

FROM ASHTON
BRANCH
DOWN – MAIN – UP
FROM BOVEY
SIDING
BAY
TO TEIGNGRACE

③ GROUND FRAME
LEVERS RELEASED
MECHANICALLY FROM
SIGNAL BOX
INTERLOCKING LEVER: 9

© SIGNALLING RECORD SOCIETY

J.P.M. 2.11.81.

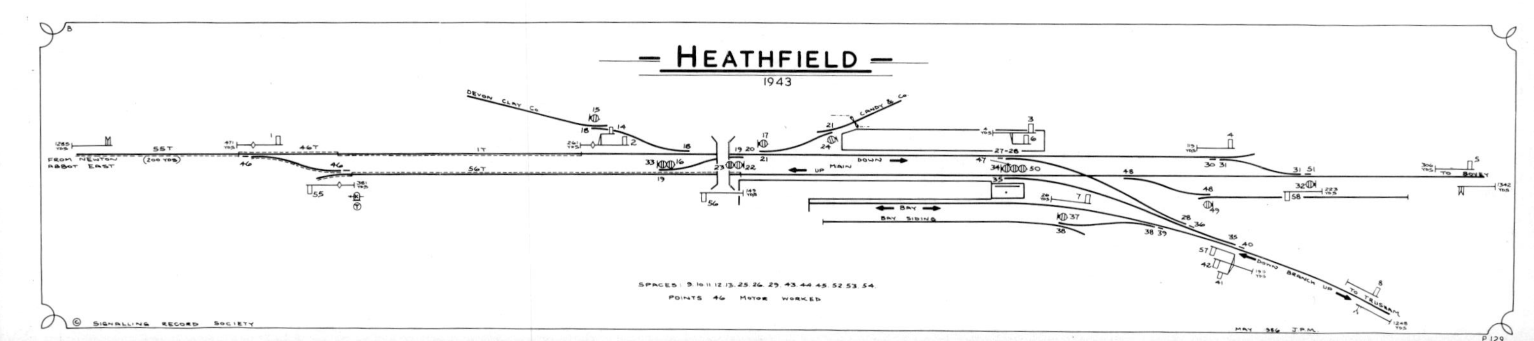

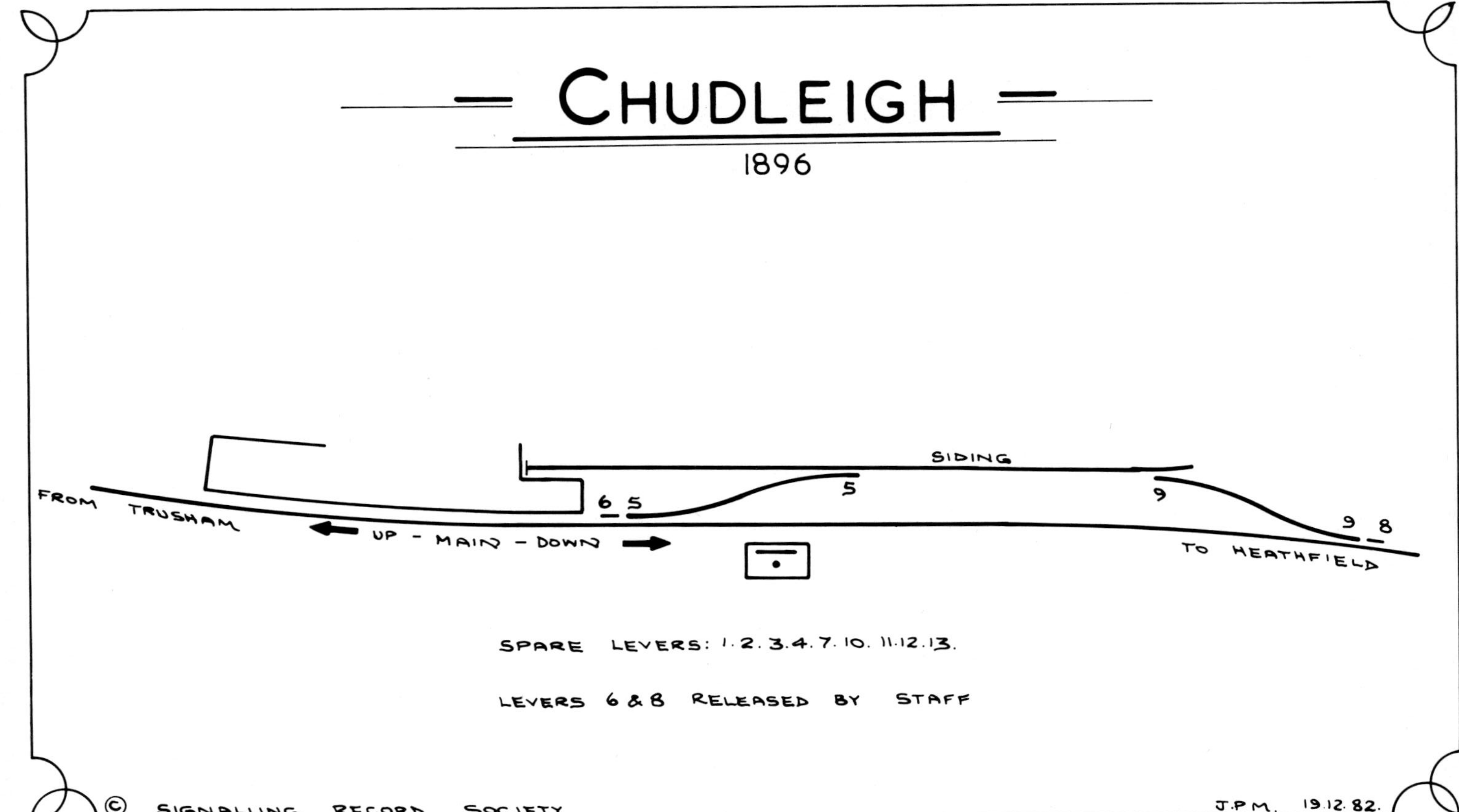
CHUDLEIGH
1896
SIDING
6 5
5
9
9 8
FROM TRUSHAM
UP - MAIN - DOWN
TO HEATHFIELD
SPARE LEVERS: 1.2.3.4.7.10.11.12.13.
LEVERS 6 & 8 RELEASED BY STAFF
© SIGNALLING RECORD SOCIETY
J.P.M. 19.12.82.

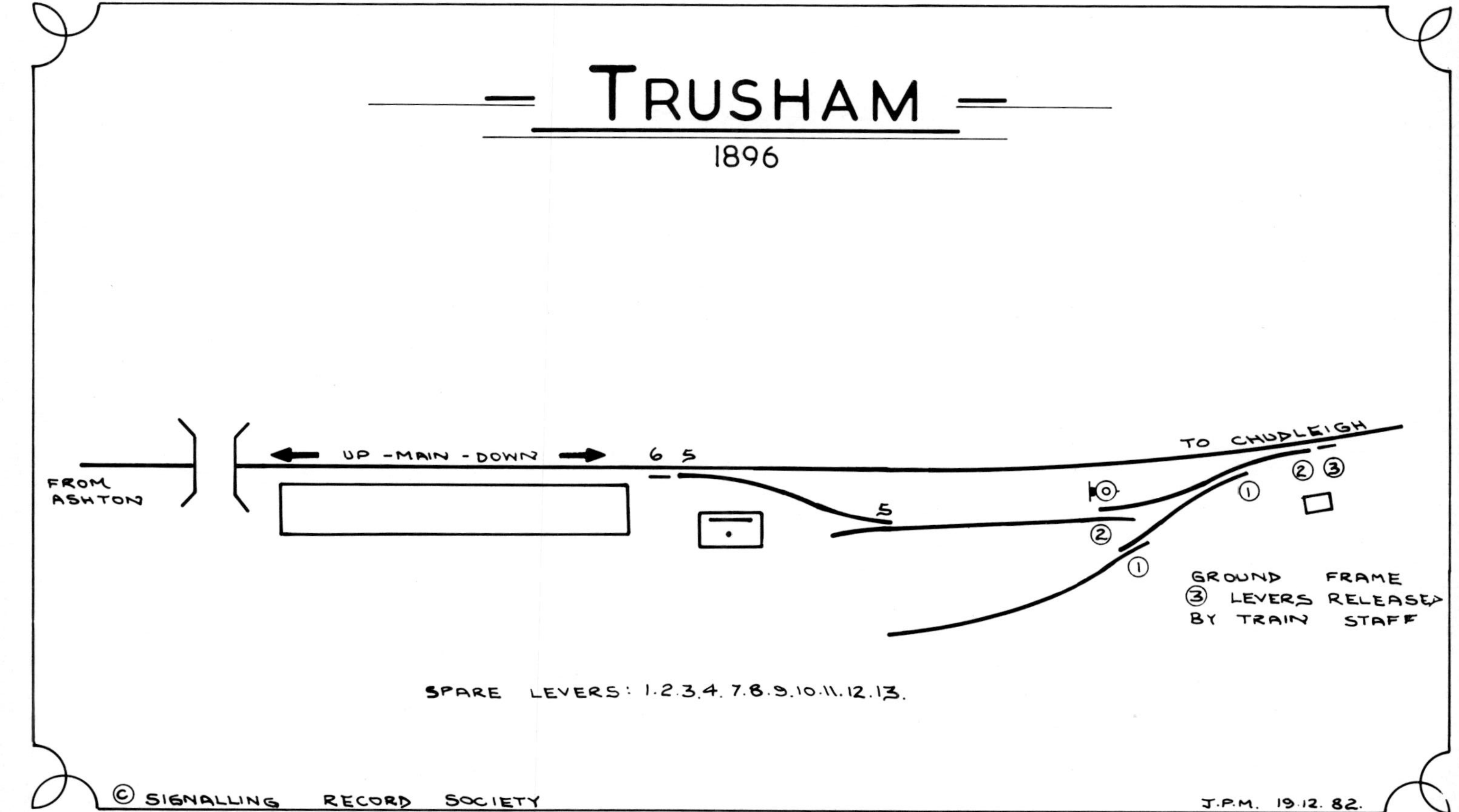
TRUSHAM
1896
FROM ASHTON
UP - MAIN - DOWN
6 5
5
TO CHUDLEIGH
2 3
1
2
1
GROUND FRAME
3 LEVERS RELEASED
BY TRAIN STAFF
SPARE LEVERS: 1.2.3.4. 7.8.9.10.11.12.13.
© SIGNALLING RECORD SOCIETY
J.P.M. 19.12.82.

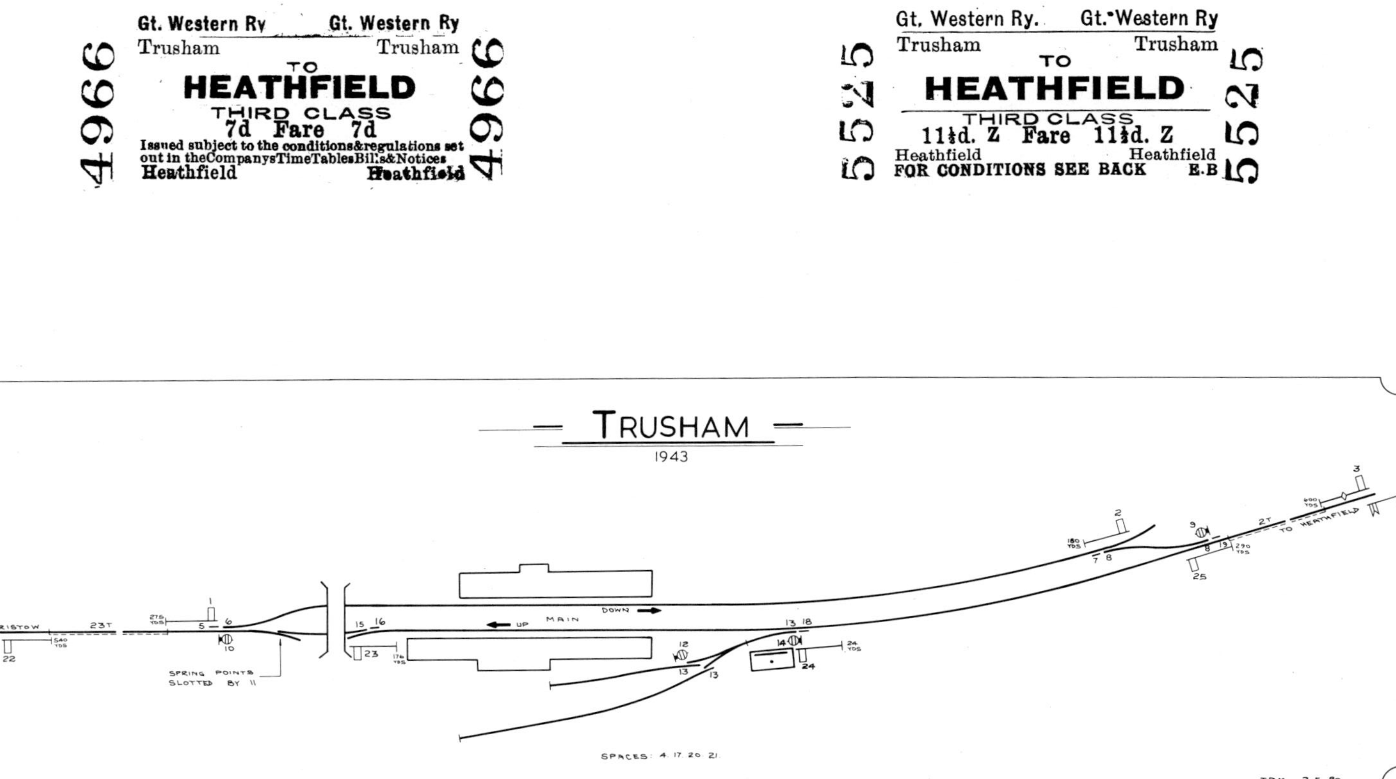
Gt. Western Ry
Gt. Western Ry
Trusham
Trusham
TO
HEATHFIELD
THIRD CLASS
7d Fare 7d
Issued subject to the conditions®ulations set out in theCompanysTimeTablesBills&Notices
Heathfield
Heathfield
4966
4966
Gt. Western Ry.
Gt. Western Ry
Trusham
Trusham
TO
HEATHFIELD
THIRD CLASS
11½d. Z Fare 11½d. Z
Heathfield
Heathfield
FOR CONDITIONS SEE BACK
E.B
5525
5525
TRUSHAM
1943
FROM CHRISTOW
TO HEATHFIELD
DOWN
UP
MAIN
SPRING POINTS SLOTTED BY 11
SPACES: 4. 17. 20. 21.
© SIGNALLING RECORD SOCIETY
J.P.M. 2.5.80
S 838

RD

ASHTON

1896

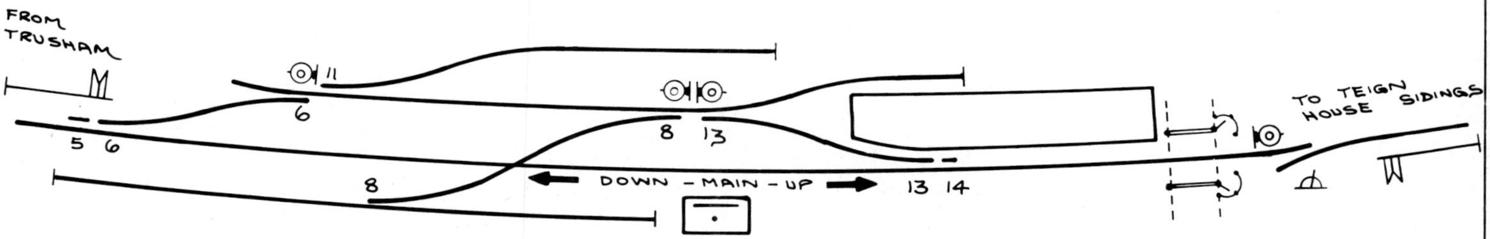

FROM TRUSHAM

11

6

5 6

8 13

8

DOWN – MAIN – UP

13 14

TO TEIGN HOUSE SIDINGS

LEVERS 5.8.14. RELEASED BY STAFF

SPARE LEVERS: 1.2.3.4.7.9.10.12.15.16.17.

GROUND LEVER WORKING CATCH POINT RELEASED BY STAFF

J.P.M. 19.12.82.

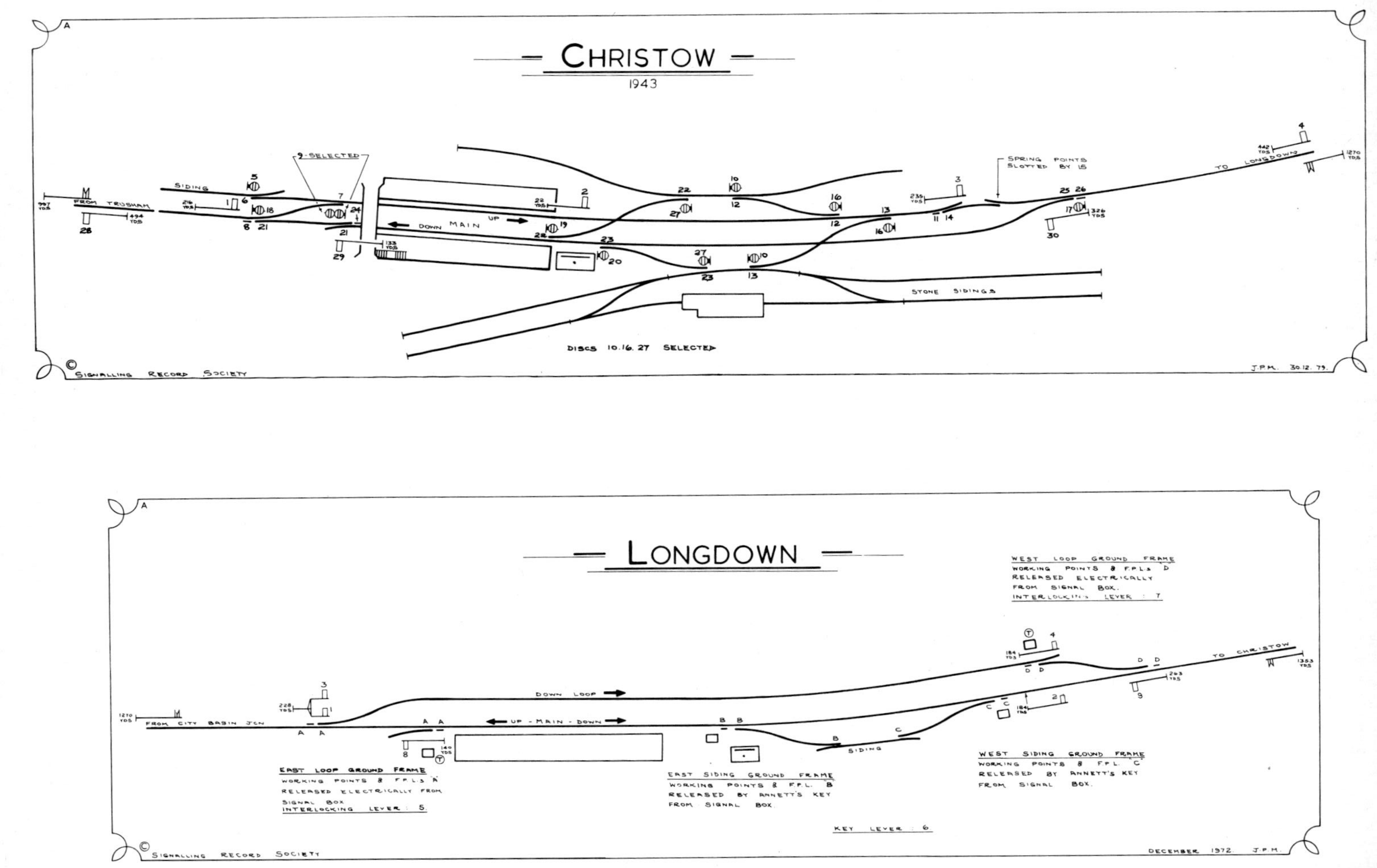
CHRISTOW
1943
FROM TRUSHAM
SIDING
9 SELECTED
DOWN MAIN UP
STONE SIDINGS
SPRING POINTS SLOTTED BY 15
TO LONGDOWN
DISCS 10.16.27 SELECTED
© SIGNALLING RECORD SOCIETY
J.P.M. 30.12.79.
LONGDOWN
FROM CITY BASIN JCN
DOWN LOOP
UP - MAIN - DOWN
SIDING
TO CHRISTOW
WEST LOOP GROUND FRAME
WORKING POINTS & F.P.L.s D
RELEASED ELECTRICALLY
FROM SIGNAL BOX.
INTERLOCKING LEVER : 7
EAST LOOP GROUND FRAME
WORKING POINTS & F.P.L.s 'A'
RELEASED ELECTRICALLY FROM
SIGNAL BOX
INTERLOCKING LEVER : 5.
EAST SIDING GROUND FRAME
WORKING POINTS & F.P.L. B
RELEASED BY ANNETT'S KEY
FROM SIGNAL BOX.
WEST SIDING GROUND FRAME
WORKING POINTS & F.P.L. C
RELEASED BY ANNETT'S KEY
FROM SIGNAL BOX.
KEY LEVER : 6
© SIGNALLING RECORD SOCIETY
DECEMBER 1972. J.P.M.

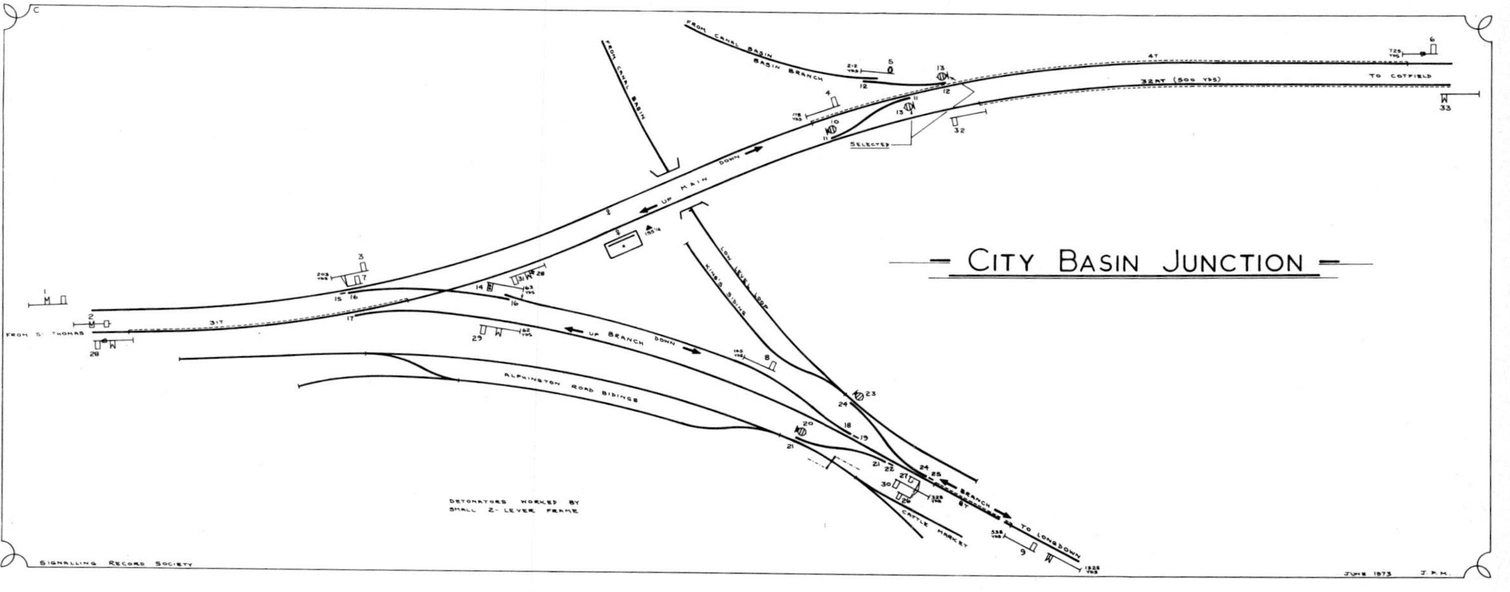
City Basin Junction
From Canal Basin
Basin Branch
From Canal Basin
To Cotfield
Selected
Up Main Down
Low Level Loop
King's Siding
Up Branch Down
Alphington Road Sidings
Branch
To Longdown
Cattle Market
Detonators worked by
small 2-lever frame
From St Thomas
Signalling Record Society
June 1973
J.P.M.

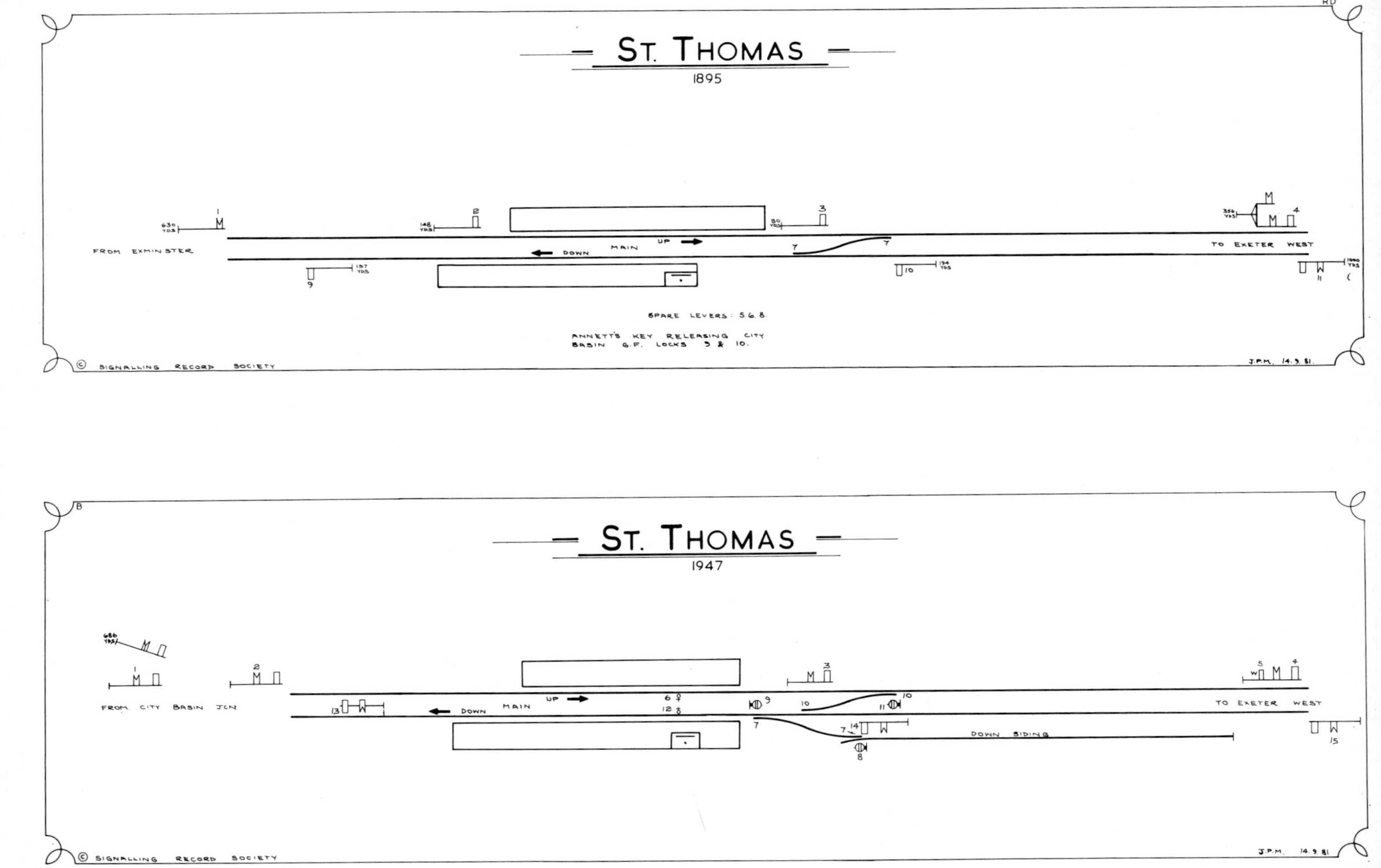

RD
ST. THOMAS
1895
630 YDS
148 YDS
80 YDS
356 YDS
FROM EXMINSTER
MAIN
UP
DOWN
TO EXETER WEST
137 YDS
194 YDS
1060 YDS
SPARE LEVERS: 5.6.8.
ANNETT'S KEY RELEASING CITY BASIN G.F. LOCKS 9 & 10.
© SIGNALLING RECORD SOCIETY
J.P.M. 14.9.81.
B
ST. THOMAS
1947
686 YDS
FROM CITY BASIN JCN
DOWN
MAIN
UP
TO EXETER WEST
DOWN SIDING
© SIGNALLING RECORD SOCIETY
J.P.M. 14.9.81

1892

TEIGN VALLEY BRANCH.

DOWN TRAINS (Week Days Only).

SINGLE NARROW GAUGE, worked by Block Telegraph and Train Staff.

Distances from Teign House. M	C	STATIONS, &c.	1		2		3		4		5		6	
			Passenger. **A**		**Goods. D**		Passenger and **Goods.**		Passenger. **A**		Passenger. **A**		Passenger. **A**	
			arr. pass.	dep.	arr. pass.	dep.	arr. pass.	dep.	arr. pass.	dep.	arr. pass.	dep.	arr. pass.	dep.
			A.M.	A.M.	A.M.	A.M.	A.M.	A.M.	P.M.	P.M.	P.M.	P.M.	P.M.	P.M.
		Teign House	......	......	......	9 30	**A**	......	......	......	......	**S**	......	......
1	42	Ashton	—	7 5	9 36	—	—	10 30	—	1 45	...	...	—	7 20
3	37	Trusham	7 15	7 16			10 40	10 42	1 55	1 56	......	......	7 28	7 29
5	26	Chudleigh	7 25	7 26	**R**	**R**	10 51	10 56	2 4	2 5	—	4 18	7 37	7 38
6	48	Knighton Crossing	—	—	......	......	—	—	—	—	—	—	—	—
7	38	Bovey Lane Crossing	—	—	...	...	—	—	—	—	—	—	—	—
7	58	Heathfield	7 35	—	......	......	11 6	—	2 13	—	4 27	—	7 48	—

UP TRAINS (Week Days Only).

Distances from Heathfield. M	C	STATIONS.	1		2		3		4		5		6	
			Passenger. **A**		**Goods. D**		Passenger. **A**		Passenger. **A**		Passenger and **Goods.**		Passenger. **A**	
			arr. pass.	dep.	arr. pass.	dep.	arr. pass.	dep.	arr. pass.	dep.	arr. pass.	dep.	arr. pass.	dep.
			A.M.	A.M.	A.M.	A.M.	P.M.	P.M.	P.M.	P.M.	P.M.	P.M.	P.M.	P.M.
—	—	Heathfield	—	8 42	......	......	—	12 18	—	3 35	**A**	6 0	—	8 48
0	20	Bovey Lane Crossing	—	—	...	**RR**	—	—	—	—	—	—	—	—
1	10	Knighton Crossing	—	—	......	......	—	—	—	—	—	—	—	—
2	32	Chudleigh	8 52	8 53	...	...	12 27	12 28	3 46	—	6 9	6 10	8 58	8 59
4	21	Trusham	9 2	9 3	......	......	12 35	12 36		......	6 18	6 19	9 8	9 9
6	16	Ashton	9 13	—	—	9 20	12 43	—	...	**S**	6 27	—	9 19	—
7	58	Teign House			9 26	—			......	......				—

S Wednesdays only and Third Tuesday in each month.

Period commencing 22nd September, 1924

TEIGN VALLEY BRANCH—*continued.*

UP TRAINS.—Week Days only.

M.P. Mileage M.	C.	STATIONS.	Ruling Gradient.	Time Allowances for ordinary Freight Trains see page 2: Point to Point Times. Mins.	Allow for Stop. Mins.	Allow for Start. Mins.	1 B Motor. arr. A.M.	dep. A.M.	2 B Motor. arr. A.M.	dep. A.M.	3 B Motor. arr. P.M.	dep. P.M.	4	5 K Newton Abbot Goods. arr. A.M.	dep. A.M.	6	7	8	9 B Motor. WFSO arr. P.M.	dep. P.M.	10
0	0	**Heathfield**	—	—	—	1	—	**8 23**	—	**10 53**	—	**1 0**		7 2	8 40				—	*3 25*	
1	9	Chudleigh Knig'ton Ht	—	—	—	—	8 27	8 28	10 57	10 58	1 4	1 5		—	—				*3 29*	*3 30*	
2	32	Chudleigh	66 F.	6	1	1	8 31	8 32	11 1	11 2	1 8	1 9		8 48	9 15				*3 33*	*3 34*	
3	75	Crockham Siding	132 R.	4	1	1	—	—	—	—	—	—		—	—				—	—	
4	20	Trusham	84 R.	2	1	1	8 37	8 38	11 7	x11 8	1 14	1 15		9 23	X•1220				*3 39*	*3 40*	
4	50	Whetcombe Siding	384 R.	2	1	1	—	—	—	—	—	—		—	—					—	
6	15	Ashton	198 R.	4	1	1	8 43	8 44	11 13	11 14	1 20	1 21		12 28	12 40				*3 45*	*3 46*	
		Christow	132 R.	4	1	2	8 49	8x50	11x19	11 28	1 26	x 1 27		12 47	•X1 40				*3 51*	x *3 52*	
		Longdown	64 R.	18	1	1	8 59	9 0	11 37	11 38	1 36	1 37		—	—				*4 1*	*4 2*	
		Stop Board 5m. 66c.	—	—	—	—	—	—	—	—	—	—		2 0	P2 3				—	—	
		Ide Halt	58 F.	12	2	1	9 6	9 7	11 41	11 45	1 43	1 44		C	R				*4 7*	*4 9*	
		Stop Board 1m. 39c.	L.	8	2	1	—	—	—	—	—	—		2 23	P2 26				—	—	
		Alphington Rd. Gds. Yd	58 F.	1	1	2	—	—	—	—	—	—		—	—				—	—	
		City Basin Junction	—	—	—	—	C	S	C	S	C	S		C	S				C	S	
		St. Thomas	—	—	—	—	9 13	9 16	11 51	11 54	1 50	1 52		—	—				*4 18*	*4 21*	
		Exeter		7	1	—	**9 19**	—	**11 57**	—	**1 55**	—		**2 35**	—				*4 24*	—	

Terminates at 7M 57C.

STATIONS.	11 B Motor. WFSX arr. P.M.	dep. P.M.	12	13 K Goods. arr. P.M.	dep. P.M.	14 B Motor. arr. P.M.	dep. P.M.	15 K Goods. arr. P.M.	dep. P.M.	16	17 B Motor. arr. P.M.	dep. P.M.	18	19 K Stone. arr. P.M.	dep. P.M.	20	21 B Auto. SO arr. P.M.	dep. P.M.	22
Heathfield	—	**3 25**				—	**5 40**				—	**7 40**							
Chudleigh Knighton Halt	3 29	3 30				5 44	5 45				7 44	7 45							
Chudleigh	3 33	3 34				5 48	5 49				7 48	7 49							
Crockham Siding	—	—				—	—				—	—							
Trusham	3 39	3 40				5 54	x 5 55				7 54	7 55		—	x 6 55		—	*10 13*	
Whetcombe Siding	—	—				—	—				—	—		C	R		—	—	
Ashton	3 45	3 46				6 0	6 1				8 1	8 2		7 3OW	7 10		*10 18*	*10 20*	
Christow	3 51	x —		—	X4 10	6 6	x 6 13				8 7	8 8		7 15	• 8 20		*10 25*	*10 26*	
Longdown				**4 30**	**4 35**	6 22	6 23				8 17	8 18		C	R		*10 35*	*10 36*	
Stop Board 5m. 66c.				**4 36P**	**4 39**	—	—				—	—		8 40P	8 44		—	—	
Ide Halt				**4 50**	**4 55**	6 29	6 30				8 24	8 25		—	—		*10 43*	*10 44*	
Stop Board 1m. 39c.				**5 5P**	**5 7**	—	—				—	—		9 4P	9 6		—	—	
Alphington Road Goods Yard				**5 8**	**5 16**	—	—	—	**7 10**		—	—		C	R		—	—	
City Basin Junction				xC	S	C	S	C	S		C	S		C	S		C	S	
St. Thomas				—	—	6 44	6 47	—	—		8 31	8 33		—	—		*10 50*	*10 51*	
Exeter				**5 25**	—	**6 50**	—	**7 20**	—		**8 36**	—		**9 15**	—		*10 54*	—	

TEIGN VALLEY BRANCH.

SINGLE LINE worked by Electric Train Staff. The Staff Stations are City Basin Junction, Longdown, Christow, Trusham and Heathfield. The Crossing Stations are City Basin Junction and Christow. When absolutely necessary two Goods Trains, or a Passenger and a Goods Train may cross at Trusham on the understanding that the Passenger Train is always kept on the Running Line, and that if the Passenger Train has to stop at Trusham, it must stop at the Platform.

DOWN TRAINS.—Week Days only.

M.P. Mileage M.	C.	Distances from Exeter M.	C.	STATIONS.	Station No.	Ruling Gradient.	Time Allowances for ordinary Freight Trains, see page 2: Point to Point Times. Mins.	Allow for Stop. Mins.	Allow for Start. Mins.	1 B Motor. arr. A.M.	dep. A.M.	2	3 K Newton Abbot Goods. arr. A.M.	dep. A.M.	4 B Motor. arr. A.M.	dep. A.M.	5	6 K Goods. arr. A.M.	dep. A.M.	7 B Motor. arr. A.M.	dep. A.M.	8	9
—	—	—	—	**Exeter**	1552	—	—	—	2	—	**7 0**		—	7 15	—	**9 30**		—	10 15	—	**10 55**		
		—	74	St. Thomas	1554	—	—	—	—	7 3	7 4		—	—	9 33	9 35		—	—	10 58	11 0		
		1	19	City Basin Junc.	1555					C	S		C	S	C	S		CS	CR	C	S		
0	19	1	38	Alphington Road Goods Junc.	1628	264 R.	6	1	1	—	—		7 24	7 35	—	—		—	—	—	—		
2	0	3	19	Ide Halt	1629	58 R.	7	1	2	7 11	7 12		C	R	9 42	9 43		C	R	11 7	11 8		
4	58	5	77	Longdown	1630	58 R.	10	1	1	7 20	7 21		7 55	8 0	9 51	9 52		C	S	11 16	11 17		
4	68	6	7	Stop Board	—	L.	—	—	—	—	—		8 2	P8 5	—	—		10 43	P10 45	—	—		
8	3	9	22	Christow	1631	64 F.	8	2	1	7 30	7 31		8 16	x9 0	10 1	10 2		10 55	—	11 26	x11 27		
		10	68	Ashton	1632	132 F.	4	1	1	7 36	7 38		9 6	9 17	10 7	10 9				11 32	11 34		
		12	33	Whetcombe Sdg.	1667	198 F.	4	1	1	—	—		—	—	—	—				—	—		
		12	63	Trusham	1634	384 F.	2	1	1	7 43	7 44		9 25•	x11 55	10 14	x10 15				11 39	x11 40		
		13	8	Crockham Siding	1635	84 F.	2	1	1	—	—		—	—	—	—•				—	—		
		14	51	Chudleigh	1636	132 F.	4	1	1	7 49	7 50		12 3	12 20	10 20	10 21				11 45	11 46		
		15	71	Chudleigh K. Hlt.	—	—	—	—	—	7 53	7 54		—	—	10 24	10 25				11 49	11 50		
		17	3	**Heathfield**	1641	66 R.	6	1	—	**7 58**	—		12 30	1 40	**10 29**	—				**11 54**	—		

Terminates at 8M. 7C.

STATIONS.	10 B Motor. arr. P.M.	dep. P.M.	11 B Motor. WFSO arr. P.M.	dep. P.M.	12	13	14 B Motor. arr. P.M.	dep P.M.	15 K Goods. arr. P.M.	dep. P.M.	16 K Goods. arr. P.M.	dep. P.M.	17	18 B Motor. arr. P.M.	dep. P.M.	19	20 B Auto. SO arr. P.M.	dep. P.M.	21
Exeter	—	**12 55**	—	*2 45*					—	2 55	—	5 5		—	**5 40**		—	*9 20*	
St. Thomas	12 58	12 59	*2 48*	*2 51*					—	—	—	—		5 43	5 45		*9 23*	*9 24*	
City Basin Junction	C	S	C	S					C	S	C	S		C	S		C	S	
Alphington Road Goods Junc.	—	—	—	—					3 4	3 10	5 15	x —		—	—		—	—	
Ide Halt	1 6	1 7	*2 58*	*2 59*					—	—				5 52	5 53		*9 31*	*9 32*	
Longdown	1 15	1 16	*3 7*	*3 8*					C	S				6 1	6 2		*9 40*	*9 41*	
Stop Board	—	—	—	—					**3 30P**	**3 33**				—	—		—	—	
Christow	1 25	x 1 30	*3 17*	—			—	4 13	**3 44P**	**x5 0**				6 11	x 6 20		*9 50*	*9 51*	
Ashton	1 35	1 37					4 18	4 20	**5 5**	**5 12**				6 25	6 27		*9 56*	*9 58*	
Whetcombe Siding	—	—					—	—	**5 17**	**5 47**				—	—		—	—	
Trusham	1 42	1 43					4 25	4 26	**5 50**	x —				6 32	x 6 33		*10 3*	—	
Crockham Siding	—	—					—	—						—	—				
Chudleigh	1 48	1 49					4 31	4 32						6 38	6 39				
Chudleigh-Knighton Halt	1 52	1 53					4 35	4 36						6 42	6 43				
Heathfield	**1 57**	—					**4 40**	—						**6 47**	—				

Period 31st May, 1948 to 26th September, 1948

UP TRAINS. TEIGN VALLEY BRANCH—continued. WEEK DAYS.

M.P. Mileage M.	C	STATIONS.	Ruling Gradient.	Point-to-Point Times. (Mins.)	Allow for Stop. (Mins.)	Allow for Start. (Mins.)	G Engine and Van. arr. a.m.	G dep. a.m.	B Auto. arr. a.m.	B Auto. dep. a.m.	B Auto. arr. a.m.	B Auto. dep. a.m.	K 7.0 a.m. Newton Abbot Freight. arr. a.m.	K dep. a.m.	K 9.30 a.m. Newton Abbot Freight. SX arr. a.m.	K dep. a.m.	B Auto. SX arr. a.m.	B Auto. SX dep. a.m.	B Auto. SO arr. a.m.	B Auto. SO dep. a.m.
0	0	HEATHFIELD	—	—	—	1					—	8 20	7 27	8 40	9 41	●10 9	—	10 45	—	10 50
1	9	Chudleigh Knighton O.S.	—	—	—	—					—	—	C	R	—	—	—	—	—	—
1	9	Chudleigh Knighton Halt	—	—	—	—					8 25	8 25½	—	—	—	—	10 49	10 50	10 55	10 56
2	32	Chudleigh	66 F.	6	1	1					8 28½	8 29	8 48	9 20	—	—	10 53	10 54	10 59	11 0
3	75	Crockham Siding	132 R.	4	1	1					—	—	—	—	—	—	—	—	—	—
4	20	Trusham	84 R.	2	1	1			—	X7 45	8 33½	8 34	9 28	9 40	10 22	X10 35	10 58	10 59	11 4	11 5
4	50	Whetcombe Siding	384 R.	2	1	1			—	—	—	—	—	—	—	—	—	—	—	—
6	15	Ashton	198 R.	4	1	1			7 50	7 51	8 39	8 39½	9 48	10 0	—	—	11 3	11 4	11 9	11 10
6	53	Ryecroft Quarry	—	—	—	—			—	—	—	—	—	—	—	—	—	—	—	—
Terminates at 8m. 7c.		Christow	132 R.	4	1	2			7 55	8 0	8 43½	8 45½	10 6	—	10 48	X11 20	11 7½	11 8½	11 14	11 16
		Dunsford Halt	64 R.	—	—	—			8 5	8 6	8 50½	8 51			—	—	11 13½	11 14½	11 21	11 22
		Longdown	64 R.	16	1	1			8 10	8 11	8 55	8 56			—	—	11 18½	11 19½	11 26	11 26½
		Stop Board 4m. 51c.	—	—	—	—			—	—	—	—			11 42	P11 46	—	—	—	—
		Ide Halt	58 F.	11	2	1			8 16½	8 17½	9 1½	9 2½			—	—	11 25	11 26	11 32	11 33
		Alphington Halt	58 F.	—	—	—			8 20½	8 21½	9 5½	9 6½			—	—	11 29	11 30	11 36	11 37
		Stop Board 0m. 22c.	L.	5	2	1			—	—	—	—			12 5	P12 9	—	—	—	—
		Alphington Rd. Gds. Y.	56 F.	1	2	1	—	7†47	—	—	—	—			—	—	—	—	—	—
		City Basin Junction	—	—	—	—	C 7	50 S	C	S	C	S			C 12	12 S	C 11	33 S	C 11	41 S
		St. Thomas	—	—	—	—	—	—	8 25½	8 27	9 10½	9 12			—	—	11 34	11 36	11 42	11 43
		EXETER	—	5	1	—	7†55	—	8 30	—	9 15	—			12 18	—	11 39	—	11 46	—

STATIONS.	B Auto. SO arr. p.m.	B Auto. SO dep. p.m.	K Freight. FO arr. p.m.	K Freight. FO dep. p.m.	B 2.55 p.m. Newton Abbot Auto. arr. p.m.	B dep. p.m.	B Auto. arr. p.m.	B Auto. dep. p.m.	K Freight. SX arr. p.m.	K Freight. SX dep. p.m.	B Auto. arr. p.m.	B Auto. dep. p.m.	B Auto. arr. p.m.	B Auto. dep. p.m.	B Auto. SO arr. p.m.	B Auto. SO dep. p.m.
HEATHFIELD	—	1 32			3 4	3 25	—	5 28			—	6 30	—	8 23		
Chudleigh Knighton O.S.	—	—			—	—	—	—			—	—	—	—		
Chudleigh Knighton Halt	1 36	1 37			3 29	3 30	5 32	5 32½			6 35	6 36	8 27	8 28		
Chudleigh	1 40	1 41			3 33	3 34	5 35½	5 36			6 39	6 40	8 31	8 32		
Crockham Siding	—	—			—	—	—	—			—	—	—	—		
Trusham	1 45	X1 48			3 38	3 39	5 40	5 41			6 44½	6 46	8 36½	8 37½	—	10 45
Whetcombe Siding	—	—			—	—	—	—			—	—	—	—	—	—
Ashton	1 52	1 52½			3 43	3 44	5 45	5 45½			6 51	6 52	8 42½	8 43	10 50	10 51
Ryecroft Quarry	—	—			—	—	—	—			—	—	—	—	—	—
Christow	1 55½	1 56½			3 47½	3 49½	5 49	—			6 56	X7 2	8 47	8 49	10 55	10 56
Dunsford Halt	2 1½	2 2			3 54½	3 55½					7 7	7 7½	8 55	8 56	11 1	11 2
Longdown	2 6	2 6½			3 59½	4 0½					7 11½	7 12	9 0	9 1	11 6	11 7
Stop Board 4m. 51c.	—	—			—	—					—	—	—	—	—	—
Ide Halt	2 12	2 12½			4 6	4 7					7 18	7 18½	9 7	9 8	11 12	11 13
Alphington Halt	2 15½	2 16			4 10	4 11					7 21½	7 22	9 11	9 12	11 16	11 17
Stop Board 0m. 22c.	—	—			—	—					—	—	—	—	—	—
Alphington Road Goods Yd.	—	—	—	3 45	—	—				5 50	—	—	—	—	—	—
City Basin Junction	C 2	20 S	C 3	47 S	C	S			C 5	52 S	C	S	C	S	C	S
St. Thomas	2 21	2 22	—	—	4 15	4 17			—	—	7 26	7 27	9 19	9 21	11 21	11 22
EXETER	2 25	—	3 53	—	4 20	—			5 58	—	7 30	—	9 24	—	11 25	—

DOWN TRAINS. TEIGN VALLEY BRANCH. WEEK DAYS.

Single Line City Basin Junction to Heathfield worked by Electric Train Staff. The Staff Stations are City Basin Junction, Longdown, Christow, Trusham, and Heathfield. Crossing Stations are Christow and Trusham. Intermediate token instrument at Chudleigh Knighton Sidings. Longdown is a crossing station, only by special arrangement during emergency working, but the Down Loop may be used, when required, for side-tracking a Freight Train.

M.P. Mileage M.	C.	Distances from Exeter M.	C.	STATIONS	Ruling Gradient.	Point to Point Times. (Mins.)	Allow for Stop. (Mins.)	Allow for Start. (Mins.)	K Freight. arr. a.m.	K Freight. dep. a.m.	B Auto. arr. a.m.	B Auto. dep. a.m.	B Auto. arr. a.m.	B Auto. dep. a.m.	B Auto. arr. a.m.	B Auto. dep. a.m.	K Newton Abbot Freight. arr. a.m.	K dep. a.m.	B Auto. SO arr. a.m.	B Auto. SO dep. a.m.
—	—	—	—	EXETER	—	—	—	2	—	7‡ 0	—	6 30	—	7 0	—	9 46			—	11 47
—	—	—	74	St. Thomas	—	—	—	—	—	—	6 33	6 34	7 3	7 4	9 49	9 50			11 50	11 51
—	—	1	19	City Basin Jct.	—	—	—	—	C 7	11 S	C	S	C	S	C	S			C	S
0	19	1	38	Alphington Road Goods Yard	264 R.	6	1	1	7‡13	—	—	—	—	—	—	—			—	—
0	62	2	1	Alphington Halt	56 R.	—	—	—			6 38	6 38½	7 8	7 9	9 54	9 54½			11 55	11 56
2	0	3	19	Ide Halt	58 R.	7	1	2			6 42	6 42½	7 13	7 14	9 58	9 58½			12 0	12 1
4	58	5	77	Longdown	58 R.	10	1	1			6 49½	6 50	7 21½	7 22½	10 6	10 6½			12 8½	12 9
4	68	6	7	Stop Board	L.	—	—	—			—	—	—	—	—	—			—	—
6	1	7	20	Dunsford Halt	64 F.	—	—	—			6 53	6 53½	7 25½	7 26½	10 9½	10 10			12 12	12 13
8	3	9	22	Christow	64 F.	8	2	1			6 58	7 0	7 31	7 33	1014½	1015½	—	11 15	12 18	12 19
Terminates at 8m. 7c.		10	29	Ryecroft Quarry	—	—	—	—			—	—	—	—	—	—	—	—	—	—
		10	68	Ashton	132 F.	4	1	1			7 4	7 5	7 37	7 38	1019½	10 20	C	R	12 23	12 24
		12	33	Whetcombe Sdg.	198 F.	4	1	1			—	—	—	—	—	—	—	—	—	—
		12	63	Trusham	384 F.	2	1	1			7 10	—	7 43	X7 44	10 25	1025½	11 25	●11 50	12 29	12 30
		13	8	Crockham Siding	84 F.	2	1	1					—	—	—	—	—	—	—	—
		14	51	Chudleigh	132 F.	4	1	1					7 48	7 49	1029½	10 30	11 57	●12 15	12 34	12 35
		15	74	Chudleigh K. Hlt.	—	—	—	—					7 52	7 53	10 33	1033½	—	—	12 38	12 39
		15	74	Chudleigh K. O.S.	—	—	—	—					—	—	—	—	C	R	—	—
		17	3	HEATHFIELD	66 R.	6	1	—					7 57	—	10 38	—	12 22	1 3	12 43	—

‡—RR to City Basin.

STATIONS.	B Newton Abbot Auto. SX arr. p.m.	B dep. p.m.	B Newton Abbot Auto. SO arr. p.m.	B dep. p.m.	K Freight. FO arr. p.m.	K Freight. FO dep. p.m.	K Newton Abbot Freight. SX arr. p.m.	K dep. p.m.	K Freight. SX arr. p.m.	K Freight. SX dep. p.m.	B Auto. arr. p.m.	B Auto. dep. p.m.	B Auto. arr. p.m.	B Auto. dep. p.m.	B Auto. arr. p.m.	B Auto. dep. p.m.	B Auto. SO arr. p.m.	B Auto. SO dep. p.m.
EXETER	—	12 50	—	1 0	—	1 30	—	1 55	—	4 10	—	4 30			—	6 30	—	9 55
St. Thomas	12 53	12 54	1 3	1 4	—	—	—	—	—	—	4 33	4 34			6 33	6 34	9 58	9 59
City Basin Junction	C	S	C	S	C 1	36 S	C 2	1 S	C 4	16 S	C	S			C	S	C	S
Alphington Road Goods Yard	—	—	—	—	1 38	—	—	—	4 18	—	—	—			—	—	—	—
Alphington Halt	12 58	12 59	1 8	1 9			—	—			4 38	4 38½			6 38	6 38½	10 3	10 4
Ide Halt	1 3	1 4	1 13	1 14			—	—			4 42½	4 43			6 42½	6 43	10 8	10 9
Longdown	1 11½	1 12½	1 21½	1 22½			C	S			4 50½	4 51½			6 50½	6 51½	1016½	1017½
Stop Board	—	—	—	—			2 22	P2 25			—	—			—	—	—	—
Dunsford Halt	1 15½	1 16½	1 25½	1 26½			—	—			4 54½	4 55			6 54½	6 55	1020½	10 21
Christow	1 21	1 25	1 31	1 35			2 36P	L2 56			4 59½	5 2	—	5 52	6 59½	X7 1	10 26	1027
Ryecroft Quarry	—	—	—	—			—	—			—	—	—	—	—	—	—	—
Ashton	1 28	1 29	1 38	1 39			—	—			5 5	5 6	5 56	5 57	7 4	7 4½	10 31	10 32
Whetcombe Siding	—	—	—	—			—	—			—	—	—	—	—	—	—	—
Trusham	1 34	X1 39	1 41	X1 49			8	7			5 10½	5 11½	6 1½	6 2½	7 9	7 9½	10 37	—
Crockham Siding	—	—	—	—			—	—			—	—	—	—	—	—		
Chudleigh	1 43	1 44	1 53	1 54			—	—			5 15½	5 16½	6 6½	6 7	7 13½	7 14		
Chudleigh Knighton Halt	1 47	1 48	1 57	1 58			—	—			5 19½	5 20	6 10	6 11	7 17	7 17½		
Chudleigh Knighton O.S.	—	—	—	—			—	—			—	—	—	—	—	—		
HEATHFIELD	1 52	1 55	2 2	2 5			3 20	X 3 30			5 24	—	6 15	—	7 22	—		

PLYMOUTH 849

D.63XX Diesel (Extract from Newton Abbot 701).

Enginemen

Newton Abbot Turn 810, 815, 818 SX, 833 SO, 851.

	arr.	dep.	
	a.m.	a.m.	
Newton Abbot Goods ..		8.30	**9D44 SX**
Heathfield	8.40		
Heathfield		8.50	**9D86 MWFO**
Trusham	9.10	9.30	**9D44**
Heathfield	10 0		
Heathfield		10.10	**9D64 SX**
Newton Abbot Goods ..	10.20		
Newton Abbot Goods ..		10.55	**9D05 MWFO**
Bovey	11.47		
	Shunt		
	p.m.	p.m.	
Bovey		2.45	**9D64**
Heathfield	3.15	4.10	
Teign Bridge Siding ..	4.16	4.36	
Newton Abbot Goods ..	4.42	4‖47	**0Z33**
Newton Abbot Shed ..	4‖52		
	a.m.	a.m.	
Newton Abbot Goods ..		10.55	**9D44 TThO**
Teign Bridge Siding ..	11.1	11.21	
Heathfield	11.27		
Heathfield		11.40	**9D05 Q**
Bovey	11.47	12.5	**9D44 Q**
	p.m.	p.m.	
Heathfield	12.13		
Heathfield		1.30	**9D86**
Trusham	2.12	2.40	**9D64**
Heathfield	3.26		
Heathfield		4.10	
Teign Bridge Siding ..	4.16	4.36	
Newton Abbot Goods ..	4.42		
Newton Abbot Goods ..		4‖47	**0Z33**
Newton Abbot Shed ..	4‖52		
Newton Abbot Shed ..		5‖25	**LD SX Q**
Newton Abbot Goods ..	5‖30	5.40	**9D78 Q**
Teign Bridge Siding ..	5.46	6.0	**9D64 Q**
Newton Abbot Goods ..	6.6	6‖15	**LD Q**
Newton Abbot Shed ..	6‖20		
Service SX	p.m.	p.m.	
Newton Abbot Shed ..		9‖40	**LD SX**
Totnes	10‖0		
0J12 Banker	a.m.	a.m.	
Dainton Siding		3‖20	**LD MX**
Newton Abbot	3‖30		
	p.m.	p.m.	
Newton Abbot		8‖40	**LD SO**
Totnes	9‖0		
0J12 Banker	a.m.	a.m.	
Rattery		1‖35	**LD Sun.**
Newton Abbot Shed ..	1‖55	2‖0	
Aller Junction . ..	2‖5		
0J12 Banker			
Rattery		5‖25	**LD**
Newton Abbot Shed ..	5‖45		

Service Sun.

For details of trains banked see pages 1 and 2

ENGINEERING AND OPERATING DATA

Pages 114 to 123 are reproduced from the Appendix to No. 5 Section of the Service Time Tables, Exeter Division, GWR — February 1947 until further notice by kind permission of British Railways Board (courtesy of L. Crosier) and, irrespective of dates, remain its exclusive copyright.

Pages 124 to 125 are reproduced from Alterations and Additions to the Appendix to No. 5 Section of the Service Time Tables, Exeter Division, GWR — February 1947 (various dates), by kind permission of British Railways Board and, irrespective of dates, remain its exclusive copyright.

Pages 126 to 128 are reproduced from the Sectional Appendix to the Working Time Tables and Books of Rules and Regulations, B.R. (W.R.), Exeter Traffic District, March 1960, by kind permission of British Railways Board (courtesy of A. R. Kingdom) and, irrespective of dates, remain its exclusive copyright.

The station nameboard at Heathfield.

E. R. Shepherd

WHERE ENGINES CAN TAKE WATER

Christow Up & Down Platforms.

LOOSE RUNAWAY CATCH POINTS OR DEAD END TRAP SIDINGS

Station or Signal Box	Up or Down Line	Where Situated	If Conn or Wkd from Box	Grad 1 in
Trusham	Up loop	138 Yds from Sig Box	Spring points Slotted	84
Christow	Up loop	242 Yds from Sig Box	Spring points Slotted	132

CROSSOVER ROADS EXIST AT THE FOLLOWING PLACES

Heathfield Station	Down to Up

SINGLE LINE CROSSING LOOPS

City Basin Junc 625 Feet Up and Down
Longdown 1100 Feet Up and Down
Christow 1100 Feet Up and Down
Trusham 1068 Feet Up and Down
Heathfield 1100 Feet Up and Down

PUBLIC ROAD LEVEL CROSSINGS

Ashton Crossing at 6M 17½C situated at the station; not a block post; Gates are worked by station staff; indicator and bell in operation; with signals and interlocking gates.

Knighton Crossing at 1M 10½C situated between Heathfield and Chudleigh; not a block post; Crossing Keeper, indicator and bell in operation; no signals.

Bovey Lane Crossing at 0M 21C situated between Heathfield and Chudleigh; not a block post; Crossing Keeper, indicator and bell in operation; No signals.

STATIONS AT WHICH SCREW COUPLINGS ARE KEPT

Christow — 1 type B
Heathfield — 1 type B

TEMPORARY RESTRICTIONS OF SPEED ON BRANCH LINES

Rule 218 — On the following branch lines Handsignalmen will be posted. Warning boards as well as 'C' & 'T' indicators will be fixed when the restriction of speed commences. The words 'Handsignalmen will not be posted' will be included in the notice posted.

On Goods and Mineral lines where a permanent speed restriction of 15mph or less is in force, further speed restrictions will not be imposed nor Handsignalmen posted in connection with Engineering work, unless arrangements are made between the Divisional Engineer and Superintendent.

WHERE RERAILING RAMPS ARE KEPT

Christow — 2 in Goods Warehouse.
Trusham — 2 in Signal Box.
Heathfield — 1 in Goods Shed.

FREIGHT TRAINS RUNNING WITHOUT BRAKE VANS (PER RULE 153)

Trusham to Whetcombe Siding (and vice versa) on a 1 in 198 falling gradient over a section of 660 Yds.

Trusham to Crockham Siding (and vice versa) on a 1 in 84 falling gradient over a section of 550 Yds.

Name of Station or Siding.	Where situated.	By whom attended.	How Locked.	Remarks.
TEIGN VALLEY BRANCH.				
Ide	East end of Siding	Guard or Porter	Key on Staff	
"	West end of Siding	Guard or Porter	" " "	
Longdown	East Loop, Up Side	Signalman	Electrically from Signal Box	
"	West Loop, Down Side	Signalman	" " " "	
"	East Siding, Up Side of Up and Down Main Line.	Signalman	Key locked in frame at Signal Box	
"	West Siding, Up Side of Up and Down Main Line.	Signalman	" " " "	
Ryecroft Siding	Siding	Guard	Key on Staff	
Ashton	East end of Siding	Guard or Porter	" " "	
"	West end of Siding	Guard or Porter	" " "	
Trusham	Whetcombe Siding	Guard	" " "	
"	Crockham Siding	Guard	Key on Token	
Chudleigh	East end of Siding	Guard	" " "	
"	West end of Siding	Guard	" " "	
Heathfield	Chudleigh Knighton Sidings	Guard or Porter	" " "	

Singles Line and How Worked—continued.

Between		Method of working the Single Line.	Where Staff, Token or Tablet kept.	Person responsible for exchanging.	Person responsible when aforesaid man is not on duty.	Remarks.
TEIGN VALLEY BRANCH.						
City Basin Junction	Longdown	Electric Staff	Signal Box	Signalman	..	
Longdown	Christow	Electric Staff	Booking Office, Longdown } Signal Box, Christow }	Signalman	..	
Christow	Trusham	Electric Staff	Signal Box	Signalman	..	
† Trusham	Heathfield	Electric Token	Signal Box	Signalman	..	

HALTS AT WHICH STAFF IS NOT EMPLOYED.

No staff is kept at the undermentioned Halts, and the supervision of them comes under the Station Masters at the Stations shewn.

The Station Masters must visit the Halts from time to time to see that the premises are in proper condition, and that notice boards, gates, shelters, seats, etc., are properly looked after:—

Name of Halt.	Station supervising Halt.
Dunsford	Christow.
Chudleigh Knighton	Heathfield.

WORKING OF FREIGHT TRAINS DOWN INCLINES.

The points at which trains must stop to release Wagon Brakes are as follows:—

Incline upon which "Stop Board" is fixed	Down or Up Trains	Point where Train must stop to release Brakes
Bampton.		
TEIGN VALLEY BRANCH.		
Longdown	Down	Christow Station.
"	Up	City Basin Junction Up Branch Home Signal.

Inclines Steeper than 1 in 200—continued.

Incline between	Length of Incline about	Gradient 1 in	Falling towards	Places at which Boards have been fixed and at which Freight Trains must stop to put down brakes.	Modifications of, or additions to, the Standard Instructions.
TEIGN VALLEY BRANCH.					
City Basin Junction and Ide	6 chains	86	Ide		
" " "	43 "	56	City Basin Jct. ..		
" " "	63 "	58	" " ..		
Ide and Longdown	2 m. 38 ch.	58	Ide		
" "	7 chains	90	"	Near Up Starting Signal for Longdown.	
Longdown and Christow	35 "	90	Christow	At 4m. 69 ch.	See Special Instructions, page 110 for assisting Freight Trains Christow to City Basin Junction.
" "	2 m. 2 ch.	64	"		
" "	40 chains	75	"		
Christow and Ashton..	4 "	132	Ashton		
" "	17 "	154	"		
Ashton and Trusham	10 "	198	Trusham		
Trusham and Chudleigh	5 "	84	Chudleigh		
" "	12 "	132	"		
" "	9 "	185	"		
Chudleigh and Heathfield	16 chains	176	Heathfield		
" "	11 "	66	Chudleigh		
" "	22 "	78	"		
" "	14 "	132	"		
" "	10 "	146	Heathfield		
" "	9 "	86	"		
" "	12 "	66	"		
" "	9 "	72	Chudleigh		
" "	10 "	88	"		

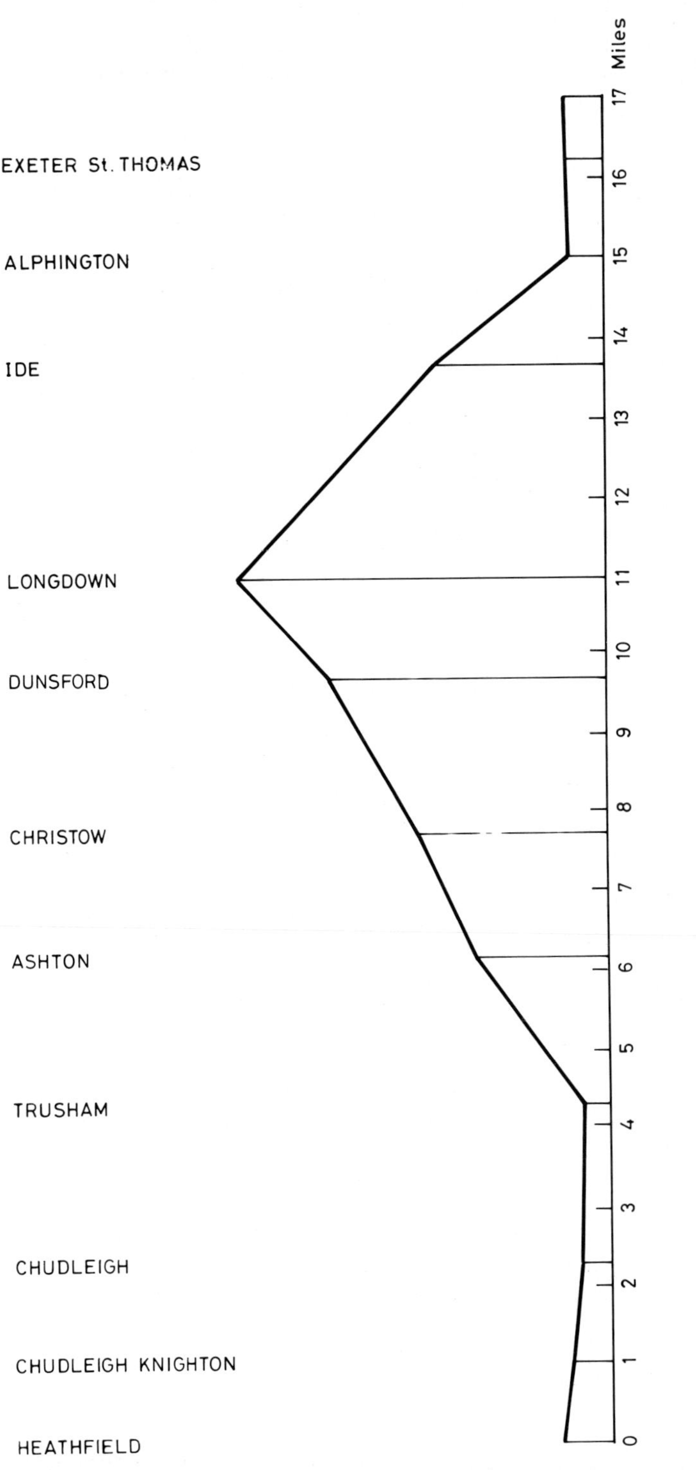

THE TEIGN VALLEY RAILWAY (GRADIENT CHART)

CROSSING OF RAILWAY BY ELECTRIC POWER LINES—continued.

Overhead Electric Power Lines cross the Line at the following Points:—

M. C.	Near	Between	Supply Co. or Authority.	Telephone No.
		TEIGN VALLEY BRANCH.		
1 10½	Chudleigh Knighton Halt.	Chudleigh Knighton Halt and Heathfield.	Teignmouth Elec. Light Co.	Bovey Tracey
2 34 } 2 52¾ }	Chudleigh	Chudleigh and Trusham.	Chudleigh Elec. Co.	Chudleigh 2144
6 18	Ashton	Ashton and Christow.	Teignmouth Elec. Light Co.	Bovey Tracey
3 70	Longdown	Longdown and Ide.	W. P. Studholme.	Exeter 3288.
— 33 } — 28 }	St. Thomas	City Basin Jct. and St. Thomas.	Exeter Gas Light & Coke Co. Ltd.	" "
— 12½	" "	" " "	Willey & Co. Ltd.	Exeter 4064.

TEIGN VALLEY BRANCH.

Motor Trolley System of Maintenance.

For general instructions see the General Appendix to the Rule Book.

The maintenance of the Branch is under the control of an Engineering Gang with Headquarters at Christow.

A small petrol motor driven inspection car is provided for the use of the Ganger. The Gang is provided with a petrol motor driven trolley capable of carrying men and a small quantity of tools.

A trailer is also supplied for the conveyance of material and tools.

Places where telephones and key boxes are fixed.

	m.	c.	
City Basin Signal Box.			
Key Box No. 1	1	9	Exeter Railway Mileage.
Key Box No. 2	2	8	
Key Box No. 3	2	75	
Key Box No. 4	3	79	
*Longdown Signal Box.			
Key Box No. 5	5	44	
Key Box No. 6	6	35	
Key Box No. 7	7	31	
†Christow Signal Box.			
Key Box No. 8	6	74	Teign Valley Mileage.
Key Box No. 9	6	2	
Key Box No. 10	5	10	

*—Control Instrument and telephone—City Basin—Longdown Section.
†—Control Instrument and telephone—Longdown—Christow—Trusham Sections.

TEIGN VALLEY BRANCH—continued.

‡Trusham Signal Box.	m.	c.
Key Box No. 11	3	22
Key Box No. 12	2	20
Key Box No. 13	1	14
Heathfield Signal Box.		

‡—Control Instrument and telephone—Trusham—Heathfield Section.

Use of Sidings by Auto Cars and Coaching Stock.

Coaching Stock and Auto Cars are prohibited from using the Sidings at the following stations:—

Ide
Longdown
Christow—beyond entrance to Cattle Pens Bank.

CITY BASIN JUNCTION.

Exchanging Train Staffs.

In those cases where Down trains are stopped at the Loop Starting Signal waiting to cross a train approaching from the opposite direction, the Guard of the train must go to the Signal Box and remain there until a Train Staff can be obtained and then take the Train Staff to the Driver.

• When the last train for the day over the Teign Valley Branch is an Up Freight train and it has arrived in the Loop, and is detained there waiting " Line Clear," the Guard must obtain the Electric Train Staff from the Driver of the Train Engine or Assisting Engine, as the case may be, and take it to the Signal Box, and the Signalman, after having obtained an assurance from the Guard that the whole of the Train with tail lamp attached has arrived, must place the Staff in the Instrument and send the " Train out of Section " Signal to Longdown.

ALPHINGTON ROAD.

Shunting.

Alphington Road Goods Yard Sidings are situated at the foot of a steep gradient falling towards the buffer stops adjacent to the public road.

Care must be exercised during shunting operations, sufficient hand-brakes being applied to prevent wagons, which are being shunted into these Sidings, coming into contact with undue force against the buffer stops or wagons standing in the Sidings.

Drivers and Guards of trains entering Alphington Road Goods Yard must have their trains under proper control.

When it is necessary for shunting purposes for the whole of an Up train to enter, and remain in Alphington Goods Yard for other Branch trains to pass, the Guard, after satisfying himself that the Line is clear, must take the Staff to City Basin Junction Signal Box, and the Signalman there, after receiving the Staff and an assurance from the Guard that the whole of the train is shunted into Alphington Yard and the Branch Line is clear, must place the Staff in the instrument and send the " Train out of Section " signal.

When a Down train is ready to leave Alphington Yard, the Guard must proceed to City Basin Junction Signal Box, so inform the Signalman, and obtain the Train Staff and hand it to the Driver, giving him any instructions which he may have received from the Signalman.

Before the Christow and Exeter Freight train leaves Christow, the Station Master must ascertain from the Guard whether he has any traffic for the City Basin Line, and, if so, the information must be telegraphed or telephoned to the Signalman at City Basin Junction Box, who will advise the Foreman at Alphington Road Goods Yard. The latter will arrange for the wagons to be placed on the City Basin Line under the Main Line overbridge and properly secured, where they will remain until picked up by the City Basin Freight train next morning. Whenever wagons for Alphington Road Goods Yard have to stand on the City Basin Line, they must be similarly placed and secured.

Before shunting over the Level Crossing situated between the Teign Valley Branch points and the Main Line overbridge, for the purpose of placing wagons in the position previously indicated, the Guard conducting the operation must satisfy himself that the Crossing is clear.

IDE.

Station is on an Incline of 1 in 60, falling towards City Basin Junction.

No vehicle must be detached and allowed to remain on the Main Line.

Before engines of Freight trains performing work are detached from their trains, the brake of the guard's van must be fully applied, and sufficient wagon brakes put down and sprags used to prevent the train moving. Any wagons shunted on to the train must be immediately coupled up.

Guards of Freight trains must fully apply the hand-brake before leaving their vans.

Six sprags must be kept, 10 yards apart, by the side of the line between the facing points and the end of the Loop.

Guards working Freight trains which call at Ide during the hours the Porter is not on duty will be responsible for working the Siding points. Traffic for Ide must be taken through to Longdown and returned to Ide by Passenger train when the Porter is on duty.

LONGDOWN.

Station is on the Summit of Inclines of 1 in 60 in both directions.

No vehicle must be detached and allowed to remain on the Main Line.

Before engines of Freight trains performing work are detached from their trains, the brake of the guard's van must be fully applied, and sufficient wagon brakes put down and sprags used to prevent the train moving. Any wagons shunted on to the train must be immediately coupled up.

Guards of Freight trains must fully apply the hand-brake before leaving their vans.

Six sprags must be kept, 10 yards apart, by the side of the line near the Signal Box.

Down Loop Line.

Longdown is normally worked as a non-crossing station but the Down Loop Line may be used when required for side-tracking a Freight train to allow an Up or Down train to pass.

During emergency working the Down Loop may be used for crossing through Passenger and/or Freight trains.

The connections at each end of the Down Loop are worked from Ground Frames released electrically from the Signal Box. Telephone communication is provided between the Signal Box and East Loop and West Loop Ground Frames.

The connections at the East and West ends of the Siding are worked from Ground Frames released by Annett's Key from the Signal Box.

CHRISTOW.

Truck Weighbridge Relief Line.

The weighbridge is situated in the Refuge Siding.

Engines must not be allowed to pass over the weighing road.

The machine has a weighing capacity up to 30 tons.

Except when it is necessary to weigh traffic, the lever controlling the points for the weighing line must be kept padlocked in its normal position, and the key kept in the Station Master's Office.

Immediately the Shunter or Porter in charge has completed weighing, the points must be reset in their normal position for the Goods Line.

The person in charge must satisfy himself from time to time that the instructions are being strictly observed.

Assisting Freight Trains—Christow to City Basin Junction.

When a Freight train requires assistance up the incline from Christow to Longdown, the assistant engine must be placed at the rear and coupled to the van, and may, if not required to return to Christow, be run through in that position to City Basin Junction. The rear engine will assist the train up the incline, and serve the purpose of an additional emergency brake when running down the incline from Longdown to City Basin Junction.

The assisting engine must be detached on arrival at City Basin Junction, and run light to Exeter.

Working of Pilot Trips between Christow and Ryecroft Private Siding.

Pilot trips may be run from Christow to the Siding without going through to Trusham, and must be dealt with in accordance with Electric Train Staff Regulation 8.A.

The trains may be propelled from Christow to the Siding during daylight at a speed not exceeding 10 M.P.H., and must not exceed 10 wagons per trip, exclusive of brake van.

The Guard or Shunter must ride in the brake van, which must be the leading vehicle leaving Christow, and the rear vehicle on the return trip. He must keep a sharp look-out, and be prepared to warn anyone on the line, and exhibit any necessary hand signals to the Driver.

The Driver must proceed cautiously and not exceed a speed of 10 M.P.H. when propelling, and be prepared to stop immediately in response to any fixed or hand signal.

This working is not permitted during fog or falling snow.

On arrival at the Siding, the brake van must be detached and left on the Main Line with brake fully applied. Out-going wagons from the Siding to be drawn out and coupled on to the brake van with sufficient brakes put down to hold them securely. Wagons for the Private Siding to be afterwards placed in position.

A man from Christow must accompany the train and assist the Guard at the Siding.

RYECROFT QUARRY.

Use of Level Crossing.

Permission to use this Crossing is given by the Signalman at Christow.

If the section between Christow and Trusham is occupied by an Up Freight train which has to perform work at Ashton Station, permission will be given for the Crossing to be used, providing the person in charge of Ashton has placed three detonators, 10 yards apart, on the Christow side of Ashton station, and he has given the Signalman at Christow an assurance that he has done so.

No Up Freight train performing work at Ashton must be allowed to leave that station until the person in charge has received permission from the Signalman at Christow for the train to proceed on its journey, and an assurance been given that the detonators have been removed from the line.

Ashton Up Distant Signal must be maintained at "Caution" for all Up Freight trains.

ASHTON.

Howard's Accommodation Crossing.

Before this Crossing is used by a heavy lorry or other exceptional traffic, as provided for in Rule 107, permission must be obtained from the person in charge of Ashton Station.

On a request being received for a crossing to be made, the Signalman at Christow must immediately be advised on the telephone what is required and his authority obtained before the crossing is permitted to take place.

Immediately permission has been obtained, the person in charge of Ashton must place three detonators, 10 yards apart, on the Trusham side of Ashton Station.

The Up and Down Distant Signals at Ashton must maintained at "Caution" during the time the Crossing is being used.

To prevent delay to the user of the Crossing, permission will be given for traffic to pass over the Crossing, if the section is occupied between Christow and Trusham, provided the person in charge at Ashton Station immediately advises the Signalman at Christow that the train has passed Howard's Crossing and the instructions above have been carried out.

When the line is again clear, the person in charge at Ashton Station must so advise the Signalman at Christow on the telephone.

BLASTING INSTRUCTIONS.

RYECROFT—WHETCOMBE—TINKLEY QUARRIES, BETWEEN CHRISTOW AND TRUSHAM STATIONS.

Blasting will be permitted at agreed times, subject to the train service and during daylight and in clear weather only.

Whenever the Quarry Company at either of the quarries requires to blast, their Foreman will apply for permission to the Signalman concerned.

Ryecroft Quarry .. .. Christow Signalman.
Whetcombe and Tinkley Quarries .. Trusham Signalman.

Immediately blasting is finished the Quarry Company's Foreman must give an assurance to the Signalman that the line is clear.

WHETCOMBE LEVEL CROSSING.

The speed over the Crossing must not exceed 15 M.P.H.

Whistle board on right hand side of line 220 yards Ashton side of Crossing.

WHETCOMBE—TEIGN VALLEY GRANITE COMPANY'S SIDINGS.

This Siding is situated 30 chains on the Christow side of Trusham Station, and the connection is controlled by a ground frame locked by a key on the Electric Train Staff of the Trusham—Christow section.

A telephone is provided between the ground frame and Trusham Station.

The gradient of the Main Line at the connection is 1 in 198, falling towards Heathfield.

Occupation of the Main Line must be given in accordance with Electric Train Token Regulation 8.A.

A Porter must assist the Guard in the work to be performed at the Siding and must accompany the trip from Trusham.

The Guard will be responsible for working the ground frame.

An engine may be permitted to propel or draw loaded or empty wagons between Trusham Station and the Siding without a brake-van.

A man must accompany the wagons, and either ride in, or walk beside, the leading or last vehicle as the case may be, and be prepared to hand-signal the Driver as required.

The number of wagons on any trip must not exceed 25, and the speed of the train must not exceed 4 M.P.H.

Whenever a propelling movement is made, the man riding in or walking alongside the leading vehicle must sound a horn for the purpose of warning any person who may be on the line or passing over Whetcombe Crossing.

CROCKHAM—TEIGN VALLEY GRANITE COMPANY'S SIDING.

This Siding is situated 25 chains on the Heathfield side of Trusham Station, and the connection is controlled by a ground frame locked by a key on the Electric Train Token for the Trusham—Heathfield Section. A telephone is provided between the ground frame and Trusham Station.

The gradient of the Main Line at the connection is 1 in 84, falling towards Heathfield.

Occupation of the Main Line must be given in accordance with Electric Train Token Regulation 8.A.

A Porter must assist the Guard in the work to be performed at the Siding, and must accompany the trip from Trusham.

The Guard will be responsible for working the ground frame.

Loose wagons must not be placed on the Main Line.

If it is necessary for any traffic to be placed on the Main Line from the Siding, it must be attached to a brake-van, and the brake-van must be firmly secured, the brakes applied to the wagons, a sprag also being placed in the wheels of the first wagon.

An engine may be permitted to draw loaded or empty wagons from Trusham Station to the Siding without a brake-van. Wagons must not, in any circumstances, be propelled from Trusham Station to the Siding.

An engine may be permitted to propel loaded or empty wagons from the Siding to Trusham Station without a brake-van. A man must accompany the wagons and either ride in or walk alongside the leading or last vehicle as the case may be, and be prepared to hand-signal the Driver as required. The number of wagons on any trip must not exceed 25, and the speed of the train must not exceed 4 M.P.H.

Three sprags must be kept on the Main Line, 10 yards apart, near the Siding connection.

The gate leading into the Siding must be closed after the shunting has been completed.

RUNNING OF TRAINS THROUGH FLOODED AREAS—TRUSHAM AND HEATHFIELD.

The following instructions apply in regard to the emergency working to be adopted when the line is flooded between Trusham and Heathfield :

The flood area between the above points usually extends from 80 yards on the Trusham side of Chudleigh Station overbridge to 150 yards on the Heathfield side of Chudleigh Station overbridge.

The Porter at Chudleigh, upon observing the area becoming flooded, must immediately get into touch with the Engineering Department.

If the area is safe for the passage of trains, immediate steps must be taken to advise the person in charge at Heathfield and Trusham, also the Exeter Station Master. Drivers of trains leaving for the flooded area must be advised to proceed cautiously.

If the Engineering Department find it necessary to prohibit trains passing through the flooded area, Down trains must work to and from the Emergency Platform on the Trusham side of Chudleigh Station, and a road motor service be maintained between Chudleigh and Heathfield, the Station Master at Christow to be responsible for obtaining a fully licensed passenger-carrying vehicle, if possible, from the Devon General Omnibus Company.

Trains working to and from the Emergency Platform at Chudleigh must be signalled in accordance with Electric Train Token Regulation 8.A., and the Driver advised that the train is to work to and from Chudleigh Emergency Platform only.

Auto trains only must work over the Branch whilst the line is flooded.

PASSENGER TRAIN WORKING—TRUSHAM, CHUDLEIGH, AND HEATHFIELD.

When it is necessary for an Auto train to work between Trusham and Chudleigh, or Heathfield and Chudleigh, it must be dealt with in accordance with Electric Train Token Regulation 8.A.

If the Auto train is substituted by an ordinary train, it must consist of engine and brake-third only, and may be propelled when empty on the return journey with the brake-compartment leading, in which the Guard must ride and keep a sharp look-out and be prepared to hand-signal to the Driver.

FREIGHT TRAIN WORKING BETWEEN TRUSHAM AND CHUDLEIGH.

A freight train working between Trusham and Chudleigh must be dealt with in accordance with Electric Train Token Regulation 8.A.

On the return journey, if necessary to do so, the brake-van may be propelled from Chudleigh to Trusham. The Guard must ride in the van, keep a sharp look-out, and be prepared to hand-signal to the Driver.

113

CHUDLEIGH KNIGHTON SIDINGS.

Connection with the Sidings is controlled by ground frame released by Electric Train Token of the Heathfield–Trusham Section.

An Intermediate Token Instrument and telephone are provided at the ground frame to permit a train to be shunted into or allowed to leave the Sidings. The Intermediate Token Instrument and telephone are fixed in a padlocked box, which can be opened by the same key as the Engineering Department Occupation Huts on the Teign Valley Branch.

The gradient of the Branch Line at the connection to the Sidings is 1 in 132 falling towards Chudleigh. All trains calling at the Sidings must be accompanied by a competent man from Heathfield to assist the Guard in the work to be performed at the Sidings. If the train is coming from the direction of Trusham, the Signalman at that place must advise Heathfield to send a man to meet the train on arrival at the Sidings.

A Freight train performing work at the Sidings may be shunted in clear of the Branch Line when necessary for another train to pass.

When a train has been so shunted and the Branch Line is clear, the Electric Train Token must be placed in the Intermediate Instrument and the Signalman at the rear advised accordingly.

When the train is ready to leave the Sidings, the Signalman at the Box in the rear must be advised, and permission asked to withdraw the Token. If permission for the train to leave the Sidings can be given, the Signalman from whom permission is asked will arrange with the Signalman at the other end of the section for a Token to be released. The Signalman in rear must be advised when a Token has been withdrawn. When the Token is handed to the Driver, the person doing so must verbally instruct him that the line is only clear to the Home Signal of the Box in advance.

For instructions as to operation of Intermediate Token Instrument see the General Appendix to the Rule Book.

Wagons must not be propelled from the Sidings to the Branch Line unless there is a Brake van at the Chudleigh end and a man in it.

If it is not necessary for the complete train to be shunted into the Sidings clear of the Branch Line, the portion left on the Branch Line must be secured in accordance with Rule 151 before the engine is detached.

2nd · SINGLE SINGLE · 2nd

5795 Heathfield to 5795

Heathfield / Heathfield

Chudl'ghK'htonH, / Chudl'ghK'htonH,

CHUDLEIGH KNIGHTON HALT

(W) 4d. FARE 4d. (W)

For conditions see over For conditions see over

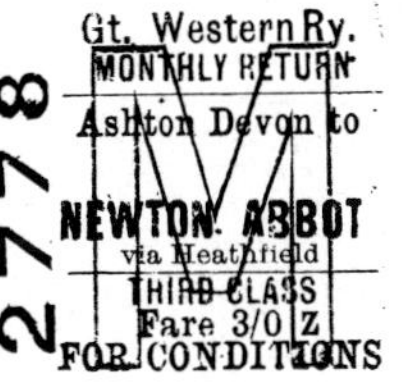

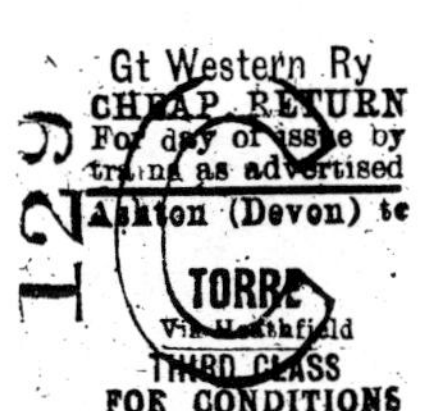

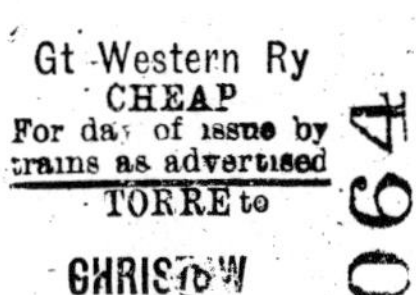

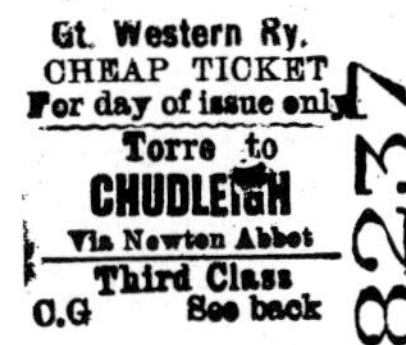

Engine Restrictions—continued

BRANCH LINES—continued.

SECTION OF LINE	ROUTE COLOUR	ENGINES AUTHORISED	PROHIBITIONS
NO ENGINE TO WORK OVER WAGON TURNTABLES.			
City Basin (Exeter) ..	Dotted Blue	All uncoloured, yellow and blue types.	
City Basin Junction : Heathfield	Uncoloured	All uncoloured types. Yellow types specially authorised. 2-6-2T. 0-6-0T. 2-4-0T. Blue types : 2-8-0 2-6-0 2-6-2T. 4-6-0 (78XX) 2-6-0 (43XX)	To be used only for shunting Alphington Road Loop and Cattle Pens Sidings. Not to pass Down Teign Valley Branch Advanced Starting Signal. Speed not to exceed ten miles per hour. Maximum speed 25 m.p.h. Note—During emergency working over this Branch see Notice No. 464.

STANDARD LOADS OF PASSENGER, PARCELS, MILK, AND FISH TRAINS FOR ENGINE WORKING PURPOSES.

The loads of all Passenger, Parcels, Milk, and Fish Trains will be calculated on the tonnage system, and the tables given on two following pages show the standard loads for the various classes of engines on the different routes.

The loads given in the tables represent the capacity of the engine if the standard point-to-point timing is to be maintained. On sections where gradients will permit, these loads may be exceeded with a suitable increase in the point-to-point timing, but on sections where there are steep rising gradients it will be necessary to provide an assistant engine.

To enable guards and others to calculate the loads of trains in tons, the tare weight of the vehicle, in 2½-in. figures, has been painted at both ends, at alternate corners, of all stock formed in trains coming within the category of those mentioned above. The loads of trains, calculated by the addition of these tonnage figures, must be ascertained by guards and the information given to drivers at the starting points and at any subsequent points at which vehicles are attached or detached.

In the case of a vehicle of another Region not marked with the tare weight, being formed in a train, the weight of the vehicle must be counted as 10 tons for a Horse Box, Carriage Truck, or other such small vehicle, 20 tons for a four or six-wheeled passenger carrying vehicle or Brake Van, 30 tons for an eight-wheeled passenger carrying vehicle or Brake Van other than 70-ft. stock, and 40 tons for a Dining Car, Sleeping Car, or 70-ft. passenger carrying vehicle or Brake Van.

LOADED VANS CONTAINING OCEAN MAILS AND BAGGAGE.

An allowance of 5 tons per vehicle must be added to the tare weight of each loaded Van of Ocean Mails and Baggage.

PARCELS AND FISH TRAINS.

Owing to the difference in the weights of loaded and unloaded Parcels Vans and Fish Trucks, it will be necessary in the case of Parcels and Fish Trains to add to the total of the tare weights shown on the vehicles an agreed figure representing the weight of the average load, for every loaded truck formed in the train. It has been decided that this fixed figure shall be one ton per vehicle for Parcels and three tons per vehicle for Fish, and, therefore, a guard, in calculating the load of his train, must multiply the number of loaded trucks by these figures and add the resulting figure to the total of the tare weights marked upon the trucks.

MILK TRAFFIC.

The weight of vehicles containing milk traffic to be computed as follows, whether the vehicles are working on passenger milk, fish, or perishable trains :—

	Empty.	Loaded.
Fixed Milk Tanks ("Miltas")	14 tons	28 tons
Road/Rail Milk Tanks ("Rotanks") ..	18 tons	28 tons

	Siphons J and BG Vehicles.	**Siphons F, G, H, and BG Vehicles.**	**Other Vehicles.**
Empty	Tare weight.	Tare weight.	Tare weight.
Loaded (Empty Churns) .	Tare weight plus 5 tons.	Tare weight plus 5 tons.	Tare weight plus 3 tons.
Loaded (Full Churns) ..	Tare weight plus 10 tons.	Tare weight plus 8 tons.	Tare weight plus 5 tons.

The weight of parcels (including stores), perishable, fish and milk trains which are run in accordance with passenger train regulations, must not exceed a gross weight of 550 tons, including brake, whether assisted or unassisted.

The following maximum loads (including Brake Van) are specially authorised for Perishables and empty and loaded Milk Trains between Newton Abbot and Paddington via Castle Cary and Newbury, viz. :—

King Class engines	=	550 tons.
Castle and 10XX Class engines	=	500 tons.
47XX Class Engines	=	485 tons.
40XX "Star", 49XX Class, 59XX, 68XX, 68XX, 79XX engines	=	465 tons.
43XX class ; 78XX engines.	=	450 tons.

When the loads exceed the governing standards shewn on page 226, the running times will be :

Exeter start to Whiteball Tunnel pass	32 minutes.
Exeter pass to Whiteball Tunnel pass	30 minutes.
Taunton start to Castle Cary pass	42 minutes.
Heywood Road Junction pass to Bedwyn pass	45 minutes.

MIXED TRAINS.

Where trains are authorised to be run as "Mixed" Trains, the total weight of the train is to be obtained as follows :—

Tonnage of Passenger Stock.
Tare Weight of Goods Brake Van (where provided).
Tonnage of Freight Vehicles to be calculated as under :

Class 1 Traffic = 16 tons per wagon. Class 2 Traffic = 13 tons per wagon.
Class 3 Traffic = 10 tons per wagon. Empties (4-wheel stock = 6 tons per wagon).

Notes.—The instructions contained herein do not in any way affect or remove the prohibition placed by the Chief Engineer on the working of certain types of engines over certain sections of line, although loadings may be given in the table for engines over portions of line which are prohibited for them.

These instructions for calculating the loads do not affect those contained in the Appendix to the Book of Rules and Regulations respecting the formation of Passenger Trains.

Empty Stock Trains must not exceed 20 8-wheel vehicles or their equivalent.

Guards must show on their train journals the number of vehicles and the actual total tonnage of the trains at starting points and on leaving subsequent stations at which vehicles are attached or detached.

Stations will, in wiring particulars of trains, give the information as shewn in the following example :—

Train 120 five late one Plymouth 34 five Penzance 179 three Newquay 100 Engine 4093 Loading moderate. When trains are not numbered the time of train must be shewn in place of number, viz., 11.0 a.m. Paddington five late, etc.

The following engines are classified as "Bulldogs" for computation of load purposes :—
3300, 3302, to 3311, 3313, 3314, 3316, 3318, 3319, 3321 to 3331, 3333, 3335 to 3350, 3352 to 3364, 3366 to 3399, 3400 to 3455.

STANDARD LOADS OF PASSENGER, PARCELS, MILK, AND FISH TRAINS FOR ENGINE WORKING PURPOSES—cont

Branch Lines.

SECTION.		CLASS OF ENGINE.										
		60XX.	10XX,	4003-4072 except 4016, 4032, 4037.	29XX. | 78XX 43XX, 53XX, 63XX, 73XX, 93XX		B.R. Standard Class 3 (2-6-2T) 3335-3455	90XX	0-6-0 & 0-6-0T.	S.R.—M 7.	2-4-0 T. Metro	0-4-2 T. 3574, 3575, 3577
			100, 111, 4000, 4016, 4032, 4037. 4073-4099, 5000-5099, 70XX	49XX, 59XX, 69XX, 79XX	31XX, 41XX, 51XX, 61XX, 81XX		4400-4410 4500-4599 5500-5574	2200-2299 32XX			0-4-2 T. 14XX, 58XX	1334, 1335, 1336.
From.	To.			68XX,	56XX, 66XX		36XX, 37XX, 46XX, 57XX, 77XX, 87XX, 96XX, 97XX.	0-6-2 T. "B" Group.	0-6-2 T. "A" Group.		844-896	
		Tons.	Tons.	Tons.	Tons.		94XX Tons.	Tons.	Tons.	Tons.	Tons.	Tons.
Exeter	Heathfield	—	—	—	280V		200	200Z	170		100	90
Heathfield	Exeter	—	—	—	300V		220	200Z	200		110	100

*—Loads for 43XX and 53XX Engines. †—The timing of "Passenger" trains on this Branch is based on a maximum of 230 tons. A S.R. "N" Class engine substituting the W.R. 43XX Class engine from Barnstaple in emergency will convey equivalent tonnage. §—Load 310 tons Minehead to Washford; 360 tons Washford to Taunton. V—Loads specially agreed for 41; 51; 43; 53; 63; 73; and 78XX Class engines between Exeter and Newton Abbot via Heathfield in connection with Diversion of Trains emergency working. Z—Loads specially agreed for 2251—2299 Class engines between Exeter and Newton Abbot via Heathfield in connection with Diversion of Trains emergency working. ‡—Allowed one minute extra running time from Paignton to Torquay when the load for "Castle" and 10XX Class engines exceeds [illegible] tons and for 49XX, etc. it exceeds 392 tons.

MAXIMUM SPEED OF TRAINS THROUGH JUNCTIONS, ETC. — continued.

Teign Valley Branch. — The speed of all Up and Down Trains between Exeter City Basin Junction and Christow must not exceed 35 miles per hour: and between Christow and Heathfield must not exceed 45 miles per hour, and be further restricted to a lower speed as shewn below:

NAME OF PLACE	DIRECTION OF TRAIN From.	To.	Miles per Hour.
Exeter City Basin Junction	All Trains to and from Main Line		15
Exeter City Basin	Branch Line to or from City Basin		10
Exeter City Basin Jct. and 1/4 m.p.Q	All Up and Down Trains		30
Alphington Road Goods	All Trains over Goods Line		10
Christow	Trains entering or leaving Station Loop		15
Ashton	All Up and Down Trains over curve through Station		35
Whetcombe Crossing at 4 m. 50 ch	All Down Trains over Crossing		15
	All Up Trains over Crossing		25
Trusham	All Trains entering or leaving Down Loop		15
West of Trusham	All Up Trains between 4 m.p. (River Bridge) and Trusham Station		25
East of Chudleigh	All Up and Down Trains between 2 1/2 m.p. and Chudleigh Station		25
West of Chudleigh	All Up and Down Trains between Chudleigh Station and 2 m.p.		30
Heathfield	All Up and Down Trains over curve between 0 m.p. and 0 m. 30 ch.		15
Heathfield (0 m.p. and 30 Ch)	Teign Valley Branch	Moretonhampstead Branch	15
Heathfield	All Trains entering or leaving Bay Line between 0 m.p. and 0 m 12 ch...		10

Q— Blue Class Engines authorised for shunting between City Basin Junction and Down Teign Valley Branch Advanced Starting Signal not to exceed speed of 10 m.p.h.

See Notice No. 464 for Speed Restrictions of additional classes of engines authorised to work over Branch in case of emergency.

TABLE J.1 (*continued*)

Incline between	Length of Incline about	Gradient 1 in	Falling towards	Modifications of, or additions to, the General Instructions for working inclines.
			TEIGN VALLEY BRANCH	
Chudleigh and Heathfield ..	10 chains	88	Chudleigh	
" " " ..	9 chains	72	"	
" " " ..	12 chains	66	Heathfield	
" " " ..	9 chains	86	"	
" " " ..	10 chains	146	"	
" " " ..	14 chains	132	Chudleigh	
" " " ..	22 chains	785	"	
" " " ..	11 chains	66	"	
" " " ..	16 chains	176	Heathfield	
Trusham and Chudleigh	10 chains	185	Chudleigh	
" "	12 chains	132	"	
" "	5 chains	84	"	
Ashton and Trusham	10 chains	198	Trusham	
Christow and Ashton	17 chains	154	Ashton	
" "	4 chains	132	"	

TABLE H.1

WORKING OF FREIGHT VEHICLES WITHOUT A BRAKE VAN IN REAR

Set out below is a list of places where freight vehicles (in accordance with Rule 153/(b)) may be worked without a Brake Van in rear.

One wagon of coal or stores for signal-boxes and stations, or the empty wagon in connection therewith, may be worked without a Brake Van between any two signal-boxes, provided the signal-boxes concerned are not more than one mile apart.

From	To	Line	No. of vehicles and special conditions
Trusham	Crockham Siding ..	Single	—

TABLE P

LEVEL CROSSING GATES—OPENING AND CLOSING BY TRAINMEN

The following is a list of level crossings where, in the absence of a crossing keeper, the gates must be opened and closed by the trainmen.

Trains must be brought to a stand well clear of the gates, after which the gates must be unlocked and opened and then locked against road traffic by the Fireman for the passage of the train over the crossing. When the train has passed over the crossing, the Guard (or Fireman in the case of a light engine) must close the gates across the railway and re-lock them, the Driver taking care not to proceed on his journey until he has received an " All Right " signal from the Guard. Enginemen and Guards concerned must see that they are supplied with keys of the gates.

Any defects in the gates or the locks securing them or in the lamps must be reported immediately by the Guard or Fireman to the Station Master concerned.

M. C.	Name of Crossing	Situated at, or between	Remarks
0 21	Bovey Lane ..	Heathfield and Chudleigh ..	Gates to be operated by trainmen. See page 90.
1 10½	Chudleigh Knighton	Heathfield and Chudleigh ..	
6 17½	Ashton	Ashton	

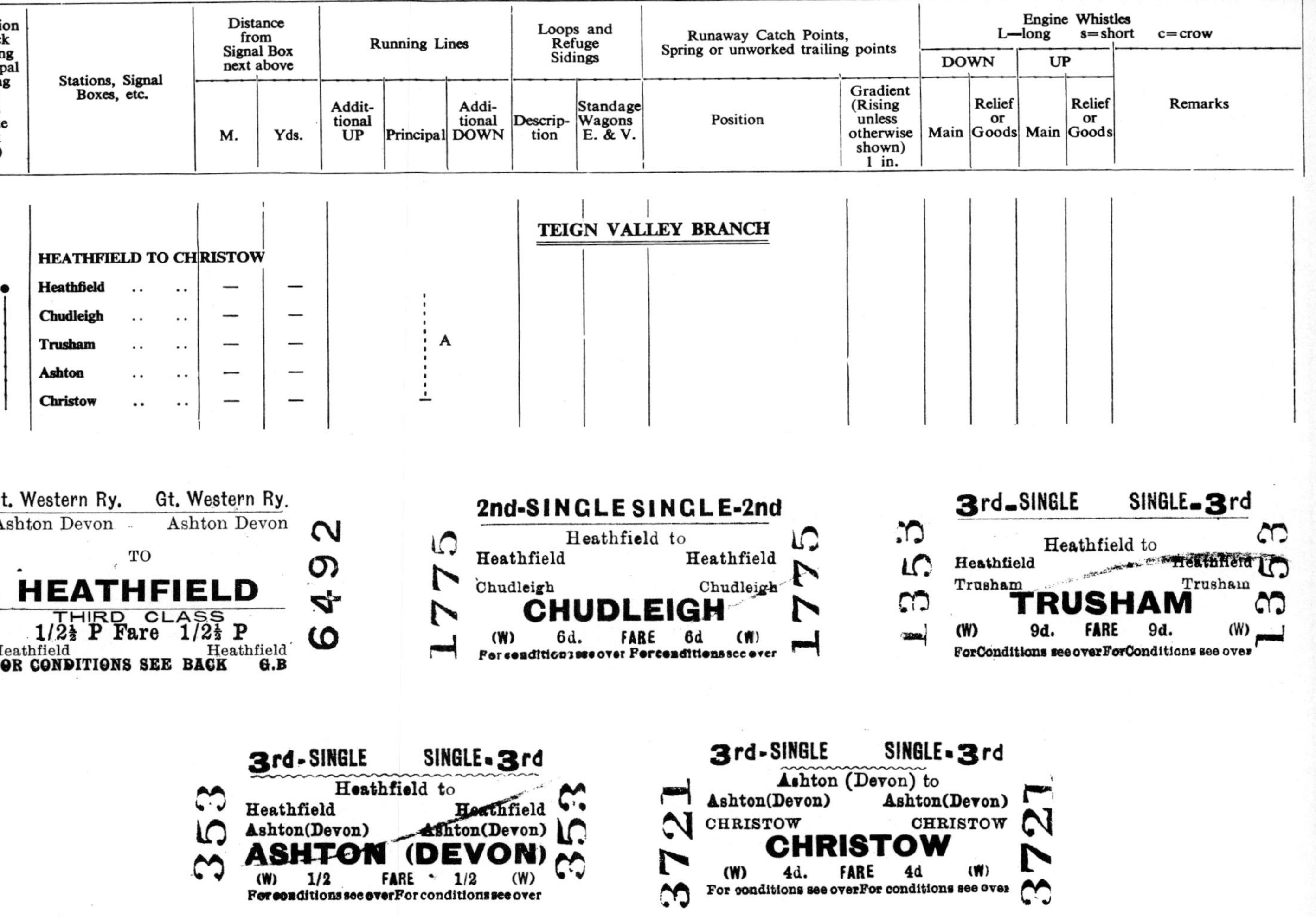

Description of Block Signalling on Principal Running Lines (Dots indicate Block Posts)	Stations, Signal Boxes, etc.	Distance from Signal Box next above		Running Lines			Loops and Refuge Sidings		Runaway Catch Points, Spring or unworked trailing points		Engine Whistles L—long s=short c=crow				
											DOWN		UP		
		M.	Yds.	Addit-tional UP	Principal	Addi-tional DOWN	Descrip-tion	Standage Wagons E. & V.	Position	Gradient (Rising unless otherwise shown) 1 in.	Main	Relief or Goods	Main	Relief or Goods	Remarks
							TEIGN VALLEY BRANCH								
	HEATHFIELD TO CHRISTOW														
One Engine in Steam	**Heathfield**	—	—		A										
	Chudleigh	—	—												
	Trusham	—	—												
	Ashton	—	—												
	Christow	—	—												

15

6492
Gt. Western Ry. Gt. Western Ry.
Ashton Devon Ashton Devon
TO
HEATHFIELD
THIRD CLASS
1/2½ P Fare 1/2½ P
Heathfield Heathfield
FOR CONDITIONS SEE BACK G.B
6492
1775
2nd-SINGLE SINGLE-2nd
Heathfield to
Heathfield Heathfield
Chudleigh Chudleigh
CHUDLEIGH
(W) 6d. FARE 6d (W)
For conditions see over For conditions see over
1775
1353
3rd-SINGLE SINGLE-3rd
Heathfield to
Heathfield Heathfield
Trusham Trusham
TRUSHAM
(W) 9d. FARE 9d. (W)
For Conditions see over For Conditions see over
1353
353
3rd-SINGLE SINGLE-3rd
Heathfield to
Heathfield Heathfield
Ashton(Devon) Ashton(Devon)
ASHTON (DEVON)
(W) 1/2 FARE 1/2 (W)
For conditions see over For conditions see over
353
3721
3rd-SINGLE SINGLE-3rd
Ashton (Devon) to
Ashton(Devon) Ashton(Devon)
CHRISTOW CHRISTOW
CHRISTOW
(W) 4d. FARE 4d (W)
For conditions see over For conditions see over
3721

TEIGN VALLEY BRANCH

Motor Trolley System of Maintenance

The Standard Instructions in connection with the Motor Trolley System of Maintenance on Single Lines worked by Wooden Staff apply.

The maintenance of the Branch is under the control of an Engineering Gang with Headquarters at Christow.

A small petrol driven inspection car is provided for the use of the Ganger. The Gang is provided with a petrol motor driven trolley capable of carrying men and a small quantity of tools.

A trailer is also supplied for the conveyance of material and tools.

Places where telephones are fixed.

Heathfield Signal box

Box No. 1	—	1 m. 14 ch.
2	—	2 m. 20 ch.
3	—	3 m. 22 ch.
4	—	4 m. 20 ch.
5	—	5 m. 10 ch.
6	—	6 m. 2 ch.
7	—	6 m. 74 ch.

Christow

89

TEIGN VALLEY BRANCH (*continued*)

Working of Level Crossing Gates—Teign Valley Branch.

The normal position of the level crossing gates at Bovey Lane, Chudleigh Knighton and Ashton is across the railway and the gates are secured in either position by standard padlock of identical pattern.

The keys are kept in Heathfield Signal Box and before proceeding on the Branch, the fireman must obtain the two keys which are suitably labelled, and hand the appropriate one to the guard.

The fireman will be responsible for returning both keys to the signalman on arrival back at Heathfield and the Signalman must see that this is done.

Unless instructions are issued to the contrary the lamps on the gates will not be lighted from 15th March until 30th September, inclusive, except during fog or falling snow.

Advice of Running

Stations Heathfield to Christow and vice versa must advise by telephone, the stations in advance the departure time of each train.

CROCKHAM—TEIGN VALLEY GRANITE COMPANY'S SIDING

This Siding is situated 25 chains on the Heathfield side of Trusham Station, and the connection is controlled by a ground frame locked by a key on the Train Staff. A telephone is provided between the ground frame and Trusham Station.

The gradient of the Main Line at the connection is 1 in 84, falling towards Heathfield.

A Porter must assist the Guard in the work to be performed at the Siding, and must accompany the trip from Trusham.

The Guard will be responsible for working the ground frame.

Loose wagons must not be placed on the Main Line.

If it is necessary for any traffic to be placed on the Main Line from the Siding, it must be attached to a brake-van, and the brake-van must be firmly secured, the brakes applied to the wagons, a sprag also being placed in the wheels of the first wagon.

Three sprags must be kept on the Main Line, 10 yards apart, near the Siding connection.

The gate leading into the Siding must be closed after the shunting has been completed.

CHRISTOW

Vehicles must not be left on the Branch Line after the freight train has departed. If it is necessary to place vehicles on the Branch line during shunting operations they must be secured by brakes and sprags.

Guards of freight trains must effectively apply the hand brake before leaving their vans.

CLOSURE AND TRACK LIFTING

By the early 1950s passenger traffic on the Teign Valley line was already in general decline as more and more people took to the motor car as a means of transport, a pattern that was developing nationwide. Moreover, little effort appears to have been made to try and counteract the effects by attracting tourists on to this very picturesque branch line located in the heart of the Devon countryside. Instead, only a limited service was provided on Saturdays, and on Sundays, the very day when ramblers and country lovers from the towns would have found it convenient, especially during the summer, no trains ran at all!

The closing down of the Bridford Barytes Mine in 1953, followed a year or so later by Scatter Rock Quarry, only served to aggravate the situation as regards revenue from the line with the result that as the losses mounted, with no obvious attempt being made to cut costs, so the likelihood of the line being closed became an increasing inevitability. However, it was not until 1957 that the first positive indications of closure came about when a public notice was issued stating that the British Transport Commission proposed, subject to the approval of the South West Area Transport Users' Consultative Committee, to withdraw the passenger train service between Exeter (St. David's) and Heathfield and to close Longdown Station for all purposes.

This was followed, in early 1958, by the issue of a further notice stating that from Monday, 3rd March, 1958, the passenger train service between Exeter (St. David's) and Heathfield Stations would be permanently withdrawn and Longdown Station, Alphington Halt, Ide Halt, Dunsford Halt and Chudleigh Knighton Halt would be closed for all purposes. After then making reference to existing passenger road services in the area, the notice went on to say that existing arrangements for the delivery and collection of parcels would continue to be maintained and that such traffic would also be accepted from or held for collection to the public at Chudleigh, Trusham, Ashton and Christow Stations. Similarly, the existing collection and delivery arrangements within the area for freight traffic in less than truck loads would be maintained and alternative arrangements for dealing with general merchandise previously dealt with at Longdown were to be available at Alphington Road Goods Depot. Facilities for dealing with freight traffic in full truck loads at goods stations on the branch, other than at Longdown, would also be maintained.

In the event, the line was granted a reprieve due to a successful protest by St. Thomas Rural District Council against the inadequacy of the bus service, and during April of that year not only was Ashton Station repainted, but three new replacement signal posts were installed at Longdown, which suggested that the line still had a future. Sadly, though, the reprieve proved to be all too brief an affair. On Monday, 9th June, 1958, the passenger service was finally withdrawn, and the section of line between Christow and Exeter closed completely, apart from the incursion into the Alphington Road sidings (now the Marsh Barton Industrial Estate) from City Basin Junction. British Rail, in a submission to the Consultative Committee, stated that on average the line

The last day of passenger services. *Top:* 0–4–2T, No. 1451 (in lined green livery), with the 12.49 p.m. train from Heathfield at Christow Station. *Lower:* 2–6–2T, No. 5530, with the 4.44 p.m. train from Heathfield at Trusham Station.

E. R. Shepherd

was used for 193 daily journeys, and that the closure would effect an estimated net saving of £15,000 per annum. In addition, a capital saving of about £30,000 was mentioned, which would be required for bridge and other repairs were traffic to continue.

On the last day of passenger services (Saturday, 7th June, 1958) the line saw its heaviest traffic for some time, and throughout most of the day trains were running with extra coaches to cope with the demand. The final train, which was shown in the timetable as the 8.00 p.m. departure from Newton Abbot, running through to Exeter St. David's, with the return journey commencing at 9.30 p.m., was no exception, although I now leave it to one of the passengers, Mr. E. R. Shepherd of Plymouth, to recount the journey:

> 'Having persuaded my wife and some friends to join me, we arrived at Newton Abbot Station at about 7.00 p.m. and found that the Teign Valley train was to leave from the isolated platform 9, situated outside the main station. Some intending passengers were already on the platform, and at 7.25 p.m. a train arrived headed by a rather dirty "Small Prairie" 2–6–2T, No. 5533, with two coaches (5077 and 5231) packed with passengers. The guard confirmed that the train had come down the valley, but thought that

2–6–2T, No. 5533, undergoing final preparations at Newton Abbot Station, flanked by a crowd of interested on-lookers, as time draws near for the last train on 7th June 1958.

Courtesy of Western Mercury News Ltd

A welcoming party awaits the arrival of the last train at Chudleigh Knighton Halt. Left to right (facing the camera) are County Counsellor George Vallance, David Agget, Mr. T. Sharp, Mr. & Mrs. Holmes, Mrs. Watts, Mrs. Hewings and Mrs. G. Vallance.

Courtesy of Mrs. D. Vallance

the final train would have more coaches. He was correct, the locomotive backed her train out, and four more coaches were shunted into the platform. Meanwhile, 5533 had run around her coaches, and then backed on to the other four, which resulted in the train formation being 5533 (running bunker first) and coaches 5231–5077–2196–6214–5713–2159.

Passengers boarded the train, which was quite well filled, but not crowded, and we pulled out 4 minutes late at 8.04 p.m. No stop was made at Teigngrace, and at Heathfield the train used the 'Down' (Candy's factory) side platform, where a small crowd was waiting. Several boarded the train, and we left at 8.13 p.m., rounding the curve onto the Teign Valley line and soon reaching Chudleigh Knighton Halt, where a handful of people were waiting. Several passengers alighted here, and this meant that the train had to stop twice to allow them to reach the short platform, losing a little more time. Chudleigh Station was quite crowded, but there were not many at Trusham; however, the platform at Ashton was well filled and a number entrained, including a gentleman with a bugle. We had to stop twice here, and eventually departed, now 12 minutes late, to a bugle fanfare, which was repeated at all subsequent stations and "en route" as well.

The residents of the Christow area were on the platform in large numbers, and we left with a full train at 8.48 p.m., having lost a further 4 minutes due to the extended station stops.

The locomotive climbed steadily up to Dunsford Halt, where four people joined the train, but the gradient and the heavy train caused some slipping as we restarted; however, the second attempt was successful and the ascent continued up to and through the tunnel to the remote Longdown Station, where, surprisingly, four people were waiting. Leaving again at 9.04 p.m. (now 19 minutes late), we passed through the second tunnel and made a restrained descent to Ide Halt, where a small group greeted the train. At the final branch platform, Alphington Halt, quite a number alighted, and we pulled out at 9.18 p.m., now 22 minutes late. Further time was lost as we were held up twice at City Basin Junction, and then at Exeter St. Thomas (where no-one was waiting), we made our last call before running in to the 'Down' Southern Railway platform at Exeter St. David's at 9.33 p.m., just 28 minutes behind time.

A crowd was waiting to greet the train here, and some flowers were laid on the running plate of the locomotive, whilst some were singing "Auld Lang Syne". She presently ran around her train, the passengers rejoined the coaches, and the final journey began, with a small crowd to bid us farewell, at 9.54 p.m., just 24 minutes after the booked time of 9.30 p.m.

At Exeter St. Thomas we collected several passengers before joining the branch at City Basin Junction, whilst several more boarded at Alphington. People were waving to the train from their gardens by the line as the daylight began to fade, and No. 5533 faced the long climb ahead. At Ide quite a crowd was there to greet us, then as darkness fell we forged slowly but steadily upwards, with someone waving a torch from a nearby farm. After running through the tunnel, and having quite a long stop at Longdown Station, which was out of sight from our coach, we restarted with a two-tone whistle from 5533, and a bugle fanfare, at 10.29 p.m.By now, we were 37 minutes late.

The descent to Dunsford Halt was taken cautiously, where we stopped at the empty platform; no-one alighted, but three people leaning on a nearby farm gate saw our train pass for the last time.

Down at Christow, lit by oil lamps, many had gathered on the platform and watched whilst our locomotive took a well-earned drink. The journey continued with several detonators exploding as we left at 10.50 p.m. — instead of at 10.01 p.m.!

At Ashton another crowd had turned out to see the train, and cars were stopped on each side of the level crossing. Our bugler departed here with a final burst of melody, and we ran on down the valley to Trusham, where, as on the outward trip, not many people had appeared to greet us.

Two stops were necessary at Chudleigh to allow passengers to detrain, then after pausing at Chudleigh Knighton Halt at 11.18 p.m., we reached Heathfield to again find people waiting to see us pass.

Leaving at 11.25 p.m., we ran non-stop to Newton Abbot, arriving at the main 'Down' platform at 11.35 p.m., just one hour late. The train was still quite full here, and after everyone had alighted, we climbed the station stairs feeling that we had said farewell to a railway which had given us much pleasure over the years, and which would be greatly missed.

As we left the station, 5533 slowly backed her train out of the station into the darkness and into history.'

Top: A typical tranquil scene between Christow and Ashton on 7th April 1958 with 2–6–2T, No. 4533, in charge of a Heathfield-bound train. *Lower:* The same stretch of line photographed on 13th March 1961, depicting the washed-out track-bed.

J. R. Besley

Also gone was the alternative route from Exeter to Newton Abbot, when the main line was affected by storm damage, and which the GWR had maintained compensated for any loss incurred on the Teign Valley line. Admittedly, for a few years, diversions could still be made on the former Southern line from Exeter to Plymouth, via Okehampton and Tavistock, but that line, too, was eventually closed to passengers. Consequently, as was the case several years ago when the track and station at Dawlish suffered considerable storm damage, passengers have sometimes had to face the inconvenience of transferring to buses for part of their journey.

For some of the local inhabitants in the villages and hamlets of the Teign Valley, too, the effects of the closure of the line to passenger traffic was traumatic, only to a far greater extent as ably portrayed by Mr. David St. John Thomas in his book, *Rural Transport Problems*. Moreover, the revised bus timetable that was introduced did little to help because, for many people, the train was the only realistic means of travelling to work, and whilst the majority did succeed in making alternative transport arrangements, at least five were known to have lost their jobs.

Meanwhile, the track was soon removed between Alphington and Christow, some of the bridges were blown up as training exercises for the Royal Engineers and the local authority, St. Thomas Rural District Council, arranged for work to commence on filling in some of the many cuttings. At the same time, however, the Heathfield to Christow section was to remain open for a few more years for the purposes of running a freight train three times a week, even though this was a somewhat costly operation: not only were level-crossing keepers retained and seven men employed on track maintenance (just four less than on the previous through line to Exeter!), but the loop at Trusham was put out of use, which meant that the train had to travel a further 3½ miles to Christow and back merely to allow the engine to change ends. Just how long such a situation would have been allowed to continue is open to pure conjecture but, whatever, in February 1961 severe flooding near Ashton washed out part of the track-bed, which led to the line being terminated beyond Trusham.

As an interesting aside, it was shortly after this occurrence that a special trip in goods brake vans (BR would not allow passenger coaches!) to travel over the surviving portion of the Teign Valley branch was organised by the South Devon Railway Society; an organisation that had been formed a few years earlier by Canon O. Jones, then Rector of Teigngrace, and Mr. E. G. Parrott of Torquay in an unsuccessful (unfortunately!) attempt to operate the Moretonhampstead branch as a preserved line after its closure by British Railways.

The date was 4th March 1961, and once again Mr. E. R. Shepherd of Plymouth was among those to join the trip and has kindly contributed the following account of it:

'On the 4th March 1961 the South Devon Railway Society organised a special trip in goods brake vans to travel over the surviving portion of the

2–6–2T, No. 4174, in charge of the SDRS 'special', photographed on the return journey to Newton Abbot at Chudleigh Knighton Halt on 4th March 1961.

E. R. Shepherd

Teign Valley branch. The train was headed by "Large Prairie" 2–6–2T, No. 4174, and consisted of eight brake vans, carrying about fifty passengers.

We left from Platform 9 at Newton Abbot at 2.00 p.m. and proceeded at a leisurely pace to Teigngrace Halt, where the Society Chairman, Canon O. Jones, and his wife joined us. The train then continued to Heathfield, where a ten-minute stop gave time for a walk around the station area.

Joining the Teign Valley line, the 'special' soon stopped to allow our fireman to open, and our guard to close, the gates of a level crossing over a minor road, and this was repeated at Chudleigh Knighton, where it was seen that the Pagoda shelter had been dismantled and the nameboard removed.

At Chudleigh signs of recent floods were evident in the erosion on the station platform; a six-minute wait here preceded our stately progress up the valley as far as Trusham, which was reached at 3.00 p.m.

The station was a depressing sight; all signals dismantled and points worked by hand levers, whilst the waiting shelter on the 'Down' (Heathfield) platform had been removed. However, the weather was fine and our locomotive, quite clean and in lined green livery, made a brave sight in the sunshine. Beyond the station, the line had been completely washed out by floods, and was never re-opened.

The return journey, once the engine had run round its train, began at 3.45 p.m., and after again stopping at all stations, we returned to Platform 9 at Newton Abbot at 4.35 p.m., having completed a very enjoyable and unrepeatable journey.'

002

2nd - SPECIAL ARRANGEMENT
MARCH 4 1961
South Devon Railway Society.

Newton Abbot (P) to
TRUSHAM
AND BACK
(W)

For conditions see over

002

043

2nd - SPECIAL ARRANGEMENT
MARCH 4 1961
South Devon Railway Society.

Newton Abbot (P) to
TRUSHAM
AND BACK
(W)

For conditions see over

043

There is little to record concerning the next four years, but in early 1965 goods facilities were withdrawn from Trusham and, on 17th May of that year, BR advised their customers that in accordance with their plan for re-shaping British Railways a freight concentration depot would be established at Newton Abbot, adding that general freight facilities would be withdrawn from Heathfield and Chudleigh as from 14th June 1965. At the same time it was stated that coal traffic would still be allowed to pass to these stations pending implementation of the coal concentration at Newton Abbot. Facilities were also to be retained for clay and private siding traffic at Heathfield, and for gas oil in tank wagons at Chudleigh.

This situation, however, lasted little more than two years. In November 1967 discussions took place between BR and Roads Reconstruction (Quarries) Ltd (now the parent company of Teign Valley Granite Company) about the volume of traffic currently passing by rail from the private siding at Crockham Quarry not being sufficient to justify the retention of freight facilities; and a month later the District Engineer of BR refused to permit wagons into the siding due to the bad state of repair. As a result, the line from Heathfield fell into dis-use. Moreover, by this time Devon County Council's plans for the Chudleigh by-pass were well advanced and, after stating that if the branch line was retained additional expenditure of around £100,000 would be involved, BR officially closed the section of line between Heathfield and Crockham on 1st July 1968.

By then, the Alphington Road sidings from City Basin Junction, at the other end of the Teign Valley line, had also fallen largely into dis-use. Some, in fact, had already been removed during the mid-sixties so that the car park for the cattle market could be extended. Nevertheless, the section of track leading towards the former site of Alphington Halt, together with a small siding, still remains to this day and is occasionally used to provide a service to a firm of scrap metal merchants.

2–6–2T, No. 4148, with the local freight at Trusham Station on 24th March 1962.

J. R. Besley

A GLIMPSE OF THE ROUTE IN 1995

Heathfield Station, with its now partially overgrown platforms, viewed from the adjoining road bridge. The track-bed of the former Teign Valley line can be seen sweeping to the right behind the now empty Geest buildings, while the section of track still remaining (part of the former Moretonhampstead branch) leads to an oil terminus, just out of the picture.

Bovey Lane Crossing, where the gate now remains firmly shut. Note the small section of track protruding through the tarmac.

Top: The bridge that carried the line over the River Bovey, on the outskirts of Heathfield. From shortly beyond this point, the track-bed has disappeared completely for some 2 miles due to clay workings and the construction of the A38 trunk road in the early '70s. The 'new' road was also responsible for the complete erasure of the former sites of Chudleigh Knighton Halt and Chudleigh Station.

Between Chudleigh and Trusham Stations the line used to cross the River Teign twice, at Huxbear Bridge (Centre) and at Crockham Bridge (Bottom). Nowadays the presence of these bridges is the only evidence to suggest that a railway ever existed in the vicinity.

Trusham Station, complete with its tin storage shed, has remained little altered over the years and has been used as a holiday home ever since the line closed.

Ashton Station, now a modern dwelling.

The final crossing of the River Teign before the line reached Christow Station. Here again, there is little other evidence to suggest that a railway ever existed in the vicinity.

Christow Station. Like Ashton Station, it is now an attractive and well-maintained modern dwelling.

Leigh Cross area: (Top) One of several stone bridges along this stretch of the old line, where the track-bed can be seen from the road over quite a considerable distance. (Centre) A photograph showing part of the track-bed and the close proximity of the adjoining road.
Bottom: The former site of Dunsford Halt — over-shadowed by trees and now just the lower part of a field!

Longdown Station. Despite the growth over the track-bed and embankments between the two tunnels, the building remains in remarkably good condition and is a gem. It is now used as a store.

The former site of Ide Station/Halt, now a cul-de-sac of modern bungalows.

The former site of Alphington Halt, lost amongst undergrowth and trees.

The last remaining section of track of the former Teign Valley line from City Basin Junction. The siding leads off to a firm of scrap metal merchants in Marsh Barton Industrial Estate.

(All photographs in this chapter courtesy of Mike Lang)

Publisher's note: Although certain sections of the track-bed can still be traced, it must be appreciated that the land is now in private ownership and no exploration should be undertaken without prior consent. For similar reasons, no attempt should be made to gain access to the former station sites still in existence or to encroach upon the privacy of the occupants.

APPENDIX I

(a) Mr. Fowler's Report

(1) The portion of the line under construction consists of a length of 7¾ miles extending from the junction with the Great Western Railway system at Chudleigh Road Station to a public road near Teign House.
(2) There are stations in progress at Chudleigh Road Junction, Chudleigh Crocombe and Ashton and there will also require to be a terminal station at Teign House or some other point if the line be extended but the site of this station has not been settled.
(3) The stations in progress are being constructed in accordance with plans signed by the authorities of the Great Western Railway and the terminal station will similarly have to be submitted to them.
(4) The main line of rails is laid throughout the entire length with the exception of the last half mile. Practically speaking the whole of the sidings at the stations remain to be done.
(5) The minor works at present in hand are being carried out by Mr. Walker, a contractor who appears to have undertaken to finish the line under a contract entered into in 1877 at which time the line had been partially completed by some other contractor. No documents appear to be forthcoming which would enable me to say what was the state of the line when Mr. Walker entered into his contract nor what sum had been expended upon it up to that date.
(6) An inspection of the line shews but too clearly that the works have been carried out without any proper engineering supervision, and by a contractor of small experience, and the result is that many of the bridges have been and are being overhauled or reconstructed. When finished as now proposed I have no doubt they will be passed by the Government Inspector and by the Great Western engineers. If the parties interested in the river objected to any of the works, which they might reasonably do since the pile piers are frequently placed almost square to the current and act like weirs, they presumably would have objected before as the bridges have been some seven years in existence.
(7) It is understood that the immediate purpose of the present report is to determine the sum required to complete the line to the satisfaction of the Great Western Railway and the Government Inspector. This it is not difficult to do if all questions be reserved of past payments and amounts due up to present date.
(8) The present contractor claims that exclusive of works in progress a sum of £4,388.15s. is due to him under the 1877 contract. The engineer's last certificate shews that the total payment authorised by him was £16,569 but the Company appear to have paid £23,622 and there is no evidence to shew who authorised the excess payment nor does there appear to be any satisfactory means of checking the accounts.
(9) The following is a Schedule of works remaining to be executed:–
Chudleigh Road Junction Station. Complete about one half platform and two thirds of approach road, construct goods shed, put in sidings, extend Great Western siding, supply 5 ton crane and sundries.

Chudleigh Station. Complete loading stage approach, road gates and sidings and supply 5 ton crane.
Crocombe Station. Complete as above.
Ashton Station. Complete as above.
Bovey Marsh Bridge to be completed with handrail.
Level Crossing Gates to be fixed.
Bovey River Bridge. Piles to be re-driven, abutment rebuilt and pitched, and superstructure re-constructed (timber is delivered).
Formation to be raised 6 inches from bridge to summit of gradient.
Flat-Topped Culvert to be constructed and drain deepened.
Wing Walls of over bridge to be secured.
Level Crossing Cottage to be built.
Cattle Creep to be lined with *new settings.*
Teign River Bridge. Piles to be re-driven, new superstructure constructed and slopes protected by kidwork or otherwise.
Bella Marsh Leete Bridge. Girder superstructure, masonry abutments and long wing walls to be constructed.
Double Culvert at Chudleigh to be completed (timber is delivered).
Teign River Girder Bridge. Timber flooring and rail guard to be constructed, piers completed and girders re-bedded on iron bed plates.
Ditto ditto.
Formation to be well drained between the two preceding bridges.
Ashton Leete Bridge or culvert to be reconstructed in masonry.
Ashton River Bridge. Girder superstructure and masonry piers and wings to be constructed.
Christow Girder Bridge. Timber flooring and guard rail to be constructed and piers completed.
Permanent Way. Materials and ballasting for 45 chains of line.
Sidings and Crossing at stations to be constructed as on signed plans.
Present Ballast to be broken and additional ballast and new sleepers supplied where necessary.
Gauge Ties to be placed on bridges and ties and guard rail round the sharp curves if required by the Government Inspector.
Wire Fencing to be completed with stranded top wire and new posts where necessary.
Slopes to be Trimmed and line drained where necessary.
Signals and Telegraph to be supplied in accordance with the requirements of the Government Inspector.
Temporary Station of a simple character to be constructed at the present termination of works.

The cost of the above works will of course be dependent to some extent upon the strictness with which the requirements of the Great Western Railway will be enforced by that Company. Having reference to the quantity of materials now delivered on the ground and to the general circumstances of the case I am of opinion that the line may be completed for public traffic for the sum of about nine thousand pounds (£9,000).

JOHN FOWLER

(b) Mr. Jenkin's Report

Liskeard, Cornwall &
5, Victoria Street, Westminster,
February 7th, 1881.

To The Directors of the Teign Valley Railway.
My Lord and Gentlemen –

In the present position of the affairs of this railway, I think it desirable to report to you shortly what has taken place since I have been acting as engineer to the Company.

At the latter end of June, 1879, I was informed by Mr. R. A. Read that an Agreement had been made with the Great Western Railway Company, under which the original line had to be completed to the reasonable satisfaction of that Company, and I was asked to superintend the works up to such completion, which I consented to do on being informed that the Company would have no difficulty in finding the money required for such completion, and that the work would probably be in hand about three months. Immediately after this I went (with the assistance of Mr. Lidstone) carefully through the whole of the work on the line, and we then found the state of things to be as follows, viz:-

We were unable to procure any plan or section of the line, so that we had to make an entirely new section of the whole line, laying out fresh gradients throughout, and raising or lowering the line to suit these gradients.

There were no plans in existence of the stations or station yards, with the exception of a plan of Chudleigh Road Junction, which was incorrect and practically of little value, so that we had to make fresh surveys with cross sections of the whole of the station yards, and to obtain the assent of the Great Western authorities to the proposed mode of laying out all the station yards.

There were no drawings of any of the bridges or other structures on the line, and as the Great Western Company required to be furnished with drawings of all the under bridges, it was necessary to prepare detailed drawings from measurement of all the river bridges, both wooden and iron, and of a number of bridges (principally of wood) across leats, etc.

When these drawings were made, it was found that there was not a single wooden bridge on the line that had been constructed of sufficient strength to bear the locomotives used by the Great Western Company, or to meet the requirements of the Board of Trade, so that it was necessary to prepare plans for the reconstruction of every under bridge, at a cost nearly equal to that of building new bridges in every case; moreover, these bridges were, in other respects, faulty in construction, and in the case of the bridge over the Bellamarsh Mill Leat the Company appeared to be under a legal liability at once to remove it, and we were obliged to prepare plans for an iron girder bridge of a totally different construction. Having thus adverted to the state of things in June, 1879, I now proceed to explain what has since been done, viz:-

The whole of the station plans have received the formal assent of the Great

Western Company, and the works shown in these plans are in an advanced state.

Working drawings of all the bridges have been prepared in accordance with the requirements of the Great Western Company and of the Board of Trade, including the girder bridge at Bellamarsh Mill Leat, one iron girder bridge over the Teign has been built, and several smaller bridges, both of masonry and of timber; and

The line has been brought to an even gradient, and ballasted through a large portion of its entire length, the amount certified by me for these works being £4,242.1s.1d., including timber, etc., delivered on the ground.

I now propose to deal with the work still remaining to be done, and in doing so I propose to take the works in order, commencing from Chudleigh Road Junction with the Great Western Railway.

Works at Chudleigh Road Junction Station. An additional platform wall has been built and the approach road more than half completed. I estimate that it will cost £500 to complete these station works, irrespective of rails and points and crossings.

Gate Keeper's House at 0M. 22Chs. This has been built during 1880, but is not quite finished. I estimate the cost of completing it at £30.

Bovey Marsh Bridge. This wooden bridge has been re-constructed to the approval of the Great Western Company. A hand-rail, etc., is still required at a cost of about £20.

Bovey River Bridge, 0M. 35Chs. The timber for this bridge is on the ground; the cost of re-constructing it will probably be £120, unless the piles are found defective, in which case this sum will be exceeded.

Gate Keeper's House at 1M. 12Chs. It may be necessary to build a house at this level crossing, in which case the cost will be about £150.

Cattle Arch at 1M. 22Chs. This will cost about £50 to alter.

Bridge Over The Teign at 1M. 27Chs. This wooden bridge over the Teign has eleven openings of about 17 feet each. Part of the timber required for its re-construction is on the ground; it must be entirely taken to pieces and the driving of the piles tested. I do not think the cost of doing it will exceed £500, even if the piles are found defective.

Bellamarsh Leat Bridge. The present wooden structure is not only too weak and badly constructed, but it interferes with the flow of the water through the Leat, and I am informed that the Company is legally bound to remove it. Detailed drawings of a girder bridge have been prepared. The cost will be about £400.

Culvert at Chudleigh. The masonry of this culvert has been built. The completion of the re-construction will cost about £25.

Chudleigh Station. The loading stage has been constructed, except the fixing of a crane; the remaining works included in the plan approved by the Great Western Company will cost about £150, irrespective of rails, and points, and crossings.

Bridge Over The River Teign at 3M. 16Chs. This is an iron girder bridge. Hand rails, guards, etc., are required, and the girders must be re-bedded. The cost will be about £120.

Bridge Over The River Teign at 4 Miles. This iron girder bridge must be completed in the same way as the last. Cost £120.

Crocombe Station. The loading stage has been constructed, and the lengthening of the platform partly completed. It will cost about £100 to complete the station works, exclusive of rails, and points, and crossings as before.

Ashton Station Works. The yard has been formed, and the sidings marked out. It will cost about £75 to complete this station, exclusive of rails, and points, and crossings.

Wooden Bridge Over Mill Leat at 6M. 40Chs. This bridge must be removed, and a masonry bridge substituted. The cost will be about £100.

Bridge at 6M. 42Chs. This timber bridge has been removed, and a masonry bridge substituted.

Bridge at 6M. 45Chs. This timber bridge has been removed, and a masonry bridge substituted.

Bridge at 6M. 50Chs. This timber bridge has been removed, and a masonry bridge substituted.

Bridge Over Teign at 6M. 53Chs. The superstructure of this timber bridge was removed for the purpose of re-construction, when it was found that the piles were resting on the hard rock beneath the bed of the river and could not be driven; it therefore became necessary to substitute an iron girder bridge, with masonry piers, which will cost about £600.

Bridge Over Teign at 6M. 79Chs. This bridge has been lately erected. It is an iron girder bridge with masonry piers. The hand-rail, guards and flooring have yet to be fixed, and the masonry tops of the piers completed. The cost will be about £100.

In addition to these works it will cost about £500 to complete the ballasting of the line, as Mr. Margary has asked to have some of the ballast broken to a smaller size and about £300 to trim the slopes and do some other requisite works, principally caused by the stoppage of the works, and £200 to complete the fencing to the satisfaction of the Great Western Railway Company, who have asked for a style of fencing much superior to that already fixed. Assuming that the rails and sleepers required for the completion of the line, and which have been purchased are not paid for, £1,000 should be put down for these and £250 for points, crossings, etc., if the same have not been already paid for, and the cost of signals will be about £2,000. To this must also now be added the cost of a temporary station at Teign House, which will cost about £800.

This makes the total cost £8,240, as set out in the accompanying schedule, and I am confident that I could get the work carried to completion for this sum.

I remain,
My Lord and Gentleman,
Your obedient servant,

SILVs. W. JENKIN.

TEIGN VALLEY RAILWAY
ESTIMATE OF COST OF COMPLETING THESE WORKS.

	Now Estimated £	Former Estimate £
Works at Chudleigh Station	500	500
Gatekeeper's House (cost of completing)	30	
Bovey Marsh Bridge	20	20
Bovey River Bridge (there is now reason to suppose that some of the piles are defective)	150	120
Gatekeeper's house (if required)	150	150
Cattle creep	50	50
Knighton River Bridge (if piles are found defective)	500	350
Bellamarsh Leat Bridge	400	400
Chudleigh Station works (including crane, &c.)	150	60
Chudleigh Culvert	25	50
Altering Girder bridges (Teign)	240	240
Crocombe Station works (including crane, &c.)	100	60
Ashton Station works (including crane, &c.)	75	50
Ashton Leat Bridge	100	100
Ashton River Bridge	600	600
Christow River Bridge	100	100
Ballasting to end of line	500	400
Cleaning and lifting line	300	150
Fencing	200	
Additional rails and sleepers	1000	1000
Points and crossings	250	
Occupation works		100
Signals	2000	2000
Temporary station at Teign House	800	
	£8,240	**£6,500**

APPENDIX II

Schedule of shareholders holding shares authorized under the scheme of 1877, as listed in the directors' report of 14th March 1881.

No. 1 preference shares – 1.5%

	Shares	£
Ashdown Mrs	200	1,000
Burkit, E.	200	1,000
Gwinner, H.	495	2,475
Jenkins, R. J.	842	4,210
Haldon, Lord	3,000	15,000
Smith, H.	200	1,000
Toogood, W.	800	4,000
Vertue, N. H.	100	500
Walker, R. and others of same name	1,641	8,205
Watts, Blake, Bearne and Co.	131	655
Holders of less than 100 shares	391	1,955
Total	**8,000**	**40,000**

No. 2 preference shares – 2.5%

Gurney S. A. and another	450	2,250
Haldon, Lord	280	1,400
Taylor, H. R.	2,400	12,000
Toogood, W.	873	4,365
Walker, R. and another of the same name.	150	750
Holders of less than 100 shares	247	1,235
Total	**4,400**	**22,000**

No. 3 preference shares – 3.5%

Ashdown, Mrs	141	705
Ellis Ed.	100	500
Gurney and another	450	2,250
Stephenson, T.	130	650
Smith, H.	100	500
Toogood, W.	827	4,135
Holders of less than 100 shares	252	1,260
Total	**2,000**	**10,000**

APPENDIX III

Lt. Col. Yorke's Report

Railway Department,
Board of Trade,
8, Richmond Terrace,
Whitehall, London, S.W.
June 12, 1903.

I have the honour to report for the information of the Board of Trade, that in compliance with the instructions contained in your Minute of the 2nd June, I have inspected the Exeter Railway.

The Railway commences by a double junction with the Great Western Railway at City Basin Junction Signal box Exeter (195 miles 11½ chains from London) and terminates by an end on junction with the Teign Valley branch of the Great Western Railway.

It is 8 miles 8.51 chains long, and is single throughout, except at the junction with the Great Western Railway at Exeter, and at Christow Station, where there is a passing loop for passenger trains.

Sufficient land has, over the greater portion of the railway, been purchased for a double line, and all the overbridges have been built for a double line.

The width at formation level is nowhere less than 16 feet, and in many places it is more.

The gauge is 4' 8½", and the interspace between the adjacent lines of rails at passing places, and between the main line and sidings is not less than 6 feet.

The permanent way is laid with steel bull headed rails weighing 77½lbs. per yard, and cast-iron chairs weighing 35¼lbs. each. The sleepers are 9' x 10" x 5" and are spaced at an average distance apart of 2' 10" from centre to centre. The chairs are fastened to the sleepers by ⅞" screw bolts, two to each chair, the arrangements being in accordance with the standard type of permanent way adopted by the Great Western Railway by which company the material has in fact been supplied.

The ballast consists partly of broken stone, or granite, and partly of gravel.

The steepest gradient has an inclination of 1 in 58 and the sharpest curve has a radius of 15 chains. The cuttings and embankments are very heavy. The most important cutting has a depth of 52 feet, the material through which it is made being shale with culmen grit, and being extremely hard. The highest embankment is 59.35 feet (or say 60 feet) high. Both cuttings and embankments appear to be standing well.

There are seven bridges over and sixteen under the line. All the overbridges are arched. The arches being of brick, and the abutments either of brick or masonry.

Six of the under bridges are constructed with steel girders and steel flooring, resting on abutments of brick or masonry. All the bridges appeared to be substantially built; the girders have sufficient theoretical strength, so far as an examination of the plans enable me to judge, and gave very moderate and uniform deflections under test. The tests were made by means of two 6-coupled tank engines (lent by the Great Western Railway) weighing approximately 44 tons each, and having a wheel base of 15' 6".

There are two tunnels of horseshoe section, one 829 yards long and the other 251 yards long. They are lined throughout, the side walls varying in thickness from 9" to 1' 10½" and the arches from 1' 6" to 1' 10½". The tunnels are fairly dry, and the workmanship appeared to be good. They are constructed for a single line only, and are provided with recesses for platelayers at 1 chain intervals on alternate sides.

There are 7 culverts, one having a span of 20 feet, the remainder having spans of 4 feet or 3½ feet. They all have brick arches, and abutments of brick, or masonry or concrete. Four of them have inverts.

There are no viaducts, and no public road level crossings, but there are three footpath crossings, and six private road or occupation crossings.

The stations on the new line are three, viz:-
Ide, Longdown and Christow.

The two first are single sided Stations, each with one platform, and they are not passing places. The platform at each station is provided with booking hall, ladies waiting room and lavatory, and conveniences and W.C.s for men. Name boards have been fixed, and clocks will be provided before the line is opened.

Christow Station is a double sided station with two platforms, and a passing loop for passenger trains. The accommodation on the up platform is similar to that provided at Ide, and Longdown, while on the down platform there is a waiting shed, and conveniences for men.

The railway is to be worked by the Great Western Railway, on the Electric staff system, and a certificate as to the mode of working will be forwarded by the Company in the course of a few days.

The line is divided into two sections, viz: from City Basin Junction to Christow, and from Christow to Heathfield, on the Teign Valley branch of the Great Western Railway.

The signalling on the line is as follows: At the junction with the Great Western Railway at Exeter, the points and signals are worked from the City Basin Junction Signal Box on the Great Western Railway, which will be separately reported on.

Near this junction there is a ground frame from which two siding connections on the Exeter railway are worked. The ground frame contains 4 levers, which are locked by the key on the electric train staff.

At Ide Station there are two ground frames each containing 2 levers, from which the points giving access to the siding are worked. The levers are locked by the key on the train staff.

At Longdown Station similar arrangements exist.

At Christow Station, there is a signal box containing 18 levers in use and 3 spare levers.

At all these places the interlocking is correct.

The railway is in good order, and on condition that the points and signals (which are at present out of use) are properly connected with their respective levers in the signal box at Christow and ground frames at Exeter, Ide, and Longdown, that clocks are provided at the stations and that the speed of trains does not for the present exceed 25 miles an hour, I can recommend the Board of Trade to sanction the opening of the line for passenger traffic.

I have, etc.
(Sd) H. A. Yorke,
Lt. Col. R.E.

APPENDIX IV

Divisional Superintendent's Office
Exeter
14th November 1945

When it is necessary for the Teign Valley Branch line to be opened specially for the diversion of traffic, without previous notice having been given, the following arrangements, which supplement those shown in Notice No. 464 dated May 1941 and Notice No. 569 dated November 1945, will be instituted by and co-ordinated from the Divisional Control Office.

It is essential that the advices shown below, which are additional to the regular departmental advices sent relative to accidents, derailments etc., should be transmitted immediately.

(1) Telephone advices to be given in the following order by Exeter Control to:

(a) Devon County Police
Superintendent, Newton Abbot, Tel. No. Newton Abbot 961, in accordance with the arrangements shown in Notice No. 569 dated 9th November 1945.

(b) Exeter City Police
Tel. No. Exeter 2224, who will on request call and convey the Longdown signalman living in Exeter to St. David's Station. (This cancels the arrangements shown in Notice No. 569)

(c) Chief Inspector Long, Tel. No. Exeter 55701.

(d) Exeter Platform Inspector, to call:
District Inspector Vickery,
14 Brunswick Street, St. Thomas, Exeter,
who, when called, should proceed to City Basin Junction signal box and report to Control.

(e) Newton Abbot Platform Inspector, to call:
(i) District Inspector Saffin,
25 Lime Tree Walk, Milber, Newton Abbot.
(ii) Asst. District Inspector Court,
17 Lime Tree Walk, Milber, Newton Abbot.

(f) Mr W. W. Box, Christow signalman, Tel. No. Christow 362 who, if available, should be asked, when proceeding to Christow Station, to advise the Christow Station Master of the proposed diversion.

Chief Inspector Long and the Longdown signalman, on arrival at St. David's Station and Inspectors Saffin and Court, if both are available, on arrival at Newton Abbot Station, to report to the Control.

(2) Chief Inspector Long, District Inspector Vickery and the Longdown signalman, if then available, to travel on the first train to be diverted over the Teign Valley Branch, or when necessary by light engine.

Inspectors Saffin and Court to leave Newton Abbot by the first 'Up' train to be diverted over the Teign Valley Branch or light engine if necessary, to ensure that the Crossing Gates at Teignbridge are secured against road traffic and the Crossing Keeper advised of the diversion.

Inspector Saffin to remain in Heathfield Signal Box until the arrival of the regular signalman and then to report to the Control for instructions.

Inspector Court to continue with the train to Trusham to ensure that the Crossing Keepers at Bovey Lane and Chudleigh Knighton have been advised

of the diversion, and that arrangements have been made for the Crossing gates to be placed and maintained across the road.
Inspector Court to take charge of the Trusham Signal Box until the arrival of the regular signalman and then to report to the Control for instructions.

(3) The Platform Inspector at Newton Abbot, when advised of the diversion to send a competent man without waiting for the first train to be diverted (in accordance with the instructions already issued) to Teignbridge Crossing to ensure that the gates at that point are placed across the road and the Crossing Keeper advised of the diversion.

(4) Chief Inspector Long to arrange for an additional man to be sent as soon as practicable to Longdown to assist the signalman at that point.

(5) The Exeter Relief Controller will be responsible, in conjunction with the Exeter and Newton Abbot Platform Inspectors, for seeing that the Guards with knowledge of the road over the Teign Valley line, are available, or have been called, at Exeter and Newton Abbot to cover diverted services, both Passenger and Freight.

(6) The following arrangements operate forthwith each night after the last train over the Teign Valley Branch line:
(a) The City Basin Junction – Longdown Staff will be drawn and kept in City Basin Junction Signal Box.
(b) The Longdown – Christow Staff will be drawn and kept in Longdown Signal Box and Points No. 25 at Christow left reversed.
(c) The Newton Abbot East – Heathfield Token will be drawn and kept in Newton Abbot East Signal Box.
(d) The Heathfield – Trusham Token will be drawn and kept in Heathfield Signal Box and Points No. 28 at Heathfield left reversed.

(7) The arrangements shown above will enable a 'down' train to proceed from Exeter to Christow and an 'up' train from Newton Abbot to Trusham pending the full Staff required (being called by the police) reporting for duty.
It should be clearly understood that the arrangements set out above are supplementary to those already in operation, whereby the Police Authorities concerned are responsible for calling the Staff required. These additional instructions are designed to enable a diversion to operate over the Teign Valley Branch whilst the Police arrangements for calling out the Staff are in process of operation and thus avoid delays occuring at Exeter and Newton Abbot pending the arrival of the Staff.

(Signed) H.A.C. Worth
Divisional Superintendent

APPENDIX V

1863 *13th July* – Royal Assent given to the Act incorporating the company.

1865 Act authorized the issue of a further share capital of £30,000, with power to borrow £10,000 and empowered company to enter into working arrangements with the South Devon Railway Co.

1867 Scheme authorized the issue of £35,000 (A) debenture stock, £10,000 (B) debenture stock and £34,000 (C) debenture stock, and annulled all borrowing powers of the company and all powers to issue shares to a greater extent than £31,000, inclusive of £20,740 already subscribed.

1868 Act sanctioned a deviation from the authorized line, and extended the time for completion.

1870 Act further extended time for completion of line.

1872 Act authorized two short extensions and an additional share capital of £72,000, with power to borrow £24,000 and annulled all powers under the previous Acts and Scheme, so far as they had not then been exercised.

1875 Authorized an extension to Crediton, an additional share capital of £150,000 with power to borrow £50,000. No capital was ever raised under this Act, and the powers to issue capital were annulled in 1880.

1877 Scheme authorized the issue of the share capital of £72,000, created by the Act of 1872 in the following manner:
£40,000 No. 1 preference shares, the proceeds to be applied to purchase of land and construction of the line.
£22,000 No. 2 preference shares, the proceeds to be applied in extinguishing the A and B debenture stock and in carrying out certain arrangements with the contractor.
£10,000 No. 3 preference shares, the proceeds to be applied in discharge of liabilities, and limited the borrowing power under the 1872 Act to £10,000.

1878 Act authorized certain deviations, and extended the time for completion of the line.

1879 Scheme authorized the issue of £14,000 in debentures, the interest of which was to be wholly borne by the No. 1 preference shares.

1880 Act authorized the abandonment of the greater part of the Crediton extension, annulled the powers to issue share and loan capital conferred by the Act of 1875, authorized the issue of £40,000 share capital, with power to borrow £13,300 and empowered the company to enter into working arrangements with the Great Western Railway Company.

1882 *9th October* – Line opened from Heathfield.

1883 Act passed authorizing the Exeter, Teign Valley and Chagford Railway to construct a railway from Exeter to Christow.

1884 *7th November* – First sod cut for new railway.

1892 Moretonhampstead line converted from broad gauge to standard gauge.

1903 *1st July* – Line opened from Exeter to Christow connecting to existing line.

1908 Ashton engine shed closed.

1916 Track alterations at Heathfield enabling Teign Valley Platform line to be used as a run-round and Teign Valley trains could run direct to and from the Moretonhampstead line platform.

1924 *24th June* – Chudleigh Knighton Halt opened.

1927 *May* – Extensions made to Heathfield Station.

1928 *16th January* – Dunsford and Alphington Halts opened.

1934 Camping coach introduced at Ashton.

1939 Camping coaches introduced at Chudleigh and Ide.

1939 *October* – New cattle market opened at Marsh Barton, Exeter.

1943 Heathfield enlarged to take additional military traffic.
Sidings laid at Chudleigh Knighton, to serve military stores.
Longdown Station made a crossing station.

1955 *7th March* –Goods facilities withdrawn at Ide.

1958 *7th June* – Last passenger train from Heathfield to Exeter.
9th June – Passenger services withdrawn.

1961 *March* – Floods damaged line between Christow and Ashton, resulting in closure of line east of Trusham.
1st May – Goods facilities withdrawn from Christow and Ashton.
3rd July – Heathfield unstaffed.

1965 *5th April* – Goods facilities withdrawn at Trusham.

1967 *4th December* – Goods facilities withdrawn at Chudleigh and Heathfield.

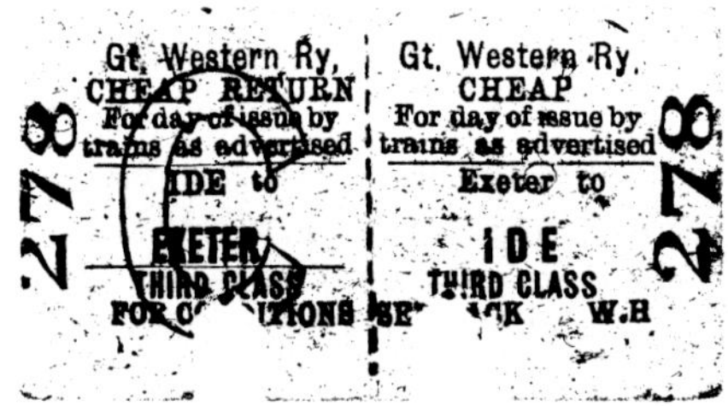

BIBLIOGRAPHY

Various books and documents have been consulted during the writing of this work, which include:

Clinkers' Register of Closed Passenger Stations and Goods Depots in England, Scotland and Wales

Contractors' Chronicle of 29th June 1903

Devon by Prof. W. G. Hoskins (Collins)

Devon Life, April 1965, March 1971 and August 1972

Exeter Flying Post

Express and Echo. 18th March 1953

Go Great Western by T. W. E. Roche (Oxford Publishing Co)

Great Western Coaches 1890–1954 by M. Harris (Ian Allan)

Great Western Engines by J. H. Russell (Oxford Publishing Co)

Great Western Engines, Names, Numbers and Classes 1940 to Preservation by B. Whitehurst (Oxford Publishing Co)

Handbook of Industrial Locomotives of S. W. England (Industrial Society)

Historical Survey of G. W. Engine Sheds by E. Lyons (Oxford Publishing Co)

Historical Survey of Selected G. W. R. Stations by R. H. Clark (Oxford Publishing Co)

History of the Great Western Railway by E. T. MacDermot

Let's Explore Old Railways in Devon by A. L. Clamp (Westway Publications)

Locomotives of the G. W. R. (R. C. T. S)

Men of the Great Western by Peter Grafton

Mid-Devon and Newton Times 11th September 1909

Private Owner Wagons by W. Hudson (Oxford Publishing Co)

Railway Modeller 1970 (page 392)

Railway Observer July 1958 – Notes by R. P. Walford – (R. C. T. S)

Railway World – February 1958 and September 1979

Regional History of the Railways of Great Britain Vol. 1 by D. St. John Thomas (David & Charles)

Register of Defunct and Other Companies from the Stock Exchange Official Year Book 1979–80

Rural Transport Problems by D. St. John Thomas (David & Charles)

Study of Rural Transport in Devon by Exeter University Steering Group 1971 (D of E)

Western Morning News 28th January and 9th June 1958

Western Times 1st November 1887

A selection of both public and working timetables and Railway Company Sectional Appendix and Notices.

THE AUTHOR

Lawrence Pomroy was born in Exeter in 1922. After leaving school, he spent two years with a local firm of accountants and enlisted in the local Territorial Army Battalion of the Devonshire Regiment. In 1940 he transferred to the Gloucestershire Regiment and later served in India and South East Asia.

Whilst spending 38 years in the construction industry, he was based in Somerset (his favourite county!), Surrey, Berkshire and Devon, and travelled extensively.

His interest in railways and travelling started at an early age with frequent train journeys to Exmouth (S.R.), Dawlish (G.W.R.) and Plymouth (S.R.). During the 1930s frequent school holidays were spent near Wells. In those days his parents would ensure a safe departure from Exeter Queen Street Station (later Central Station), on the former Southern line to Waterloo, and Lawrence would subsequently change trains at Templecombe, on the Somerset and Dorset Line.

The journey, from Shepton Mallet, would then be completed on an old Bristol Tramways bus to Dinder.

Service in India involved travelling great distances, mostly by train. One of many long train journeys was on the old Assam and Bengal Railway to Dibrugarh, close to the northern terminus and the North East Frontier with Burma and China.

In more recent years travelling has involved visits to the Continent, with many memorable rail journeys in Switzerland. Although having visited Venice, his ambition to travel there on the Orient Express has yet to be fulfilled.

In his spare time Lawrence enjoys reading, crosswords, gardening, model railways (G.W.R.) and researching old country railways. He and his wife now live in Wiltshire.

Lawrence W. Pomroy